I0011903

StartupPro: How to set up and grow a tech business

Practical guidance on how to turn your passion, idea, and technical skills into a successful business

Martin Zwilling

Impackt Publishing
We Mean Business

StartupPro: How to set up and grow a tech business

Copyright © 2014 Impackt Publishing

All rights reserved. No part of this book may be reproduced, stored in a retrieval system, or transmitted in any form or by any means, without the prior written permission of the publisher, except in the case of brief quotations embedded in critical articles or reviews.

Every effort has been made in the preparation of this book to ensure the accuracy of the information presented. However, the information contained in this book is sold without warranty, either express or implied. Neither the author(s), nor Impackt Publishing, and its dealers and distributors will be held liable for any damages caused or alleged to be caused directly or indirectly by this book.

Impackt Publishing has endeavored to provide trademark information about all of the companies and products mentioned in this book by the appropriate use of capitals. However, Impackt Publishing cannot guarantee the accuracy of this information.

First published: November 2014

Production reference: 1221114

Published by Impackt Publishing Ltd.
Livery Place
35 Livery Street
Birmingham B3 2PB, UK.

ISBN 978-1-78300-142-2

www.Impacktpub.com

Credits

Author
Martin Zwilling

Reviewers
Fan Du
Jay LeBoeuf

Acquisition Editor
Nick Falkowski

Content Development Editor
Sweny M. Sukumaran

Copy Editors
Karuna Narayanan
Alfida Paiva
Faisal Siddiqui

Project Coordinator
Venitha Cutinho

Proofreaders
Simran Bhogal
Maria Gould
Ameesha Green
Paul Hindle

Production Coordinator
Melwyn D'sa

Cover Work
Simon Cardew

About the Author

Marty Zwilling has a passion for nurturing the development of entrepreneurs by providing first-hand mentoring, funding assistance, and business plan development. He is the Founder and CEO of Startup Professionals, a company that provides products and services to startup founders and small business owners.

He writes a daily blog for entrepreneurs, and dispenses advice on the subject of startups to a large online audience of 750,000 Twitter followers. He is also a regular contributor to Forbes, Entrepreneur Inc, Business Insider, and the Huffington Post. He also has published two other books, *Do You Have What It Takes To Be An Entrepreneur?* and *Attracting an Angel*.

He has a 30 year track record of demonstrated results as an executive in general management, computer software development, product management, and marketing, as well as in leading technical business transformations, conducting due diligence for investors, mentoring new technical executives, and overseeing business development, customer service, and outsourcing both onshore and offshore.

Marty began his career with IBM, holding an array of positions including executive roles in software development and professional services. Prior to beginning his career, Marty obtained a Bachelor of Science degree in Accounting and a Minor in Computer Science from the University of Illinois in Champaign-Urbana.

A resident of Fountain Hills, Arizona, Marty is also an active member of the local Angel investment group (Arizona Technology Investor Forum), an advisor to the Arizona State University Venture Catalyst program, Executive in Residence at the Thunderbird School of Global Management, and member of the Advisory Boards for several startups in the area.

About the Reviewers

Fan Du is a Ph.D. student in the computer science department of University of Maryland. He received his bachelor's degree at Zhejiang University with honors. He has worked as a software engineer intern in top companies including Alibaba, Tencent, and IBM Watson. He was the founder and CTO of WaiMai Online, a startup company that provides an online ordering system for more than 40 restaurants.

Jay LeBoeuf is a technology executive and entrepreneur in the media creation and production industry. Jay is the President/Executive Director of Real Industry—a nonprofit organization transforming how students learn about the real world and how products go from an idea through to the process of commercialization.

Jay led R&D, IP, and technology strategy as Strategic Technology Director at iZotope. He founded and was CEO of an intelligent audio technology company Imagine Research, which was acquired by iZotope in March 2012. While creating *Google for Sound*, Jay was recognized as a Bloomberg Businessweek Innovator, and was awarded $1.1M in Small Business Innovation Research grants by the U.S. National Science Foundation, and interviewed on BBC World, Science 360, and other major media outlets. Prior to founding Imagine Research, Jay was a researcher in the Advanced Technology Group at Digidesign (Avid Technology) in charge of innovations for the industry-standard Pro Tools platform. He lectures on Real Industry and music information retrieval at Stanford University's Center for Computer Research in Music and Acoustics (CCRMA), and is on the Board of Advisors for music startups Chromatik and Humtap.

Contents

Chapter 6: After the Funding, How Do You Survive the Execution Risks?   123

Chapter 7: Are You Ready for All the Leadership and Team Challenges?   143

Chapter 8: Do You Understand How Social Media is Changing the Business Landscape?   165

Chapter 9: If You Build It, Will They Find You, and Will They Use It?   183

Chapter 10: Can You Build the Relationships Needed to Succeed in Business?   203

Preface

The purpose of this book is to address the needs of every technical entrepreneur who dreams of turning their passion and application ideas into a successful business. They need to know where to start in taking the idea from a concept to a product, incorporating the business as an LLC or C-corporation, finding the funding required to complete development and roll out the product, and how to build the team they need for all the marketing and delivery tasks, and all the details in between.

Equally important, the book will provide tips on how to network for partners and investors, communicate effectively with customers and employees, organize your business infrastructure, and have fun at the same time.

The entry cost for technical entrepreneurs to develop new applications is at an all-time low, with inexpensive yet powerful new software toolkits and hardware platforms. With the advent of smartphones and new web technologies, the application opportunities are huge.

At the same time, crowd-funding is adding a whole new dimension to the funding challenge. Old and new funding sources are discussed in detail, including the new alternatives with crowd-funding, as well as the implications of Angel funding, Super-Angels, and VCs.

The guidance is intended to be pragmatic and practical, rather than theoretical, based on my own many years of experience working as a developer, small software company executive, large company executive, mentor for startups, and Angel investor.

What this book covers

Chapter 1, Do You Have What It Takes to be an Entrepreneur?, sets the context for the book by providing you with a profile of entrepreneurs, who are markedly different from technical geeks that can write code in their needs and expectations and how they network and communicate. Through the more detailed discussion, readers have an opportunity to reflect on their own interests and passions, their strengths and weaknesses, and their ultimate success and happiness with the entrepreneur lifestyle.

Chapter 2, Does Your Dream Idea Have the Potential to be a Business?, helps you bridge the gap between a great idea and a great startup. I'm sure you all realize that there could be quite a distance between a great idea and a great startup. However, many people don't have a clue on how to bridge the gap. Some entrepreneurs are so caught up in their dream that they jump immediately into implementation with no focus on strategy and tactics first. The result is that when they hit the first obstacle (and there will be many), it seems like the end of the road. They don't have any idea which way to turn.

Even when your startup is a one-man show and lots of fun, a "business" needs some discipline and controls to keep it from being defined as a hobby by investors, and to assure some financial return.

Chapter 3, When, Where, and How Do You Formalize a Technical Business?, introduces you to the practical requirements you need to understand and execute to start a business. These include naming your company and product, the formalities of incorporation as an LLC or C-corporation, tax and liability considerations, and creating a website. In today's environment, this also includes how to use social media, writing a blog, creating an account on LinkedIn and Twitter, and an introduction to marketing.

Chapter 4, Does a Technical Entrepreneur Really Need a Business Plan?, discusses all the pros and cons of a business plan, and then tells you how to build one with all the basics, including surrounding elements such as a financial model and elevator pitch, without a huge cost or investment in time. The thought of preparing a business plan for the first time can be very intimidating. There are many "moving parts," and it's easy to get lost in the details. In reality, if you are not looking for investors, no business plan is expected by anyone. Yet I would suggest that creating one is still a valuable exercise since you need the plan as the blueprint for your company, team communication, and progress metrics, unless your management style makes this a waste of time.

Chapter 5, When and How Do You Find Funding for a Technical Business?, explores the most common and most productive approaches to get your startup moving forward. Of course, every approach has pros and cons. For example, with any outside investment, you give up some ownership and control, and with bootstrapping, your growth curve will likely be longer and more organic.

Money to build the business is the number one challenge for most startups. Don't believe the urban myth that you can sketch your idea on a napkin and professional investors will throw money at you. In reality, only 3 out of 100 companies who apply are successful with Angels, and the success rate with VCs is even lower. A large percentage of startups never apply to either.

If you are new to the entrepreneurial world of startups, you are likely confused by the terminology of seed-stage, lean startups, micro-VCs, and Super Angels. Don't be embarrassed since even professional investors are often confused these days by the new terms as well as old terms used with new meanings. In any case, this chapter looks at the options you really have and how to make them happen.

Chapter 6, After the Funding, How Do You Survive the Execution Risks?, covers details about patents and other intellectual property. A large portion of every startup's competitive advantage and potential value to investors is the size of your intellectual property portfolio. When someone says Intellectual Property (IP), most entrepreneurs think only of patents. In reality, patents are only one of many items that should be in your IP portfolio. This chapter explores the range of these items, helps readers understand the pros and cons of each, discusses cost issues, as well as value to investors, founders, and customers.

Chapter 7, Are You Ready for All the Leadership and Team Challenges?, explores the fact that creating and building a business is not a one-man show, even though it usually springs from the mind and determination of one person—committees don't start successful businesses. But turning an idea to a business success requires many people to work together effectively, and that requires entrepreneurial leadership.

Leadership is not a skill one is born with, but it can be learned and honed from experience and failures. Startups also require many different leadership skills, from technical to financial, so an entrepreneur needs to understand how to build the right team, work will all kinds of people, and provide communication and motivation to all.

Chapter 8, Do You Understand How Social Media is Changing the Business Landscape?, tells a new entrepreneur where and how to start using social media, as well as how to measure the impact, and make the required trade-offs between cost and value received.

Everyone is talking about how social media can help you jumpstart your business at no cost, and experts are springing up on all sides to help you do it at a high cost. So who do you believe, and what are the keys to success for any startup?

If your startup can't be bothered with social media or has no plan to take advantage of it, then you are definitely at risk these days with the new generation of customers. But simply jumping in is not enough. Before you start spending money and time being a user, you need to understand how it can help you and your business.

Chapter 9, If You Build It, Will They Find You, and Will They Use It?, focuses on the requirement for marketing in general, as well as the new rules required by social media and the overload of information bombarding potential customers via the Internet and traditional marketing sources.

Marketing is everything these days. You can have the best technology, but if customers don't know you exist or they don't know how your technology solves a real problem for them, your startup will fail. Yet I see many entrepreneurs that focus on the basics of marketing too little and too late.

Chapter 10, Can You Build the Relationships Needed to Succeed in Business?, explores the fine line between competitors and partners, and provides guidance on where, when, and how to find the right partners for growth and strength, without unduly risking your position with competitors.

New entrepreneurs are usually so focused on selling more of their branded product or service to their own customer base (organic growth) that they don't consider the more indirect methods (non-organic growth) of increasing revenue and market share. Non-organic growth would include OEM relationships, finding strategic partners, "coopetition," as well as acquisitions.

In all cases, the challenge is the same, of finding people that you can work with and enjoy in the business relationship. The relationship has to have trust, communication, and respect in order to work. Otherwise, like a marriage, it will be doomed to constant conflict, second guessing, and unhappiness.

Who this book is for

This book is targeted to young and first-time entrepreneurs who have a technical background and training, a great idea for an enterprise software product, but don't have experience or training in setting up a business, marketing a product, and managing the finances required.

Conventions

In this book, you will find a number of styles of text that distinguish between different kinds of information. Here are some examples of these styles and an explanation of their meaning.

New terms and **important words** are shown in bold. Words that you see on the screen, in menus or dialog boxes for example, appear in the text like this: "Clicking the **Next** button moves you to the next screen."

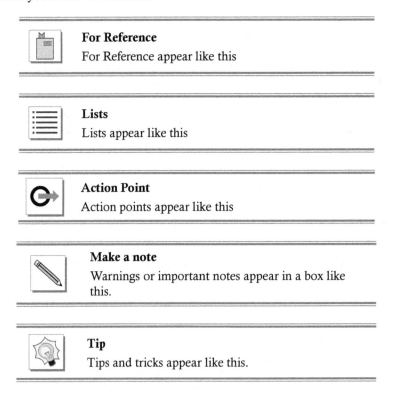

For Reference

For Reference appear like this

Lists

Lists appear like this

Action Point

Action points appear like this

Make a note

Warnings or important notes appear in a box like this.

Tip

Tips and tricks appear like this.

Reader feedback

Feedback from our readers is always welcome. Let us know what you think about this book—what you liked or may have disliked. Reader feedback is important for us to develop titles that you really get the most out of.

To send us general feedback, simply send an e-mail to `feedback@impacktpub.com`, and mention the book title via the subject of your message.

If there is a book that you need and would like to see us publish, please send us a note via the **Submit Idea** form on `https://www.impacktpub.com/#!/bookidea`.

Piracy

Piracy of copyright material on the Internet is an ongoing problem across all media. At Impackt, we take the protection of our copyright and licenses very seriously. If you come across any illegal copies of our works, in any form, on the Internet, please provide us with the location address or website name immediately so that we can pursue a remedy.

Please contact us at `copyright@impacktpub.com` with a link to the suspected pirated material.

We appreciate your help in protecting our authors, and our ability to bring you valuable content.

Do You Have What It Takes to be an Entrepreneur?

We already know that you are a technical superstar, with a passion for creating an innovative product that will be a paradigm shift in the technology you love. This is a necessary capability, but not a sufficient one, to be an entrepreneur. According to Wikipedia, entrepreneurs are people who create new and innovative businesses. Innovative products do not necessarily lead to innovative businesses. However, obviously, people who can do both are the most likely to be successful and happy.

Most experts agree that creating an innovative business is at least equal in difficulty to creating an innovative product or service. It requires a unique set of skills, personal attributes, and a mindset that many people don't have or don't choose to learn. In fact, just like many don't choose to build and nurture their technical skills, you might not want to develop the business and personal attributes associated with entrepreneurs.

Technical entrepreneurs often believe that great products will ultimately lead to a successful company, and good business skills only accelerate this process. In fact, there are tradeoffs involved between a focus on the technical aspects and a focus on the business aspects. The best entrepreneurs are able to find the right balance—technical perfectionism will kill you, just like minimal focus on building the business will kill you, even with a strong product.

Let's take a look at the personal attributes that differentiate non-entrepreneurs from the great ones, and help you achieve that balance!

Personality traits of great technical entrepreneurs

A while back, when a technical startup founder mentioned to me that he wasn't sure he had the personality to be an entrepreneur, I realized how important this insight was. My first thought is that if you are more annoyed than energized by expert advice, team suggestions, and customer input, then you should probably avoid this line of work.

Actually, it's more complicated than that, but that's a good start. After working with entrepreneurs for more than a decade, I have developed a good "radar" to quickly recognize the mentalities that will likely pass the test of investors, employees, and customers.

However, it's easier for me to look in from the outside than it is for you to look out. So, here is a list of mentality characteristics, which I believe are absolutely necessary for you to see in yourself as an entrepreneur. On the other hand, if any of these characteristics cause you stress and discomfort, you probably won't be happy in the role of an entrepreneur:

> ➤ **You enjoy being the visionary leader**: Being able to envision what the business and industry will be like in years to come is a skill that can guarantee that you will be around for the long haul. What makes most success stories in business is not totally reinventing the wheel, but leading the charge to make the current wheel better or applying the existing wheel to a new market opportunity.

> ➤ **Sometimes you are creative, sometimes logical**: A successful entrepreneur has to come up with innovative ideas but also turn them into a value-creating profitable business. This requires a good amount of both left-brain and right-brain activities, with enough common sense to find the balance.

> ➤ **Risk energizes you**: To really enjoy the ride in the world of entrepreneurship, you need to be able to sustain yourself outside of your comfort zone and have a sense of adventure. Startups never go as you anticipated. This is why you need to be ready to go "off the script" and improvise, and enjoy the thrill of victory when it works.

> ➤ **Actively seek others' input**: The quicker you learn not to take it personally (and it's hard when it's your business and your creation), the more successful you will be. You will always come across people who will criticize you, no matter how great or valuable your product or service may be.

> ➤ **Motivated yet patient**: When you start a business, you need to have the frame of mind that this is what you want to do for the foreseeable future or at least until your current goals are achieved. Most people want financial freedom, but they want results immediately, and this is not the case 99 percent of the time. Most successful entrepreneurs understand that success does not come overnight; it takes years.

> ➤ **Jack of all trades**: When running a business, you'll be doing a little bit of everything. You have to be good but not an expert at everything you do, and you have to know when to be flexible and when to ask for help. If you want to specialize in just one thing, then running a business might not be for you.

If you don't fit into everyone's personal view of an entrepreneur's mentality, don't be totally discouraged, and don't worry about someone else's view. Winning businesses have been started by people of every type. Yet, overall, the facts are that about two-thirds of startups fail as a business (which means they are not sustainable financially), so think hard before you ignore warning signs.

I'm convinced that if entrepreneurs spent half as much time evaluating themselves and what makes them happy, as they do writing business plans and visiting attorneys and accountants, they would be winners far more often.

Finally, don't forget that the most important thing is to always do something that you enjoy. Life is too short to be going to work every day unhappy. Beyond that, I believe success is a state of mind derived from confidence, self-esteem, and what you really want in life. How strongly do you really want to manage a startup versus continuing to build great products for someone else to manage and sell?

Are all technical entrepreneurs natural-born?

Some people assert that technical entrepreneurs with the personal attributes discussed earlier have to be "natural-born," and you either are one or you aren't. I concede that good, natural-born entrepreneurs do exist, but more often, I tend to agree with Peter Drucker, who said "It's not magic, it's not mysterious, and it has nothing to do with genes. It's a discipline, and like any discipline, it can be learned."

On the natural-born side, some entrepreneurs seem to have a strong vision and the ability to inspirationally lead others based on their background, upbringing, and early experiences. It is this vision that is the beacon to drive the right people behavior, leading to the success of the business. If you don't have a vision in your heart or if you don't have the strength to inspire people, entrepreneurship is probably the wrong road for you.

If you feel you do have the right characteristics, you can still benefit from learning some skills and disciplines that improve the success and the impact of every technical entrepreneur. Here are some of the key ones, assembled from an old interview with Herb Kelleher (http://searchcio.techtarget.com/news/924412/Entrepreneurs-Born-or-made-A-conversation-with-Herb-Kelleher-of-Southwest-Airlines) of Southwest Airlines and other executives:

> **Ability to set priorities and focus on goals**: Many people allow themselves to be driven by the crisis of the moment. Personal discipline is the key word here. Set yourself some priorities and goals, and live by them.

> **Ability to identify important issues**: Some people call this common sense; others call it 'street smarts.' In the normal startup environment, there are multiple forces that compete for your attention every day, and you need to learn to delegate or ignore many. It relates back to experience and knowledge, more than genes.

> **Conviction to be a passionate advocate**: When you believe in something enough to turn your passion into action, you have become an advocate. This power and voice is then used to persuade others to make the correct decision. An effective advocate requires conviction, usually acquired during related first-hand experience or training.

> **Broad knowledge and experience**: Experience allows one to tackle challenges with confidence, in a given area. Broad knowledge facilitates the same success in other business areas. Entrepreneurs need this, because their challenges are across the spectrum, from technical to legal, operational, financial, and organizational.

➤ **Active listening skills**: Above all, the ability to listen and understand the real meaning of what people are saying (and not saying) is paramount, because the most important information never arrives in reports or via e-mails. Some people pick this up from experience, and others find classroom courses most helpful in setting the focus. The best experience is getting outside the building and talking to real customers.

➤ **Sound judgment**: I don't think anyone is born with sound judgment; it has to be learned but can be started at a very early age. Every entrepreneur must have the capacity to assess situations or circumstances shrewdly and to draw proper conclusions.

➤ **Pleasant skepticism**: Skepticism is not doubting but applying reason and critical thinking to determine validity. It's the process of searching for a supportable conclusion opposed to justifying a preconceived conclusion. It is a learned skill.

All these characteristics revolve around the larger theme of team building. In short, to succeed, the entrepreneur must see and articulate a vision in order to attract and motivate a team and then be able to identify the key issues, challenge the views held within the team, and make judgments from among the varying perspectives in the team.

Every technical entrepreneur enters the game with a unique combination of genes and skills. If the things mentioned here feel natural to you and if you are young at heart (optimistic and fun loving) and have a healthy curiosity and zest for life, the entrepreneurial world may have a place for you too. Give it a try. If you start having fun, you probably have what it takes.

Every entrepreneur needs multiple intelligences

Whether natural-born or learned, the best technical entrepreneurs have a range of skills and insights across many fronts, from business to technical to interpersonal. I used to call this range of insights 'street smarts', but recently, I found a better explanation called multiple intelligences. Successful entrepreneurs always seem to be adept in several of these areas.

The theory of multiple intelligences was developed way back in 1983 by Dr. Howard Gardner (http://www.amazon.com/Multiple-Intelligences-Theory-Practice-Reader/dp/046501822X), at Harvard University. He suggests that the traditional notion of intelligence, called the Intelligent Quotient (IQ), is far too limited. Instead, he now accepts at least eight different intelligences that cover a broad range of human potential. These include the following:

➤ **Linguistic intelligence (word smart)**: Linguistic intelligence is the ability to think in words and use language to express complex meanings. Linguistic intelligence is the most widely shared human competence, most evident in poets and novelists. It is also evident in entrepreneurs writing good business plans and convincing investors.

➤ **Interpersonal intelligence (people smart)**: Interpersonal intelligence is the ability to understand and interact effectively with others. It involves effective verbal and nonverbal communication, sensitivity to moods and temperaments, and the ability to understand multiple perspectives. Entrepreneurs, particularly, need interpersonal intelligence.

➤ **Intrapersonal intelligence (self-smart)**: Intrapersonal intelligence is the capacity to understand oneself and to use such knowledge in planning and strategy. Intrapersonal intelligence involves not only an appreciation of the self, but also of the human condition. It is evident in psychologists, spiritual leaders, and business leaders.

➤ **Bodily kinesthetic intelligence (body smart)**: Bodily kinesthetic intelligence is the capacity to manipulate objects and use a variety of physical skills. This intelligence also involves a sense of timing and the perfection of skills through mind–body union. Inventors and people who provide mechanical products need this intelligence.

➤ **Logical-mathematical intelligence (number/reasoning smart)**: Logical-mathematical intelligence is the ability to calculate, quantify, and think logically. This intelligence is usually well developed in mathematicians, technologists, and computer programmers, and it is usually associated with traditional IQ.

➤ **Naturalist intelligence (nature smart)**: Naturalist intelligence designates the human ability to discriminate among living things as well as sensitivity to other features of the natural world. I believe that good entrepreneurs use this to discriminate among consumer needs and pick the most marketable products to offer.

➤ **Musical intelligence (musical smart)**: Musical intelligence is the capacity to discern pitch, rhythm, timbre, and tone. This intelligence enables us to recognize, create, reproduce, and reflect on music interests and needs, as demonstrated by composers, conductors, musicians, vocalists, and sensitive listeners. There is a known correlation between engineers, software developers, and those with strong musical smarts.

➤ **Spatial intelligence (picture smart)**: Spatial intelligence is the ability to think in three dimensions. Core capacities include mental imagery, spatial reasoning, graphic and artistic skills, and an active imagination. Sailors, pilots, sculptors, painters, and architects all exhibit spatial intelligence. It's easy to see how this is important to entrepreneurs who design and build physical products (nonsoftware).

Robert L Schwarz once said, "The entrepreneur is essentially a visualizer and an actualizer. He can visualize something, and when he visualizes it, he sees exactly how to make it happen." This is a combination of intelligences many people don't have. If you have it, flaunt it and enjoy your foray into the entrepreneurial lifestyle.

Technical entrepreneurs have to love learning more than money

Over the years, I've had the privilege of working with some of the best technical entrepreneurs in Silicon Valley and elsewhere. On the average, the entrepreneurs I know are living on Ramen noodles. However, one thing they all seem to have in common is a love for learning and change. They rush in with a passion to better the world, and money is just an indication of their progress.

The successful ones then invest their time and money in furthering their knowledge base. I'm not talking about academic classes, because at best, these only teach you how to learn. In these days of rapid change, I believe that most of the facts that college students learn as a sophomore are obsolete before they exit their senior year.

Learning should be viewed as an ongoing part of everything you do and as one of the most important things. It's an unfortunate artifact of our educational system that young people spend a dozen years focused more on memorizing facts than the learning process and then thinking that they will have all they need to know for the rest of their lives by the time they graduate.

In business, as in most other disciplines, there are practical steps towards learning what you need for the next stage of your company and your life. These include the following:

> **Networking with people who know**: A question I sometimes get from startup founders is, "What do I talk to these guys about?" I say you can't learn much if you are doing all the talking. Just ask investors what they look for in successful companies. I've never known any successful entrepreneurs or investors who were not happy to share their insights.

> **Read entrepreneur stories**: Most successful entrepreneurs have been written about on the Internet, in magazines, or books. Spend some time with these biographies, and soak up the insights offered and take inspiration from them. Follow-up online with social networking to make contacts, dig deeper, and maybe even line them up a mentor.

> **Adopt a mentor**: Boomers and other former executives who have "been there and done that" make great mentors. They have the time and interest in "giving back" some of what they have learned to the next generation. Gen-X executives may be too busy running their own companies to be mentors. A mentor is someone who doesn't let ego or money get in the way of helping.

> **Formal learning**: Some formal learning is always advisable, but go beyond university MBA courses to professional seminars and case studies. Formal courses work best for basics, such as a business startup course or financial accounting. Go with topics you are interested in and need now.

> **Volunteering with local organizations**: This type of work is highly valuable in any environment, including universities and professional organizations. The payback is that you can get experience for free while working on real stuff. I've done business plan judging at local universities and learned more than I contributed.

> ➤ **Just start a business**: There is no better way to learn about being entrepreneurial than starting a business. No matter how much advice and counsel you have been given, I guarantee that you will encounter new challenges daily to enhance your learning opportunities.

If you are one of those people who likes structured classes to learn and counts on spending at least 2 weeks per year in the classroom to "catch up," this is laudable, but don't try to start a business at the same time. It won't happen.

If you have decided to become a technical entrepreneur solely to make more money, you are also likely to be disappointed. It's that double challenge of learning to overcome all obstacles while still surviving on the financial front that keeps a good entrepreneur motivated to face a new day.

Technical entrepreneurs learn best from business networking

I would recommend business networking as the most effective way for a technical startup founder to find investors, advisors, and even key executive candidates. However, what if you are an introvert or new to this game and don't know where or how to start?

The answer is still the same, but I have learned over the years that there is etiquette to this process, just like there is for social networking. Here are a few of the "do's":

> ➤ **Post your profile on LinkedIn and Twitter, and join in startup discussions**: Of the 200 or so social networks that are now recognized by Wikipedia, there are other social networks, such as Orkut, Netlog, and Sina Weibo, that entrepreneurs use for networking, depending on where you are in the world. Talking to friends on Facebook probably won't help you. Reading and posting on Hacker News is popular, especially in the San Francisco Bay Area.

> ➤ **Join and actively participate in local business organizations**: Business groups such as TiE-The Indus Entrepreneurs (https://www.tie.org/) and EO-Entrepreneurs Organization (http://www.eonetwork.org/Pages/welcome.aspx) are places to meet people you can help as well as people who can help you. Remember that it helps to give a little to get something back. Another place to start is the local Chamber of Commerce.

> ➤ **Get introductions from existing business contacts**: Start with the people you know, who know your work, and would recommend you to others. It isn't always the first introduction but the friend of a friend who may be the one that pays dividends.

> ➤ **Volunteer to help out with entrepreneur activities at your local university**: All universities love and need to get help from people in the "real world" to coach and judge activities in their Entrepreneurship and MBA programs. In return, you will meet or be connected to many people who can help you.

> ➤ **Attend an investment conference**: These events are swarming with potential investors, and this is the forum where they are actively soliciting new opportunities. So, don't be shy about handing out your business card at breaks, lunch, mixers, or scheduled activities.

> ➤ **Offer to give back where you can**: Ask every potential investor and mentor how you can help them. You may be able to contribute services, provide connections, or generally support their efforts in some way. It's a great way to generate goodwill.

Join a local investment group. If you can meet the SEC "accredited investor" criteria ($1M net worth or $200K annual income), this is a great way to be seen by potential investors as peers before you need money. In addition to this, you will see how the process really works from the other side of the table—the best preparation you could have for your own approach later. In most cases, these groups don't require that you invest in others, as a condition of membership.

If all of these are obvious to you, then you are already on the right track, and you probably wouldn't consider doing any of the "don'ts":

> ➤ Don't do cold calls or e-mail blasts of your resume and business plan to potential investors. It's a waste of their time as well as yours and is an annoyance to many.

> ➤ Don't corner and barrage that heavy hitter you heard about with your life history at a social gathering.

> ➤ Don't send your unfinished business plan unsolicited to every VC or investment group you can find on the Internet just to see whether they like the concept.

> ➤ Don't hand out your business cards to everyone in the room in the hope that one will be impressed with how unique and expensive it looks.

> ➤ On LinkedIn, don't complain to everyone that you are limited to only 3,000 invitations and request them to send you an invitation to become friends. LinkedIn only allows you to send 3,000 new invites per membership. (How many friends do you need?)

Back on the positive side, I like to say, especially for us introverts, that networking is more about listening than it is about talking. Believe it or not, most successful investors have big egos and will probably remember you better if they do most of the talking at first. Nevertheless, have your 30-second pitch honed, and don't be shy about giving it. Don't forget your enthusiasm, and have fun, but remember your manners!

A technical entrepreneur must build relationships

You can't win as a technical entrepreneur working alone. You need to have business relationships with team members, investors, customers, and a myriad of other people. This doesn't mean you have to be a social butterfly to succeed or introverts need not apply.

It does mean that you need to look, listen, and participate in the business world around you and network through all available channels such as business-oriented social networks online, local business organizations, and events or conferences in your domain.

I hope all this seems obvious to you, but I still get a good number of notes from "entrepreneurs" who have been busy inventing things all their life but can't find a partner to start their first business, and others trying to find an executive, an investor, or a lawyer.

What these people need is more relationships, not more experts, more blogs, or more books. So, I thought I would explore some essentials in building and nurturing business relationships (most of these apply to personal relationships as well):

> **Build your network**: These are people of all levels who have been there and done that, which means people who know something that you need to know. See the previous section on how and where to get started. You don't need a thousand friends, but a few real ones can make all the difference.

> **Give and you will receive**: Relationships need to be two-way and can't be just all about you. If you are active in helping others with what you know, they will be much more open to help you when you need it. The more you give, the more you get in return, both literally and figuratively.

> **Work on your elevator pitch**: This is a concise, well-practiced description of your idea or your startup, delivered with conviction to start a relationship in the time it takes to ride up an elevator. It should end by asking for something to start the relationship.

> **Don't skip all business social settings**: Face time is critical, even with the current rage on social networks, phone texting, and e-mail. Studies show that the majority of communication is body language. This is usually the important part of the relationship.

> **Nominate someone as your mentor**: Build a two-way relationship with several people who can help you, and then kick it up a notch with one or more by asking them to be your mentor. Most entrepreneurs love to help others and will be honored to help you.

> **Cultivate existing allies**: These are people who already know and believe in you but might not be able to help you directly in your new endeavors. However, don't forget that each of these allies also has their own network, which can be an extension of yours if you treat them well.

> **Nurture existing relationships**: We all know someone who claims to be a "close friend" but never initiates anything. They never call, never write, and wait for you to make the first move. If you don't follow-up on a regular basis with someone, then there is no relationship, only a former acquaintance.

On the positive side, many attributes of an introvert lead to better business decisions, such as thinking before speaking, building deep relationships, and researching problems more thoroughly. Mark Zuckerberg, Facebook founder, is currently the most famous introvert entrepreneur, so don't let anyone tell you it can't be done.

One of Mark's secrets seems to have been to surround himself by extroverts such as COO Sheryl Sandberg and people who have a complementary energy. However, working alone doesn't get you very far. It takes a team to win the game of business, so take a look around you to see how you are doing so far.

Attributes to work on for entrepreneurial success

In my experience, it always helps to look at both sides of every coin. So far, we have primarily highlighted the positive attributes that an aspiring technical entrepreneur needs to look for in himself or herself and in the people around them. Now, let's focus on the other side of the coin; we need to identify the negatives for potential entrepreneurs.

First of all, people who find it a struggle to manage their own lives don't make good entrepreneurs, and they won't enjoy the challenges. Small businesses require multitasking, work prioritization, and decision-making, with no entourage of assistants and specialists. That's why Fortune 500 executives usually don't survive as startup CEOs.

In all cases, you have to learn to accept total responsibility for things that happen to your business, just like you are responsible for everything in your personal life. Maybe you are comfortable with having a spouse in control of your personal life, but couples running a business are high risk.

If you recognize yourself in the following points and don't believe you will change, you probably won't have as much fun running a startup as serial entrepreneur Sir Richard Branson always seems to be having. You don't even have to try the entrepreneur lifestyle to know whether these points are likely to be a problem for you:

- ➤ **You often feel overwhelmed and out of control**: There is always more to do than the time to do it. Usually, the stress people feel does not really come from having too much to do but from having to make decisions on what to do first and not setting reasonable targets.

- ➤ **Starting many things, but completing few**: Productivity is all about the ability to complete tasks. It requires tradeoffs and decisions to declare that something is finished. Get in the habit of finishing what you start. Perfectionists are often frustrated in startups, since nothing is ever perfect enough for them.

- ➤ **You like to defer big things until later**: If you catch yourself deferring important tasks in favor of smaller, easy things, that's a management problem. Adopt a "do it now" motto, and tackle your to-do list in order of priority.

- ➤ **Over-thinking and second-guessing**: If you spend more time thinking and worrying about a task than doing the task, then you are not managing yourself. Don't waste your precious creative energy. Finish items, and get them off your mind.

> ➤ **You get defensive at the slightest criticism**: Some people feel pain and high stress with any negative feedback or suggestions for improvement. They react quickly and emotionally with rationalizations and justifications for their actions and find active listening very difficult. You need a thick skin to be an entrepreneur.

> ➤ **Avoiding new opportunities due to fear of failure**: Real entrepreneurs look at every new opportunity as an exciting and new life experience. They are energized by the risk and learn from every failure.

> ➤ **Always counting your weaknesses**: Good business leaders never criticize themselves for their weaknesses. Smart ones recognize their undeveloped skills and higher potential, but they are confident that they can change and constantly work at it.

> ➤ **Lack of confidence and enthusiasm**: If you have a "downer" day at least once a week and can't remember the last time you were truly enthusiastic about something in your life or work, you are not ready to manage a business. Self-confidence is the key to success.

> ➤ **You like to work alone**: Every business and every relationship is a team effort. Loners tend to hide from others to be more comfortable, or because working alone gives them more control. Make an effort to network with others to stay informed and contribute, but not dominate.

> ➤ **Admit to being a control freak**: Believe it or not, many people who don't manage themselves very well are control freaks when it comes to their business and other people. Practice the art of delegating and the joy of being spontaneous.

Managing yourself effectively is the best form of preparation for managing a new business. It means you understand yourself and are likely able to read other people and understand them. This leads to a trusting relationship with your team and customers.

All entrepreneurs are survivors, never victims

People with a "victim" mentality should never be entrepreneurs until they overcome their fear. We all know that the role of starting and running a business is unpredictable and has a high risk of failure. For people with a "victim" mentality, this fear of failure alone will almost certainly make it a self-fulfilling prophecy.

I'm sure you all know someone who is the perennial victim. The problem is that most of these people aren't likely to accept your assessment, so it's hard to help them. They don't see themselves as others see them, and many simply refuse to accept the reality of the world in general.

According to an article by Karl Perera, called *Victim Mentality - You Don't Have to Suffer!* (http://www.more-selfesteem.com/victim_mentality.htm), there are many indications of a "victim" mentality in a person's thought process. Here are some key ones he mentioned, applied to the technical entrepreneur environment:

➤ *"When things don't work, I secretly believe I'm the cause":* Victims act as though each business setback is a catastrophe and create stress for themselves. These people feel more importance and ego when relating problems rather than successes.

A survivor believes that bad things are an anomaly to be brushed off or just another challenge to overcome. In fact, they look forward to the challenges and get most of their satisfaction from declaring success.

➤ *"When I talk to myself, I never have a positive discussion":* Second-guessing every decision affects mood, behavior, and happiness and is likely to cause or intensify a "victim" mentality. If you are negative, you cannot see reality. This leads to more bad decisions, confirming that you are indeed a victim.

Survivors continually relive their positives and see themselves as miracle workers. They live in the present or the future and rarely dwell on mistakes of the past. They have faith in themselves and life as a whole.

➤ *"When others put me down, I'm wounded to the soul":* Negative comments from others are devastating to a victim. Offensive behavior towards you actually says more about the other person. However, if you have a negative mentality, you will just take what they say or do at face value and believe that you deserve to be the victim.

The survivor always stands up and fights negative comments, and usually turns the blame back on the deliverer. They are quick to counter with all their positives. They build boundaries around negative or toxic people and avoid them at all costs.

➤ *"I believe in fate, even though it's unfair":* If you succumb to fate, then you think you are responsible for all the bad things that happen to your business. The victim feels that he or she has been treated unfairly but is trapped. There seems to be no way out.

Survivors believe that they can make things happen rather than let things happen to them. They accept random turns in their life as new opportunities rather than unfair punishment.

➤ *"Everyone is punished for a reason":* Religious beliefs can have a positive or negative effect on your life. If you believe in a supreme being who is responsible for everything, it's easy to believe that your pain and misery is punishment for something you did wrong.

Survivors obviously take it the other way. They enjoy a personal relationship with the supreme being of their understanding and feel gratitude for everything positive in their life. They may ask their supreme being for help but rely on themselves for results.

This "victim" mentality is not a good thing under any circumstances, but it's particularly lethal when applied to an entrepreneur. If you would like to be an entrepreneur, remember that you don't have to be a victim. Take a good look in the mirror. Truly, the only one who makes you feel like one is the same person who can make you a survivor—you!

Test the startup lifestyle before jumping into it

A *lifestyle entrepreneur* is an individual who creates a business with the purpose of altering their personal lifestyle and not for the sole purpose of making profits. A lifestyle entrepreneur focuses more on the life rewards provided to people who enjoy and have a passion for what they are doing. By definition, a lifestyle entrepreneur truly enjoys the startup lifestyle.

Until the recent recession, market research (`http://ecopreneurist. com/2008/08/14/operating-a-small-sustainable-business-resources- for-ecopreneurs/`) indicated that as many as 90 percent of the roughly 20 million American small-business owners were motivated more by lifestyle than growth and money. Since 2008, the desire for profits has trumped passion in 54 percent of new startups according to a more recent study (`http://www.symantec.com/about/news/ release/article.jsp?prid=20120613_01`). It seems that everyone wants to make a quick buck these days.

Being called a technical entrepreneur should be a compliment, not an insult. The term applies to anyone who places passion before profit and intends to combine personal interests and talent with the ability to earn a living. This usually means not taking money from equity investors, as investors want fast growth, high profits, and a public offering or sale strategy to allow investments to be recouped.

Of course, even lifestyle entrepreneurs want to be happy and want their business to be successful. According to William R. Cobb and M. L. Johnson, in their book, *Business Alchemy: Turning Ideas Into Gold*, these different success expectations are what separate a lifestyle entrepreneur from a growth entrepreneur:

> ➤ **The owner is the only one "in charge"**: Every lifestyle entrepreneur starts their business to be their own boss and follow their passion, so they don't even think about having investors, a board of directors, or going public. If you think corporate bosses are tough, wait till you start spending investor money or try satisfying Wall Street and stockholders.

> ➤ **Insist on being engaged at the transaction level**: If you are living your passion, you want to interact with customers and "touch and feel" the product every day. Growth entrepreneurs find that this fun world quickly changes to managing personnel problems, tuning organizational structures, and dealing with testy investors.

➤ **The income generated is part of the owner's personal income**: The legal structure of these startups is usually a sole proprietorship, a **Limited Liability Corporation** (**LLC**), or a subchapter "S" Corporation. Under all of these, net income flows easily into your personal income. Corporate versus personal growth really becomes a lifestyle decision.

➤ **Startup funding comes from personal savings and family**: There is no free money from any source. Nonequity funding has to come from personal sources, government grants, or bank loans. This doesn't dilute the owner's equity, but it might well limit you to organic growth versus international rollouts and acquisition options. Grants have their own price in time and effort for complex applications.

➤ **Business model to maintain the lifestyle is the primary driver**: The lifestyle entrepreneur chooses a business model to make a long-term, sustainable, and viable living, working in a field where they have a particular interest, passion, and talent. They operate the business to sustain a minimal level of cash flow necessary to support the lifestyle.

➤ **Maximizes the owner's personal tax privileges**: This means that owners can look for every opportunity to get a personal tax advantage from the business, such as charging vehicle operating costs to the business, renting facilities from themselves, or managing business and personal travel.

➤ **Enjoy being visible and active in the local community**: Lifestyle business owners usually benefit and enjoy being a part of the local Chamber of Commerce, Rotary, and other civic organizations. These can become part of balancing your lifestyle rather than part of the stress of business-driven networking.

➤ **No exit planned until retirement**: A lifestyle business becomes an integral part of an entrepreneur's identity and their life. If, and when, the time should come to "exit" from the business, they will often seek to transfer it to a family member or simply close it down.

In my view, lifestyle entrepreneurship should be growing in popularity rather than shrinking, as technology provides startups with the cheap digital platforms needed to reach a large global market. Also, more women have been jumping into entrepreneurship, and they have long wanted to make their business and personal lives and aspirations work more in harmony.

Younger Gen-Y entrepreneurs also tend to be more passionate, idealistic, and not driven by money, so I would expect to see them trend up in lifestyle entrepreneurship. I'm told that Mark Zuckerberg of Facebook started out as a lifestyle entrepreneur. Obviously, he has now *graduated* to corporate executive status in a large public company. That's a totally different role, about as far away from the entrepreneur lifestyle as you can get. Except for the money, I suspect he liked the previous role better. What do you think?

Missteps to avoid for aspiring technical entrepreneurs

Many people, especially those who have spent years struggling up the corporate ladder, dream of jumping ship as a technical professional and becoming an entrepreneur. However, every job move is fraught with risk, and the move from technical employee to entrepreneur is on the high end of the risk curve. This is a big jump, especially in an unstable economy, so do your homework first on this one.

According to an article in the Harvard Business Review, *Five Ways to Bungle a Job Change*, there are at least five common missteps that professionals make when moving to a new job. I will assert that each of these has a comparable relevance for those of you contemplating leaving a company employee role to create or join an entrepreneurial startup. They are as follows:

> ➤ **Not doing enough research**: When moving to a new company, you need to ask questions about expectations, financial stability, cultural fit, and role responsibilities. All of these apply directly to starting your own company. Test your "dream" startup plans on some experienced entrepreneurs to get a reality check before you leave your current job.

> ➤ **Leaving for money**: Remember, the grass always look greener on the other side of the fence. Making more money in the short term is unlikely as an entrepreneur. In fact, most startup founders pay themselves no salary for the first year or two, and investor money is hard to find. I tell new entrepreneurs not to quit their "day job" until they have real revenue.

> ➤ **Going "from" rather than "to"**: If you are desperate to get out, you may just be lurching into entrepreneurship, only to find it more stressful and unsatisfying. People who feel competent but unsatisfied or bored in their current job make better entrepreneurs than people who feel overworked, underappreciated, and over stressed.

> ➤ **Over-estimating yourself**: Search consultants say that many job seekers have an unrealistic view of their skills, prospects, and culpability. If you have had problems with several companies, you may be part of the problem. This part will be amplified in any startup, as you are now the company, so the blame stops with you.

> ➤ **Thinking short term**: Moving from an employee to an entrepreneur is a lifestyle change as well as a career change. Don't make the misstep of assuming it is a short-term move to riches or an escape from a problem. Starting a business is hard work, requires a lot of learning, and only pays off in the long term.

These missteps are obviously interdependent. When people overvalue themselves, they are prone to stress from job performance feedback and dissatisfaction with compensation. This leads them to jump, without real consideration of the fit and opportunity, into the entrepreneurial world, where they could be even unhappier.

Every employee needs to evaluate these challenges, as the average baby boomer will have switched jobs 10 times, according to the U.S. Bureau of Labor Statistics. The days are gone when we commit early in life to a lifetime career with one company or a lifetime of entrepreneurship. The business landscape is changing rapidly these days, so we need to be willing to change as well.

A good question to ask before finalizing a change is, "What if I'm wrong?" Be ready to cut your losses and move on. Jumping repeatedly to another bad situation is not the answer. In every case, take a hard look at your real strengths and weaknesses. Be willing to listen to an advisor or mentor on how others perceive you and be willing to work on those weaknesses. In later sections of this book, you will also find more insights on assessing and managing risks.

The most important element is to understand for yourself what elements of a job role are the most satisfying to you and what constitutes a healthy work-life balance for you. You spend most of your adult life at work. Life is too short to let career missteps make it unhappy.

Customers and investors like ideas, but measure you on their execution

Your technical idea and vision may be great, but after the idea, it's all about execution. I often hear from investors that a great idea is necessary but not sufficient. The most important thing is a proven team led by an experienced entrepreneur, which means one who has built a startup before and has experience with the execution process in this domain.

I talked earlier about the best personality traits for a good entrepreneur, but I've never talked about the importance of the process. Yes, even entrepreneurs need to follow a disciplined execution process if they want to maximize their probability for success.

Even though in his book, *Awesomely Simple*, John Spence was talking about larger organizations, I think his concepts adapt equally well to a startup. Here is my adaptation of the key steps to ensure a winning execution in any business:

> ➤ **Create a vision and instill values**: The vision may be yours alone, but the communication has to include your team, potential investors, and customers. For most people, the communication is the hard part—written, verbal, over and over again.

> ➤ **Define a focused strategy**: Limit the focus to a few critical areas that will yield the highest possible return. If your strategy has more than five elements, it's not focused. Not everything can be a priority. Do not spend any time on unimportant goals.

> ➤ **Get stakeholders' commitment**: People who are not committed cannot be held accountable for delivering ambitious results. The guiding coalition must demonstrate 100 percent unity, or there will be a mutiny. The worst case is a silent mutiny.

> **Align the objectives of principals**: I have seen startups implode when principals were pitted against each other on mutually exclusive objectives, such as adding more technology versus keeping costs down. Quantify time and cost goals early, make sure everyone agrees, and measure results regularly to verify alignment.

> **Every process needs a system**: Once a process is complete and working successfully, it's time to define it formally. Then, use only well thought out systems, manual or automated, to ensure repeatable success of every key process. The most basic element of every startup system is a written, agreed, and measurable business plan or Business Model Canvas (`http://en.wikipedia.org/wiki/Business_Model_Canvas`).

> **Manage priorities**: You must relentlessly communicate the current priorities to all constituents and keep the total to a manageable number. One of the biggest mistakes I see in startups is a new and larger set of priorities every week, causing the team to lose momentum and commitment.

> **Provide team support and training**: People are your most valuable asset, so start with the right ones and make sure they have the tools and training to deliver the results you are asking for. Don't assume they know everything you know or can learn as fast as you do.

> **Assign and orchestrate actions**: Leaders must make sure that all team members are taking the right actions (and behaviors) on a daily basis to deliver long-term performance. Even after all the previous steps, great leaders can't afford to merely be observers. Lead by action.

> **Measure, adapt, and innovate**: Things change in a startup, and things will go wrong. You won't notice if you don't measure. Measure four or five key drivers, not 20 or 30 things. Motivate everyone with an insatiable curiosity to make things 1 percent better every day (kaizen).

> **Reward and punish**: What gets measured and rewarded, gets done. Be exceedingly generous with praise, celebration, recognition, small rewards, and sometimes, money. Set high standards for performance, and use the three Ts (train, transfer, or terminate) to deal with people unable to effectively execute the plan.

I'm not suggesting that your task execution will be perfect if you follow these steps precisely. There are far too many pitfalls and risks in a startup to imply that they can all be avoided. However, if you adopt this blueprint, it's much less likely that when things get tough, your investors will be thinking of an alternate meaning for the term "execution."

Succeeding as a technical entrepreneur is really about you

Being a good technical entrepreneur is all about you, not your technology. If you expect to succeed in the thrill-a-minute, rollercoaster ride of a startup, let me assure you it takes more than a good technical idea, a rich uncle, and luck. In fact, the idea is often the least important part of the equation. Most investors tell me that they look at the people first, then at the business plan, and only then at the idea.

If you want some specific tips to beat the odds, take a look at the following concepts adapted from Richard C. Levy's book, *The Complete Idiot's Guide to Cashing in On Your Inventions* (http://www.amazon.com/Complete-Idiots-Guide-Cashing-Inventions/dp/0028642201). He was talking about inventions, but I think his concepts apply perfectly to any technical entrepreneur starting a business:

- ➤ **Don't take yourself too seriously**: Don't take your idea too seriously. The world will probably survive without your idea. You may need it to survive, but no one else does. However, there is no excuse not to love and laugh at what you are doing. I'm convinced that people who love their work are more innovative as well as happier.

- ➤ **The race is not always for the swift, but for those who keep running**: It's a mistake to think anything is made overnight other than baked goods and newspapers. You win some, you lose some, and some are rained out, but always suit up for the game and stick with it. It's not speed that separates winners from losers; it's perseverance.

- ➤ **You can't do it all by yourself**: Entrepreneurial success is almost always the result of unselfish, highly talented, and creative partners and associates willing to face the frustrations, rejections, and seemingly open-ended time frames inherent to any business startup with you.

- ➤ **Keep your ego under control**: Creative and inventive people, according to profile, hate to be rejected or criticized for any reason. An out-of-control ego kills more opportunities than anything else. While entrepreneurs need a healthy ego for body armor, it can quickly get out of hand and become arrogance if not tempered.

- ➤ **You will always miss 100 percent of the shots you don't take**: Don't be afraid to make mistakes. If you don't put forth the effort, you won't fail, but you won't succeed either. Inaction will keep opportunities from coming your way.

- ➤ **Don't start a company just for the financial rewards**: We all want to make money. That's only natural. However, you should be motivated by the opportunity to "make meaning" as well. People who do things just for the money usually come up shortchanged.

- ➤ **Be prepared for criticism**: Not every idea or decision works. For every action, there is always someone who will challenge and second-guess you. Odds are, you'll encounter far more criticism than acceptance. Don't be defensive, learn from your mistakes, and don't blame someone else.

- ➤ **Learn to take rejection**: Don't be turned off by the word "No," because you'll hear it often. Rejection can be positive if it's turned into constructive growth. My experience is that ideas get better the more they are presented. "No" means "not yet."

- ➤ **Believe in yourself**: One of the first steps toward success is learning to detect and follow that gleam of light, which Emerson says flashes across the mind from within. It's critical that you learn to abide by your own spontaneous impression. Allow nothing to affect the integrity of your mind.

> ➤ **Sell yourself before you sell your ideas**: Be concerned about how you are perceived. You may be capable of dreaming up ideas, but if you cannot command the respect and attention of associates and investors, your proposal will never get off the mark, and you may not be invited back for an encore.

As with all the other "principles of success" guidance I have seen, you should take these tenets with a grain of salt. Yet, I'm betting that every technical entrepreneur out there can relate to these principles and practices, and most of the long aspiring and unhappy entrepreneurs have broken one or more of them. Don't be afraid to learn from your mistakes, forget the past, and go for the trophy anyway.

Summary

The purpose of this chapter has been to give you an overall perspective on the personal attributes and traits that are the key to the success of every technical entrepreneur. I'm certainly not trying to characterize any of them as "good" or "bad" in general—that's for you to decide.

Before you start down a long hard road, it's worthwhile to do the introspection, based on what you have read so far, to see whether you already have the entrepreneur mindset or have the interest and desire to acquire it. In my experience, the people who don't have it and don't want to change, probably won't be happy in the role of an entrepreneur. If you are not happy in the role, you probably won't do the job well, and you will have a tough time succeeding.

I want you to succeed and to have fun doing it. In that context, all the following chapters will focus on the specifics of doing it right, avoiding the mistakes that many others before you have made, and helping you make the right decisions.

The first of these decisions is to pick the right dream to start a business from. In the next chapter, I will outline all the ways that you need to take a hard look at your idea before assuming that everyone will love it as much as you and many customers are willing and able to buy your solution. Not every good idea is a good business.

Every technical entrepreneur I know has a wealth of good ideas. This is all about picking the right one for your first step into the business world. Enjoy!

>2

Does Your Dream Idea Have the Potential to be a Business?

Now that you understand the mindset and best attributes of a technical entrepreneur, you need to look just as hard at the attributes of your technical product or service before you assume it's a great entrepreneurial opportunity. In other words, just because you love it and can build it, that doesn't mean that everyone will love it and buy it.

It's better to take a hard look at the idea *before* you have spent your life savings (and the hard-earned money of others), rather than later. These "reality checks" may seem like common sense, and they are, but I've seen too many technical entrepreneurs suffer the painful consequences of following their passion and ignoring reality.

Of course, passion is what real technical entrepreneurs live for, and they sometimes assume it can take them anywhere they want to go. However, those who continually temper their passion with reality principles and adjust their course are much more likely to see success in getting there. Like the line from a country song, "If you don't know where you're going, you might end up somewhere else."

How to perform a reality check of your opportunity

For example, I have a certain technical friend who called me a while back, all excited about his latest vision to solve a pet peeve of every computer and Internet user. "What if you could enter your sign-on password just once when powering on your system, and it was able to remember and supply that password to all your applications without user intervention? I'm going to write the software to offer this service!"

I'm sure you all realize that there could be quite a distance between a great idea and a great implementation, and an even greater distance to a great startup. However, many people don't have a clue on how to bridge the gap. So, trying carefully not to rain on his parade, I suggested that my friend complete the following analysis as due diligence on the idea before quitting his day job to create and roll out the solution:

> **Are you ready for the startup lifestyle?** We covered this in *Chapter 1, Do You Have What It Takes to be an Entrepreneur?*, but it's still the number one reality check. If you are currently an employee of another company, then starting your own company as an entrepreneur is a big lifestyle change. Starting a business is hard work, requires a lot of determination and learning, and only pays off in the long term. Take an honest look at yourself before leaping.

> **Are there customers with real pain and money?** Your own conviction that if you love the idea then everyone will love the solution is necessary but not sufficient. Customers may "like" a product, but will generally only pay for things they "need," physically or emotionally. Or maybe, the people who really need the product don't have any money. Talk to experts in this domain (IT consultants or application designers), and listen for hidden requirements and challenges. Ask yourself questions like the following:

>> What value do we deliver to the customer?

>> Which one of our customers' problems are we helping to solve?

>> What bundles of products and services are we offering to each customer segment?

>> Which customer needs are we satisfying?

>> Do you actually understand your customer and which segment it appeals to?

>> Who are we creating value for?

>> Who are our most important customers?

> **Is the market opportunity large and growing?** Again, don't trust your own judgment and passion on this one. Look for market analysis data from a "credible unbiased third party"—which means a nationally-known market research firm such as Gartner, Forrester, IDC, industry trade organizations, or many others.

> **Is this a crowded space already?** Use Google or one of the many other search engines to search for existing solutions to this problem. A search argument such as "single sign-on, multiple applications" might be the place to start. If you find ten competitors who already have this offering, it's probably not worth going any further.

> **Does your solution have hidden dependencies or costs?** Many products fail because of "dependencies" and hidden costs. For example, automobile engines that burn hydrogen are easy and great for the environment, but getting service stations around the world and new safety legislation takes decades. Make sure you understand all the potential costs, sales channels, marketing requirements, and cultural issues.

> **Do you have intellectual property to defend against competitors?** Your solution has probably not been commercialized yet, but a patent may have been submitted by someone else, putting your idea in jeopardy. Another series of searches on Google Patents, the US Patent Office site, and "Free Patents Online" is in order at this point. Of course, you could pay a Patent Attorney a few thousand dollars to do the same search", but this is an additional cost.

> **Can you build a motivated and qualified team?** It's hard to build a business as the lone ranger. You need to assemble, motivate, and manage a team—development, sales, partners, and customers. Startups are tough on even the most dedicated and passionate founders—some founders will likely fail and be unhappy. Headstrong introverts probably won't do well here.

> **Have you looked realistically at the costs?** Passionate entrepreneurs tend to develop rose-colored plans, overestimating early sales and underestimating costs. To convert your passion into a tangible business value, write a business plan that makes financial sense for the needs and future goals of your startup, and have it checked by an expert.

> **Do you have stamina and skills?** As a startup founder, remember that the buck always stops with you. There is no room for the blame game. Contributing factors aside, most startups fail because they just give up, not because they run out of money or time. Focus on building personal staying power, and maximize learning and improvements. If you have had problems with several companies in the past, you may be part of the problem.

> **Are you going "from" rather than "to"?** If you are desperate to get out of an existing role, you may just be lurching into entrepreneurship, only to find it more stressful and unsatisfying. People who feel competent but unsatisfied or bored in their current job make better entrepreneurs than people who feel overworked, underappreciated, and overstressed. Remember, the grass always looks greener on the other side of the fence. I tell new entrepreneurs not to quit their day job until they have real revenue from the startup.

From bitter experience, every experienced entrepreneur I know could add additional "idea due diligence" items, which I've neglected to mention. By the way, if team experience and resources are the only limitation, it is better to give your idea away to a qualified group rather than selfishly sit on it, or run it and yourself into the ground trying to make it work. Nobody wins with that approach.

In case you are wondering what happened to this single sign-on idea, try the search I suggested and you will find a dozen sites that already claim this capability. There is even a Wikipedia page that outlines more than 30 of the most common ones. Needless to say, after I did the work, my friend decided to quit talking about this idea.

However, he will be back with ideas, just like you should be, and one of these days, he may find an idea that someone can make a reality. It won't happen for him, because just talking about an idea doesn't start any business.

Recognize the entrepreneur passion trap

Jumping into the technical entrepreneur role with just a dream and a prayer, and without the reality checks discussed in the preceding section, is called a **passion trap**. Most experts agree that entrepreneurial success has a lot to do with your level of passion, determination, and innovation, but these have to be tempered with some strong business principles to keep the focus on reality.

According to Small Business Association figures, about six million Americans a year make the bold leap onto the startup path, with many more worldwide, and many have no corporate safety net to fall back on. Unfortunately, less than half of these new ventures survive beyond a few years. The passion trap is just one of the downfalls.

I'm sure we have all seen entrepreneurs with high levels of passion and confidence touting an idea that seems to make very little sense to us. Of course, we never see ourselves in this mode, yet we need to recognize that all humans see reality differently through a built-in set of cognitive biases based on their own unique background of experiences, training, and mental state.

These biases are good in that they allow us to quickly filter and make decisions in the constant barrage of information we face each day, but bad because they often lead to errors in reasoning and emotional choices. The worst case is the "passion trap," where a pattern of beliefs, choices, and behaviors feel good and become self-reinforcing, but lead to disaster.

John Bradberry, in his book *6 Secrets to Startup Success* (http://www.amazon.com/ Secrets-Startup-Success-Entrepreneurial-Thriving/dp/0814416063), identifies five key biases that sabotage many passionate entrepreneurs in their startup decision-making. I challenge any entrepreneur to honestly tell me that they have never fallen victim to any of these while making startup decisions:

> ➤ **Confirmation bias**: This refers to the human tendency to select and interpret available information in a way that confirms pre-existing hopes and beliefs. The antidote is to look for dissenting views that seem to form a pattern of concern. Then, what you perceive as isolated exceptions might indeed appear as a clear majority.

> ➤ **Representativeness (belief in the law of small numbers)**: Many entrepreneurs tend to settle on conclusions they like, based on only a small number of observations or a few pieces of data. The new founder who hears positive reviews from three out of four friends may assume that 75 percent of the general population will react similarly.

> ➤ **Overconfidence or the illusion of control**: Overconfidence leads founders to treat their assumptions as facts and see less uncertainty and risk than actually exists. The illusion of control causes startup founders to overrate their abilities and skills in controlling future events and outcomes. Both result in "rose-colored" plans rather than realistic ones.

> **Anchoring**: This refers to our mind's tendency to give excessive weight to the first information we receive about a topic or the first idea we think of. It encourages founders to cling to an original idea or, if pressed, to consider only slight deviations from the idea instead of more radical alternatives. The ability to pivot sharply and timely is at risk here.

> **Escalation of commitment ("sunk cost" fallacy)**: Startup founders often refuse to abandon a losing strategy in an attempt to preserve whatever value has been created up to that point. They feel that they have put so much money, time, and energy into an idea or plan, that it must be the best idea. Investing more into a bad idea doesn't make it good.

Bradberry defines these biases leading to the passion trap as a self-reinforcing spiral of beliefs, choices, and actions, causing critical miscalculations and missteps, which result in rigidly adhering to a failing strategy until it's too late to recover. Entrepreneurs who fall into this trap usually don't even see it coming.

Bradberry defines some useful principles to help enthusiastic technical entrepreneurs squeeze the most out of their passion, while not being trapped by it. These principles will help keep you from falling into the passion trap, so every existing and budding entrepreneur should internalize them:

> **Ready yourself as a founder**: Too often, passionate entrepreneurs leap headfirst into a venture before thinking it through. To improve your readiness to succeed as a startup founder, take an honest look at yourself as a founder before leaping. Perform a reality check on your goals, and then focus on ways to leverage your skills, assets, resources, and relationships.

> **Be attached to the market, not your idea**: Passion is an inner phenomenon, but all healthy businesses are rooted outside the founder, in the marketplace instead. To turn your passion into profits, put your emphasis on the market, and always think about your business relative to the customers you serve. Know your markets and execute your market opportunity by placing a priority on your customer's experience and perception of value.

> **Ensure that your passion adds up**: Passionate entrepreneurs tend to develop rose-colored plans, overestimating early sales and underestimating costs. To convert your passion into a tangible business value, write a business plan that makes financial sense for the needs and future goals of your startup and have it checked by an expert.

> **Execute with focused flexibility**: No amount of startup planning can accurately predict the unexpected twists and turns imposed by reality. To succeed, a new venture needs both iteration and agility. Establish an ongoing process to translate ideas into actions and results, followed by evaluation. A startup will face countless opportunities and a possible death by a thousand distractions. Most startups that I have worked with were plagued with a lack of laser-sharp focus on achieving a few (1-3) goals.

> ➤ **Cultivate integrity of communication**: Passionate commitment to an idea can breed reality distortion, that is, aspiring entrepreneurs often see only what they want to see and rely on "feeling good" about their venture as their only measure of success. Commit to building the skills essential for high-integrity communication, such as curiosity, humility, candor, and scrutiny. The best communication relates observable metrics that a founder can use to evaluate the health, strength, and growth of their business.

> ➤ **Build stamina and staying power**: Contributing factors aside, most startups fail because they run out of money or time. To lengthen and strengthen your venture's runway, aim to launch close to the customer and raise more money than you think you'll need. Focus on building personal staying power, and maximize learning and improvements.

Every entrepreneur needs to be on the lookout for early warning signs of biases and passion traps that signal they are in danger of undercutting their odds of startup success. Some obvious warning signs are founders who are thinking or saying, "This is a sure thing," or executives losing patience with advisors who point out risks or shortcomings in their plan. A good mentor can also help beginners to avoid these traps.

Optimism, for example, is a typical entrepreneurial trait that improves performance, but only up to a point. In fact, moderately-optimistic people have been shown to outperform extreme optimists on a wide range of task and assignments. There are a number of similar entrepreneurial characteristics that are recognized as good, but can be amplified to unhealthy levels, resulting in passion traps or so-called "Icarus qualities."

In my experience, a great startup is more about great execution rather than a great idea. It's about converting your passion into economic value. To counter-balance the biases in your passion, the best approach is to look beyond your own mind and actively listen to your customers, your advisors, and your team. Your goal must be to balance your own perception of needs and wants with real market-driven requirements data.

The difference between entrepreneurial requirements and engineering perceptions

Every engineer who has invented some new technology, or is adept at creating solutions believes that is the hard part, and that it should be a short step to take that solution to the market as a technical entrepreneur. In reality, that short business step embodies far more risk, and a poor technology solution is not near the top of most lists on common reasons for business failures (http://www.moyak.com/papers/small-business-failure.html).

In fact, a Duke and Harvard survey (http://blogs.berkeley.edu/2011/03/22/engineering-vs-liberal-arts-who%E2%80%99s-right-%E2%80%94-bill-or-steve/) of over 500 technology companies showed that only 37 percent of their leaders even have Engineering or Computer Science backgrounds. Clearly, engineers should think twice before assuming they have an advantage over the rest of us towards being an entrepreneur.

A good Engineering or Computer Science background does not necessarily build good leaders, and leadership is a critical skill needed to build a business.

Now, there are many resources out there to help engineer entrepreneurs, such as the book by Krishna Uppuluri, *Engineer to Entrepreneur: The First Flight* (http://www.amazon.com/Engineer-Entrepreneur-The-First-Flight/dp/0983613648). He identifies the key business misconceptions of most engineers and provides a workbook approach to provide a quick start on various business life cycle topics. I've summarized his points and added my own, as follows:

> ➤ **"Everyone loves cool ideas and new technology":** Before investing a lot of time and money into any idea, entrepreneurs should assess its commercial viability. This means evaluating third-party market research, getting real customer feedback from prototypes, and listening to the concerns of successful executives in the same business area.

> ➤ **"I need to go-it alone to assure quality and elegance":** Engineers assume that the business issues can be resolved later. Working alone or with other engineers is great for the average engineer introvert, gives them better control, and minimizes distractions. A team with diverse skills is harder to manage but is more likely to build a thriving business.

> ➤ **"Marketing is fluff and selling is black magic":** The old adage, "If we build it, they will come" came from engineers. In reality, simply building a solution won't make it connect with customers, manage competition, or communicate and proselytize the offering in the industry. With today's information overload, selling is always required.

> ➤ **"We need to get functionality maximized before we focus on customers":** The business reality is that you can't engineer the functionality right until you focus on customers. Superfluous functionality, from a customer's perspective, is a failure. The mantra for an entrepreneur today should be to ship fast, make changes, and iterate.

> ➤ **"A good engineer hates unpredictability and risk":** A good entrepreneur embraces risk as an opportunity, whereas most engineers are risk-averse and cautious. The result is that engineer-driven solutions often are too little and too late, if they ever ship, in today's fast-moving market. Managing risks is good; eliminating all risk is bad for startups. Staying in a totally-known and safe territory minimizes innovation and opportunity.

> ➤ **"We can't worry about making money until we get it built":** If you can't make money, it isn't a business. Business constraints, such as market size, customer demographics, manufacturing, distribution, and support costs need to be set, or there is no context for getting it right. Getting it right at the wrong cost will get you no customers.

> ➤ **"Outside funding causes loss of control and undue pressure to deliver":** Funding is like a turbocharger for a startup company if used correctly. Investors love to fund the growth and scaling of a proven business model for entrepreneurs, and they avoid funding research and development for engineers at all costs. Hence, the pressure to deliver.

Certainly, there are many examples of great companies led by engineers, including Microsoft with Bill Gates, Oracle with Larry Ellison, and Google with Larry Page. This is strong evidence that it is possible to make the step from an engineer to an entrepreneur, or team up with someone who can provide the complementary skills and perspective.

In fact, as Krishna says in his book, the stars are uniquely aligned these days for engineers to be entrepreneurs, if they follow the guidance given in this book. The Internet is a great equalizer, allowing all of us to develop broad as well as deep skills and insights quickly.

Assess the opportunity and the risks with a startup incubator

There is nothing like a group of peers and a few sage advisors to help you zero in on the real challenges of your dream. Before you finalize your course in building a technical solution and commit your resources to the entrepreneurial effort, it makes sense to visit and perhaps join one of the local startup incubators in your community or university.

First, however, let me put your expectations and their role into proper perspective. More and more technical entrepreneurs are telling me about the successful graduates and investors queued behind a few well-known startup incubators, including Y Combinator, TechStars, and the Founder Institute. They dream of appearing at the door with their idea on the back of a napkin and popping out a few months later with investors' money to burn. The reality is far different. More often, aspiring entrepreneurs pop out with the realization that their dream is not really the opportunity for them.

By definition, a business or a startup incubator is a company, university, or another organization that provides resources to nurture young companies, usually for a share of the equity, hoping to capitalize on their success, or at least strengthen the local economy. According to the **National Business Incubator Association (NBIA)**, there are currently over 1250 incubators today in the US alone.

The good news is that a few of these do have an envious success record with the entrepreneurs they choose to accept. Y Combinator, led by Paul Graham, recently claimed success with 172 companies over 7 years, which now have a combined value of $7.78 billion. Founder Institute, led by Adeo Ressi, claims the most graduates, with over 650 companies, and 90 percent of these companies are still running.

Yet, success is really not the best indicator of help received, since once could argue that the really great entrepreneurs didn't need any help from the incubator, and might have been even more successful without it. All the rest of us might be the real beneficiaries, with a lot more to learn. Here are several key lessons I assert you can learn from a good incubator:

> **Aptitude reality check**: Adeo Ressi believes that his preliminary test of applicants is predicting more and more accurately whether you have the DNA of an entrepreneur, before even being accepted. His tests focus on personality traits alone (ignoring your startup idea), looking for fluid intelligence, openness, and agreeableness. Why spend years struggling and all your money if entrepreneurship is just not your thing?

> **Initial funding**: Many incubators do provide seed funding for selected entrepreneurs, usually in small amounts ranging from $10,000 to $20,000, and usually taking 5 percent to 15 percent of your equity in return. This investment can get your startup off the ground in an otherwise impossible financial situation, but this should not be viewed as the main reason for joining.

> **Expert mentoring and training**: In my view, the quality of incubator leadership is the single biggest potential value provided, along with it being a learning opportunity for entrepreneurs. Every successful incubator has strong leadership in addition to staff that has business and investment credentials. Skip the ones who only seem to be offering you space and facilities.

> **Peer support**: In addition to the formal mentoring, the peers you'll be working alongside at startup incubators provide much more than emotional support. You will find expertise in areas you need, as well as quick advice from entrepreneurs just ahead of you in every phase of the business cycle.

> **Facilities support**: Of course, you can't eliminate the value of affordable office and meeting space, administrative support services, and advanced communication technology for struggling entrepreneurs. However, don't believe the myth that incubators are all about "cheap rent," and avoid business incubators in otherwise vacant buildings.

> **Learn by doing**: An incubator allows entrepreneurs to get their ideas out of their mind and out of the classroom, while still retaining a modicum of structure and discipline. This is as close as possible to real experience, and there is no teacher like experience. It's an opportunity to succeed or fail fast, with a minimal investment of time and money.

> **Follow-on funding and connections**: Success in an incubator means likely access to venture capital, and connections to industry gurus and business opportunities. About 80 percent of TechStars' startup graduates go on to raise venture capital or a significant Angel funding round, versus maybe 1 percent of all startups that seek funding (http://www.forbes.com/sites/tomiogeron/2012/04/30/top-tech-incubators-as-ranked-by-forbes-y-combinator-tops-with-7-billion-in-value/).

The bad news is that the odds of getting in are still hugely stacked against even the most dedicated entrepreneurs. At Y Combinator, an average of only 2.5 percent of applications are accepted per cycle, and more than half of these fail to complete the program (http://www.effective-altruism.com/author/ryan-carey/). You can get into less famous incubators more easily, but the learning and chance of getting funded at the end go down accordingly.

Of course, incubators usually have other costs as well. Incubators often take 10 to 15 percent of a company as part of the investment deal. Entrepreneurs need to be sure they are comfortable with giving away part of the business, and they need to do the due diligence on the past success and leadership reputation. Every incubator is different and may not match your culture or needs.

You may also be hearing more about "business accelerators" as an alternative or improvement on the incubator model. The key difference between them, according to purists, is that accelerators compress the timescale for startups in order to drive entrepreneurs from ideas to marketable products in a matter of months. Overall, the learning opportunities are essentially the same.

My conclusion is that the best incubators can really help every technical entrepreneur, but there are no shortcuts or substitutes for the right mindset, hard work, and a real solution to a real problem with a big opportunity. Here are some questions to ask yourself before choosing an incubator or accelerator:

> ➤ How much are you willing to spend?

> ➤ Does their business area focus match your needs?

> ➤ What references do they have?

> ➤ What is the quality of peer startups you would be working with there?

The following sections of this chapter will cover a few of the specific lessons that you might learn from an incubator. Thus, I'm not suggesting that every technical entrepreneur needs to join an incubator, but they are productive if you find that the first-hand feedback from peers and advisors helps to make the lessons stick.

The importance of frequent tuning and daily determination

Most of the technical entrepreneurs I know are classic proof of the old adage that people tend to overestimate what they can do in a short period, and underestimate what they can do over a long period. They become frustrated when they are unable to build their startup in a weekend, and give up way too soon when the path to real success seems to be interminable.

Both problems can be mitigated by learning the power of frequency, as defined in a recent book by Jocelyn K. Glei, *Manage Your Day-to-Day* (http://www.amazon.com/ Manage-Your-Day-Day-Creative/dp/1477800670), which asserts that working consistently and frequently on something makes it possible to accomplish more, with greater originality, than spasmodic bursts of effort. A successful startup needs to be a daily task with consistent focus.

I suggest that the following key reasons from Glei for how the habit of frequency fosters both productivity and innovation in general, apply especially well to an entrepreneur starting a new business:

➤ **Frequency makes starting easier**: Getting started is always a challenge. It's hard to convert an idea into a business, and it's also hard to get back into the groove with all the distractions of other activities and your "real job." If you block out your time every day to focus on your startup, you keep your momentum going and start seeing long-term progress.

➤ **Frequency keeps insights current**: You're much more likely to spot opportunities for innovation and see new trends in the marketplace if your mind is constantly humming with issues related to the startup. Frequent discussions with peers and customers on open questions will keep you from being led astray by your own biases.

➤ **Frequency keeps the pressure off**: If you're producing just one page, one blog post, or one sketch a week, you expect it to be good and final, and you start to worry about quality. It's better to write 100 lines of new code every day, recognizing that you will have to iterate to perfection, rather than expecting a week of work to happen all in one night.

➤ **Frequency sparks creativity**: You might be thinking, "Having to work frequently, whether or not I feel inspired, will force me to lower my standards." In my experience, the effect is just the opposite. Creativity arises from a constant churn of ideas, and one of the easiest ways to get results is to keep your mind engaged with your project.

➤ **Frequency nurtures frequency**: If you develop the habit of working frequently, it becomes much easier to sit down and get something done even when you don't have a big block of time; you don't have to take time to acclimate yourself. The real enemy of progress is the procrastination habit, which should be replaced with the frequency habit.

➤ **Frequency fosters productivity**: It's no surprise that you're likely to accomplish more if you work daily. The very fact of each day's accomplishment helps the next day's work come more smoothly and pleasantly. By writing just 500 words a day in a blog, I suddenly realized that I had enough for a book in just a few months.

➤ **Frequency is a realistic approach**: Frequency is helpful when you're working on a startup idea on the side, along with pressing obligations from a job or your family. It's easier to carve out an hour a day, than to set all else aside for a week in the early stages of your startup.

Don't be like many of the people that we all know who feel like they are working at a breakneck pace all day, every day, but have very few tangible results to show for their efforts. Every entrepreneur needs to build a proactive daily routine while being able to field a barrage of messages, and still carve out the time to do the work that matters.

Another enemy of progress in startups is the curse of perfectionism. Some entrepreneurs never start, waiting for that ideal moment when there are no distractions. Some are lost in the middle, obsessing over every step, and some never finish, always refining and adding, rather than learning from a minimum viable product; thus the need to combine frequency with pragmatics.

If you can manage your day-to-day routine with frequency, rather than letting reactive chaos manage you, you will find that your creative mind is sharpened, and your focus on the new technical venture will generate the *change the world* results that attracted you to this technical entrepreneur opportunity in the first place.

Feature creep can turn your leading edge into the bleeding edge

Even if you have that day-to-day focus on building and honing your product, every technical entrepreneur needs to face the challenge of knowing when to stop building and perfecting your product, and start selling it, even if building it is more fun than the business side.

Scope creep (or **feature creep**) is an insidious disease that kills more good startups than any other, especially high-tech ones, and yet most founders (who may be the cause) never even see it happening. This term refers to the penchant to add just one more feature to the product or service before its first delivery, just because you can, or you perceive the customer needs to have it. Other excuses often given are to occupy the market as soon as possible, or to collect feedback from customers and improve the product.

The instigators are all well-intentioned—executives talk to potential customers who "must have" a few more things, or the technical team prescribes some "technically elegant" options that they can't resist adding before the release. The result is a bloated first product, which finally collapses under its own weight, or it is too late or too expensive for the intended customer.

The best product is one that is highly focused and has the absolute minimum number of features to do the job. The solution is to do the right job up-front on requirements, as well as documenting and approving specifications, and having the toughest person you know to do the project management. Here are five basic rules to live by:

> ➤ **Document the requirements**: A well-run requirements phase is your best chance to ensure that the scope creep will be recognized when it happens, and it will. If initial requirements are not documented, then there is no base, and no one can recognize that the stack is getting higher as time passes.

> ➤ **Lock down the sign-off authority**: In all documents, clearly define who must sign off on the content and provide business-side feedback. If you do the sign-off, don't be afraid to say "no." Draw the line between need versus want. Founders who constantly give in to changes will get more until the startup breaks.

> ➤ **Final features approval event**: Make a visible event at the executive level out of the final specification approval, detailing features, costs, and time frames. Make sure everyone knows that changes after this point will have personal consequences and will delay the product and increase the cost.

> **Define milestones for cost review and sign-off**: Milestones are for early warnings, because there is no recovery when you are out of time and money. Good milestones include the completion of specifications, a prototype, beta testing, final documentation, and final delivery.

> **Implement and enforce a change process**: Changes will be required to every project, so plan for them. The market changes, executives learn new things, customers demand changes, and technology changes. Change requests should be documented and sized, and tradeoffs should be presented for approval or disapproval. There are several formal development processes, such as Scrum (`http://en.wikipedia.org/wiki/Scrum_(software_development)`), which facilitate changes without scope creep.

Efforts to discourage scope creep are not designed to punish creativity. Rather, team members should be encouraged to contribute to a database of additional features that they think would be interesting and useful, and submit them as change requests on a weekly basis.

Change requests must be visibly reviewed by executives frequently. Potential customer user interviews are also useful in determining the real need and value of marginal change requests. If the features are interesting but not necessary for initial release, they can be scheduled for further development on later releases of the project, be it new software, a car, or any other sort of device.

There's always going to be something newer, faster, and bigger, and the perfect product is a never-ending chase, but only if you allow it to be. Remember that in new product development, as in writing, *addition by subtraction* is the Golden Rule.

Scope creep causes your project to become slowly less elegant and very "un-simple", which is a startup's worst nightmare. Technical entrepreneurs need to know when to stop chasing the leading edge, or they will be cursed to live and die on the bleeding edge.

Early adopters don't make your market

When you think about going to market, or even look hard at the market, the customers that technical entrepreneurs most easily relate to and depend on are **early adopters**. The conventional wisdom is that early adopters are the ideal target for new products, to get business rolling. Early adopters are great, but I see two pitfalls with any conclusions based primarily on early adopters; first, the size of this group may not be as large as you think, and secondly, their feedback may lead you directly away from your real target market of mainstream customers.

The term "early adopters" relates to the people who are eager to try almost any new technology products, and originates from Everett M. Rogers' book, *Diffusion of Innovations* (http://www.amazon.com/Diffusion-Innovations-5th-Everett-Rogers/dp/0743222091). Early adopters are usually no more than 10 to 15 percent of the ultimate market potential, and marketing tothem may be necessary but not sufficient in marketing to the mainstream. Witness the market struggle for 3DTV acceptance over the past couple of years.

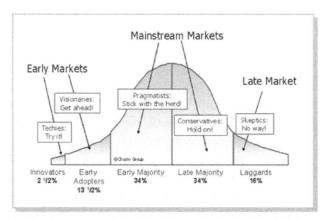

Technology adoption life cycle: groups are distinguished from each other based on their characteristic response to discontinuous innovations created by new technology (http://readwrite.com/files/files/files/images/tech-adoption-lifecycle.jpg)

The good news is that these people will readily provide candid feedback to help you refine future product releases, and push towards new features, increased control, and interoperability. The bad news is that they hardly ever push towards simplicity and increased usability needed by the masses.

The result can easily be the classic death spiral, driven by a small but vocal portion of your market, for more and more features, when you can least afford it in time or money. Equally bad is the implementation of input from a few early adopters, which can actually prevent your products from being adopted by the majority, as follows:

> ➤ **Minimizing the value of usability features**: The features you designed for average users, such as wizards for configuration, and simple buttons to eliminate complex processes, will get no feedback or removal recommendations. Early adopters like to see tricky and elegant details rather than general usability.

> ➤ **Increased control and flexibility**: Product suggestions by early adopters often ask for increased user control over details of the technology. However, each increase in the control that you hand over to the users also increases user interface complexity and the opportunity for pitfalls for the average user.

> ➤ **Emphasis on engineering robustness**: Early adopters love technology, sometimes to a fault. Technical issues such as execution speed, file size, and memory usage are typical examples that always need further optimization. At some point, it becomes compulsive engineering rather than engineering to increase the value for the average user.

> **Higher product price**: Users want new features that automate complicated but obscure tasks. These features will likely be used by only a tiny fraction of the entire user base, but will increase the complexity for everyone. Early adopters are normally less price-sensitive, so this may mislead you in finalizing your pricing model.

The dilemma that we all face is that the most valuable customers might be the least vocal (the silent majority). The users who scream the loudest are usually a minority segment. The challenge of every business is to proactively seek out a cross section of core users and ask them for feedback, rather than responding to random noise.

I'm certainly not suggesting that you ignore early adopters. Simply recognize them as a specific and important small market segment, and treat them with respect. Early adopters have money, and if they like your product, they're generally very vocal about it and provide invaluable word-of-mouth press, and spread the word about your product on social websites. You need their evangelism and passion to get enough momentum to start attracting mainstream consumers.

So don't be lulled into complacency by early adopters as your first customers. Temper your feedback assessments, product changes, and marketing strategy to the mainstream market. Ten percent of your projected market won't make you or your investors very happy. Thus, a perceived huge opportunity may have just become a small one.

Check your alignment with today's customer buying habits

Technical entrepreneurs always work hard to create an innovative product or service, but often count on standard seller marketing for sales. However, the reality is that sellers are no longer in charge of the customer-buying process. Current reports (http://chiefmarketer.com/online_marketing/0329-consumer-power/) suggest that 90 percent of today's shoppers skip marketing pitches, research online before they buy, and over 50 percent check user reviews before making a decision.

The Internet and smartphones have changed everything. Kristin Zhivago, in her book, *Roadmap to Revenue* (http://www.amazon.com/Roadmap-Revenue-Sell-Your-Customers/dp/0974917923), makes the point that the selling system is broken, since sellers no longer sell the way customers are buying. Here is my summary of her detailed roadmap to get you back on the right track with a "customer-centric" approach rather than a "company-centric" approach:

> **Find out what customers want and how they want to buy it**: The best way to do this is with real customer interviews. Customers will tell you things when being interviewed that they will never tell you while you are selling to them. She recommends phone interviews by you, by appointment, with structured questions, and you document results.

> ➤ **Debate and adjust your offering to better match what customers want**: Distribute an executive summary and recommendations report, as well as transcripts of your interviews, to all the key players in your company. Schedule and run the necessary sessions to update strategic product offerings, processes, and marketing programs.

> ➤ **Align your business model to how your customers want to buy**: Don't start from how you want to sell. Start with a new understanding of the real customer need, their search process in finding you (referral, website, or social media), and the most desired payment model, for example, one-time payment versus subscription, or lease versus purchase.

> ➤ **Integrate the customer buying process into your support operation**: Decide which parts can be automated, the people resources required, and customer service points of contact. All of these processes should be documented, and should explicitly include the customer buying process and perceptions as the base. Their perception is your reality.

> ➤ **Build and deploy a revenue growth action plan**: This is your rollout of the new product offerings, business model updates, and process changes to map to the new understanding of the customer buying process. Include planned measurements and metrics. Start where the customer wants you to be and work backwards.

For more details, I also recommend a good book by Steve Blank that addresses the customer-centric development process, titled *The Four Steps to the Epiphany* (`http://www.amazon.com/Four-Steps-Epiphany-Steve-Blank/dp/0989200507`).

As you start making the shift to customer-centric, if your team doesn't "get it," then you haven't communicated effectively. Communicating change is always hard, so pay careful attention to the central message, repetition opportunities, and "walking the talk". People are quick to make things up to fill a vacuum, and rumors or myths die hard.

Make sure your own motivation is strong, and don't let anyone view these efforts as a one-time push. It has to be managed and sold internally as a culture change, requiring everyone's help. Experience has shown that the best way to change a process is to set up a new way of doing things, and then flip the switch (flip method) rather than making incremental changes (drip method).

Every business needs to take advantage of the new tools and technologies, which can assist you in making this shift in strategy and measuring effectiveness. These range from basic search engine optimization (SEO) tracking, with tools like Google Analytics, to a new generation of marketing platforms, including HubSpot.

There are multiple benefits to both you and your customer. The customers will get what they want, when they want it, and you will see more revenue, greater brand loyalty, real relationships, and a competitive edge. This sounds to me like the recipe for business success that every technical entrepreneur is looking for.

Winning customers from big business brands

You can't succeed as a technical entrepreneur if you can't win customers, and the new Internet-empowered or enterprise customers are tough. They are in control, and they no longer care where or from whom they buy, so here is your chance to win. They do have a specific purchase progression with key milestone moments that determine your win or loss outcome in every transaction.

I agree with the premise in a recent book by the widely-respected expert on business growth, Robert H. Bloom, in his book, *The New Experts* (http://www.amazon.com/New-Experts-Empowered-Customers-Marketing/dp/1608320243), which states that today's customers are armed with three lethal weapons:

➤ Instant access to information about every potential purchase

➤ Immense choice

➤ Real-time comparison of competitive prices

They don't care about customer loyalty, and all that matters is that you deliver what matters most to them, when it matters most. If you are a new entrepreneur, your business life depends on using the following four decisive moments in their buying process:

➤ **Your now-or-never moment**: This is your buyer's all-too-brief first point of contact with your business. You have to create customer preference at this moment or the customer will vanish—probably forever. The key lesson here is to think like a buyer, and not a seller. The first priority must be to get your prospect to know you and trust you.

➤ **Your make-or-break moment**: This refers to the often-extended period of consideration, negotiation, and decision to purchase, during which far too many transactions fall through. You win here by remaining consistently engaged with real interaction and involvement, and by knowing their needs and values better than any competitor.

➤ **Your keep-or-lose moment**: This moment is the period when your customer is actually using your products and services. Rather than heaving a sigh of relief at the sale, you must redouble your efforts to improve the relationship while the customer is first using, consuming, enjoying, and relying on the product or service they purchased from you.

➤ **Your multiplier moment**: This is the moment when you can convert a one-time customer into a repeat customer and an advocate and referral source for your company. These are the transactions that require far less investment and will create far more profitable revenue. You need a reliable system of metrics to measure your performance here.

While this is viewed by customers as a blessing, this buyer empowerment is seen by many businesses as a curse. Some won't change, and they will die. As a startup, you at least don't have to overcome the inertia of how things have always been done in your company, but you do have to recognize the new reality and use it to your competitive advantage.

A simple recommendation is that empowered customers have to be met by your empowered employees, using the same Internet technologies to keep up. After you embrace the new reality, the first thing you need to do is get the new requirements ingrained in your most innovative employees. Then, you have to trust them.

Trust them to think and act independently on behalf of your startup and your brand. Clear a path for them, see what they come up with, provide resources, and support them. When they make mistakes, highlight the learning experience, pick them up, and get them innovating again.

The other things that your whole team needs to do are reduce complexity and deliver a consistent customer experience. This allows your startup to handle new input, resolve customer issues, and move forward more swiftly. Entrepreneurs that recognize this empowerment and the importance of delivering a positive, consistent customer experience will gain and maintain the competitive advantage.

Because it's a wide-open market, the latest technology often comes to consumers first. As a technical entrepreneur assessing the opportunity of your dreams, you need to understand and capitalize on the decisive moments of empowered customers now or never.

Women technical entrepreneurs have some unique challenges

Women entrepreneurs are starting small businesses at approximately twice the national average for all startups, and many of these are technical entrepreneurs. Despite some inaccurate stereotypes, the evidence is that these are in every industry, from small technical consulting firms to medical high technology. As a result, there has been a lot of focus on any possible unique challenges for women, while trying to assess the opportunity, and beyond.

In most cases, the business questions asked and the answers given are essentially the same for all entrepreneurs, whether they are men or women. However, according to a couple of articles I've seen recently by Peri Pakroo, J.D., who just published a book titled *The Women's Small Business Startup Kit* (http://www.amazon.com/Small-Business-Startup-Step-Step/dp/1413316840), the road to success for women does involve its own unique set of hazards. Peri keys off the messages from Sheryl Sandberg in her bestseller, *Lean In* (http://www.amazon.com/Lean-In-Women-Work-Will/dp/0385349947), which examines why women's progress in achieving leadership roles has stalled, explains the root causes, and offers compelling, common sense solutions that can empower women to achieve their full potential.

Surveys of women entrepreneurs show that women's business concerns tend to skew towards issues such as finding work-life balance, startup financing, and marketing. Here are some tips and resources from both of us to address these concerns:

➤ **Always start a business that fits with your personal life**: There are no rules as to what a "real" business looks like. For most men and some women, success might mean a huge international operation with millions in revenues. For others, a consulting or artisan business with a healthy return and generous personal freedoms would be the pinnacle of success.

➤ **Keep the organization formalities simple**: You can usually start a sole proprietorship or a partnership for less than $100 by registering with just one government office. There are many step-by-step guides available, like the one referenced above for women. The real challenge in all cases is a sound business idea and some management acumen.

➤ **Plan for funding requirements**: Starting a business without enough money to ride out the early lean days is still a common reason why businesses fail. Beyond self-funding and banks, two resources that women should definitely look into are Women's Business Centers (WBCs) and community development financial institutions (CDFIs).

➤ **Network like a social butterfly**: This is one of the best ways to market your business and create profitable opportunities. It is always best to forge relationships with contacts before you need help from them. Networking does not require unsavory schmoozing or pandering to get to know potential partners, investors, and customers.

➤ **Utilize online support sites**: There are many good support sites springing up, such as Ladies Who Launch, National Association of Women Business Owners (NAWBO), eWomen Network, and the Center for Women's Business Research. These can also provide coaching, marketing, and other important resources.

➤ **Women learn from women**: Successful women entrepreneurs, even more than men, are usually anxious and willing to connect with, support, and learn from other emerging and established female business owners. Find them by attending local business organization meetings, including the Chamber of Commerce.

➤ **Dream bigger**: The value of setting high goals for yourself and your business is not just a motivational myth. Many experts believe that this is the key reason that the average revenues of women-owned businesses are still only 27 percent of the average of men-owned businesses. Change your mindset to increase your focus on growth.

In the past, women have often come to entrepreneurship with fewer resources available to them than men. With these tips and resources, women should be able to achieve a higher threshold for technical entrepreneurs, and will enjoy their full potential as business owners.

Summary

An entrepreneur's overall evaluation of an opportunity operates off a set of tenets that are built into their psyche, or drilled into them from training and mentors. These are often represented by sayings like "You never get anywhere unless you take a chance" and "Passion and persistence are the keys to success." In my experience, these don't always work, so don't rely on them totally to validate your entrepreneurial dream and passion.

Real technical entrepreneurs must have three things: the ability to identify or recognize an opportunity, the ability to review or assess an opportunity, and last but not least, the ability to successfully execute and realize an opportunity. While these tasks seem straightforward on paper, the skills you need for each one are very different, and it is difficult to be good at all of them. To be a successful technical entrepreneur, you need to have all three, in the right order and at the same time.

The people who typically excel at opportunity recognition are the right-brain creative type people, which many technical people are not. These people are clever and look at the same situations that everyone else does, but envision something different. They see new angles, new possibilities, and new ways to do things. Take a hard look in the mirror on this one.

The opportunity review phase is where left-brain people generally stand out in the entrepreneurship process. The opportunity review is when the analytical assessment of the opportunity that was recognized occurs. During this stage, an entrepreneur must assess potential strategies and business models as well as conduct market and economic analyses in order to establish an answer to the question: Can I bring this idea to the market in an economically successful way?

Now that you have validated your idea as a great business opportunity, it's time to execute it. The next chapter addresses the specifics of formalizing your business and turning your dream into reality. If you have come this far and your vision still makes sense, then I think you will enjoy the rest of the journey. Let's take the next step.

>3

When, Where, and How Do You Formalize a Technical Business?

The intent of this chapter is to provide recommendations on how to address all the practical requirements of starting a technical business, including ones with web apps, smartphone apps, computer software products, or any high-tech hardware. These requirements include picking a location for your operation; incorporating the business, tax, and accounting considerations; and the implications of timing on the various steps involved.

In the U.S., I recommend that technical businesses be formally registered with one of the States, either as a Limited Liability Corporation (LLC), where income and losses are merged with owners' personal income tax returns but liability is kept separate, or incorporated under United States federal income tax law, and taxed separately from its owners (C-Corp). Most other countries have similar mechanisms. Tradeoffs will be discussed in this chapter.

Besides incorporating as an LLC or C-corporation, starting a business really requires that you create an online presence for both you and your business. In today's environment, this also includes getting a website domain name, getting started with social media, writing a blog, creating an account on LinkedIn and Twitter, and getting an introduction to the marketing expectations of customers today.

Not all of these decisions have to be made at the same time, but you will see that you need to first think about all of them together before you spend time and money getting halfway down one road before you realize it's the wrong one. Starting a business is all about execution, and it's a lot harder to pivot such an execution than it is to pivot on the ideas while they are still in your head. Now, it's time to really get your business started.

Startup location – a critical success factor

Even in this age of globalization and virtualization, the geographic area where you choose to live and work on your startup can still make any business a success or failure. I still have to tell some technical entrepreneurs that even with the best idea, they should consider moving to Silicon Valley to find the investors they need, or they need to move to the U.S. to get the attention of the market they choose.

For example, if you are building the next great social network to replace Facebook and need funding, you probably won't find any interested and focused VCs or Angel investors in Phoenix, Arizona, where I live. Also, investors from the super-hubs (Silicon Valley, New York, or Boston), won't assume that anyone outside their domain is savvy and has the resources to make it happen.

On the other hand, if you are into solar technologies, there is probably an advantage of being in Phoenix or a similar location in the southwest U.S. Having a great idea in the wrong place won't get you the funding you need, the experienced domain experts you want, or the pilot market results you need for survival. You need to move to the right location and get connected before you ask for help.

Thus, if you need to move, do it first, rather than waiting and hoping that you can earn money at home first. You really need to make connections at the new location to get you started on the right foot. Also, you may think that your current location has few competitors, but in reality, we are in a world market via the Internet, so competitors can find you anywhere. Hiding from competitors doesn't work these days.

Of course, there are always exceptions, but how much added risk do you need for your startup? Maxwell Wessel, in a recent article (http://blogs.hbr.org/2013/11/three-questions-to-consider-before-deciding-where-to-locate-your-startup/) in the Harvard Business Review on this subject, points out the exceptional successes of Zappos in Las Vegas, Sendgrid's massive growth in Colorado, and RightNow's $1.5 billion dollar sale to Oracle from Bozeman, Montana.

For your own startup location positioning, I recommend his four key questions that every entrepreneur should contemplate before resigning themselves to failure or deciding where to move to improve their odds of success:

> ➤ **What's your city's advantage?**: Today, Silicon Valley is the consumer and enterprise software capital of the world. Finance has homes in New York, Hong Kong, and London. Energy is still the domain of Houston and Dubai. The list goes on and on. Most cities have something that they are particularly good at. Find yours if you want to stay at home.

> ➤ **How can you get exposure:** Finding talent and financing isn't the only hurdle to overcome on the road to startup success? It's just the first of many. Exposure is another key ingredient. Exposure to customers, incumbents, and competitors all drive success. Exposure instills the fear and urgency you need to deliver the right competitive solution.

➤ **What will set your business apart:** No one can tell you what to do to create your edge, but it is important that you figure out how you can. Being in the right location helps you maintain pace because of access to skilled and experienced people. Being close to your customers, your vendors, or even your competitors can make all the difference.

➤ **Are you sure you can't move:** Moving might not be easy. However, it is one of the simplest things you can do to improve the odds that your business takes off. If you're about to devote your professional life to building a business and are ready to sacrifice the blood, sweat, and tears it requires, seriously consider this question. It's very important.

Also, you need to consider the costs and potential impacts of creating and building your startup in secondary markets, usually meaning not in Silicon Valley or one of the other super-hubs, as correctly summarized by Wessel:

➤ **It takes longer to raise money than you expect**: Raising capital isn't the be-all and end-all of startup success. However, it is an important metric for firms in pursuit of explosive growth. Raising capital is a necessary step and survival time without it grows short or interminably long. The extra two months spent in traveling to raise funds is two months of your business falling behind. In addition, scheduling and traveling are a problem since fundraising usually occurs over three or more meetings. These include very casual meetings over coffee, where cancellations and rescheduling are common.

➤ **It is harder to find the talent you need than you anticipate**: The primary startup hubs are more amenable to the risky yet flexible lifestyle of startups and the concept of working for equity. It is expensive and time-consuming to recruit the right technical and executive skills in a secondary market.

➤ **It decreases your odds of being bought**: When it comes to the technology ecosystem, clusters are vital. Wessel measures (http://blogs.hbr.org/2013/10/dont-build-your-startup-outside-of-silicon-valley/) a 39 percent acquisition advantage to being in-state. Tech companies see engineers move frequently, integrate their products tightly, and often find themselves acquiring or merging with counterparts. Personal relationships do count.

➤ **It decreases your odds of success**: If you judge entrepreneurial success as surviving or selling (including raising follow-on funding, being bought, or a successful Initial Public Offering (http://en.wikipedia.org/wiki/Initial_public_offering)) as no doubt your investors do, then your odds of success are 10-15 percent higher inside the realm of the super-hubs. That's not a big margin, but every little bit counts in this space.

From my perspective, these are the right questions and the right considerations, but there are no absolutes. Being in the right place is important, but it doesn't ensure success. It still takes entrepreneurs with real passion, determination, and a viable solution to have any positive outcome.

This measurable difference in outcomes, however significant, is not stopping aspiring entrepreneurs from building businesses where they live today. There are many good reasons to do so. Entrepreneurs cite family roots, a sense of neighborhood responsibility, existing professional networks, and more.

In fact, since the recent recession, startups are mushrooming everywhere. From 2006 to 2011, the number of startups founded and funded outside of California, Massachusetts, and New York, according to Wessel, has grown by almost 65 percent. Key new startup hubs include Boulder, Denver, and Austin.

So location isn't everything, but you need to go in with your eyes open. It takes more than a dream and passion to build a business.

No matter where you are physically located, you can choose to incorporate in any state. It used to be true that *everyone* incorporated in Delaware due to its more favorable terms, but many of these terms simply don't apply to technical startups, or the differences don't exist anymore. Most business professionals now recommend that your first choice should be your home state, or the state where your startup resides.

Every state will highlight its advantages, like the following points that I found for a state where I lived and where I was considering incorporating one of my businesses:

➤ Incorporation fees are low

➤ The process is simple, including the convenience of geographical proximity

➤ Local attorneys, if required, are more familiar with local laws

➤ Your startup automatically gets an intrastate securities law exemption

➤ There is no need to register as a "foreign" corporation in the state of operation

Still, there are business considerations that might override low cost and simplicity. For example, if your business is likely to get venture capital soon, have a large number of shareholders, or you have a high probability of going public, it might still be a good idea to incorporate in Delaware or Nevada due to these two states' more size-friendly laws. The same applies if you are a foreign startup that needs to incorporate in the U.S. to operate with American customers.

For the rest of us, there are distinct advantages to staying close to home. As an example, let's take a closer look at the specifics for my case in Arizona:

➤ **Arizona's incorporation fees are low**: Filing fees vary from state to state, but will fall anywhere from $50 in Mississippi to $410 in Nevada, including administration fees. Arizona is close to the bottom, with statutory fees of only $60. Even if you choose to add the expedite fee of $35 and consider another $100 for publication requirements, the costs to incorporate in Arizona are very reasonable.

> ➤ **The process is simple, including the convenience of geographical proximity**:
> To incorporate a corporation in Arizona, you are required to file Articles
> of Incorporation with the Arizona Corporation Commission, publish the
> incorporation filing in a newspaper of general circulation three times, and submit
> an affidavit of publication back to the Commission. You could also visit their
> offices in Phoenix or Tucson for personal assistance.

> ➤ **Local attorneys, if required, are more familiar with Arizona laws**: If your
> company needs a complex structure, organizationally or financially, the
> assistance of a local attorney may be required. They will be familiar with any
> unique Arizona requirements for organizational structures, record keeping,
> capitalization, debt financing, roles of shareholders, distributions, personal
> liability, and state tax considerations.

> ➤ **Your startup automatically gets an intrastate securities law exemption**:
> To qualify for the intrastate offering exemption, a company must be incorporated
> in the same state where it is offering the securities and carry out a very significant
> amount of its business in that state. If you incorporate and do business in
> Arizona, this item alone can save you a significant amount of management time,
> paperwork, corporate tax, and legal fees.

> ➤ **No need to register as a "foreign" corporation in the state of operation**:
> Most states have laws that require entrepreneurs to re-register a Delaware
> company in the state where it is actually doing business, and unfortunately,
> re-registration involves more than a few hours of paperwork.

This is definitely not an advertisement for incorporation in Arizona, since most states
have similar points to attract new companies to their state. My only point is that every
entrepreneur should look hard at the potential advantages of incorporating in his home
state, rather than assuming that Delaware and Nevada are the only rational choices.

However, don't forget that forming the new corporation is just the "tip of the iceberg"
with respect to operating a business in the corporate form. Although it is relatively
easy and inexpensive to incorporate a business in Arizona, I recommend that you don't
hesitate to consult an Arizona corporate attorney when incorporating for issues that may
require legal advice and action. With a little luck, your new startup entity should be up
and running in 30 to 60 days.

The net of this section is that picking a physical location is the hard part, but following
through with the creation of the proper business entity is also critical to your long-term
success. Waiting too long on either of these decisions will cost you more time and money
later, and dramatically increase your risk.

Most investors won't even consider supporting a company that is not firmly located and
incorporated as an LLC or C-corp. So make your decision now, and build the specifics into
your rollout plan. Last minute emergency changes and associated legal fees are no fun.

Picking the right company name

Every technical startup needs a name! This may seem a silly and frivolous task, but it may be the most important decision you make. The name of your business has a tremendous impact on how customers and investors view you, and in today's small world, it's a world-wide decision.

A big red flag is to talk to an investor or show him a business plan with TBD (to be determined later) or NewCo (a common name placeholder) in the title position. Right or wrong, the name you choose, or don't choose, speaks volumes about your business savvy and understanding of the world you are about to enter.

It's not that hard to get started by making a list of potential names from a scan of the Internet, combining relevant words, or looking through a dictionary. Then, it's time to look for the characteristics that experts and investors look for in a name, with some help from Alex Frankel (http://www.igorinternational.com/press/b202-company-names-identity.php) and others:

> **Unique and unforgettable**: In the trade, this is called stickiness. However, the issue of stickiness turns out to be kind of, well, sticky. Every company wants a name that stands out from the crowd, a catchy handle that will remain fresh and memorable over time. That's a challenge because naming trends change, often year by year, making timeless names hard to find (remember the dot coms). Of course, the name needs to be unique, so be sure to use Google or another search engine to check for duplicates worldwide.

> **Avoid unusual spellings**: When creating a name, stay with words that can easily be spelled by customers. Some startup founders try unusual word spellings to make their business stand out, but this can be trouble when customers "Google" your business to find you, or try to refer you to others. Stay with traditional word spelling, and avoid those catchy words that you love to explain at cocktail parties.

> **Easy to pronounce and remember**: Forget made-up words and nonsense phrases. Make your business name one that customers can pronounce and remember easily. Skip the acronyms, which mean nothing to most people. When choosing an identity for a company or a product, simple and straightforward are back in style and cost less to a brand.

> **Keep it simple**: The shorter the length, the better. Limit it to two syllables. Avoid using hyphens and other special characters. Since certain algorithms and directory listings work alphabetically, pick a name closer to A than Z. These days, it even helps if the name can easily be turned into a verb, like "Google me".

> **Make some sense**: Occasionally, business owners will choose names that are nonsense words. Quirky words (Yahoo, Google, and Fogdog) or trademark-proof names concocted from scratch (Novartis, Aventis, and Lycos) have their own risk, even though they may sound cool and seem easy to remember. Always check the international implications. More than one company has been embarrassed by a new name that had negative and even obscene connotations in another language.

> ➤ **Give a clue**: Try to adopt a business name that provides some information about what your business does. Calling your landscaping business "Lawn and Order" is appropriate, but the same name would not do well for a handyman business. Your business name should match your business in order to remind customers what services you provide.

> ➤ **Make sure the name is available**: This may sound obvious, but a miss here will cost you dearly. Your company name and Internet domain name should probably be the same, so check out your preferred names with your State Incorporation site, Network Solutions for the domain name, and the U.S. Patent Office for Trademarks.

> ➤ **Favor common suffixes**: Everyone will assume that your company name is your domain name minus the suffix ".com" or the standard suffix for your country. If these suffixes are not available for the name you prefer, pick a new name rather than settling for an alternate suffix such as ".net" or ".info." Get all three suffixes if you can.

> ➤ **Don't box yourself in**: Avoid picking names that don't allow your business to move around or add to its product line. This means avoiding geographic locations or product categories to your business name. With these specifics, customers will be confused if you expand your business to different locations or add on to your product line.

> ➤ **Sample potential customers**: Come up with a few different name choices and try them out on potential customers, investors, and coworkers, or do some pilot studies. Skip your family and friends who know too much. Ask questions about the names to see if they give off the impression you desire.

If you are still unsure of yourself, you should know that there are many dedicated firms, such as *Igor International* and *A Hundred Monkeys*, which can relieve you of $1 million of your hard-earned funds to come up with just the right appellation. Hmmm, I wonder how much they spent on their own names.

Paying for a domain name

Before you incorporate with your ideal company name, make sure you can get the same or similar Internet domain name for your website and email address. There is nothing more frustrating than finding and incorporating your company with a great name, only to find that the domain name you need to match is already taken or parked and is for sale to you for more money than you want to pay.

The right place to start is to target today's average of approximately $8-$10 per year for a .com domain name from GoDaddy or one of the hundreds of other domain name registrars. Certain extensions such as .tv and .vs range between $20 to $40 for a year's registration, but you can find sales on certain extensions for as little as fifty cents per year.

But amazingly, most of the *good* names have already been bought by speculators (domain name investors), who are just looking for someone like you to really need the name, and be willing to pay extra for it.

Who owns all of these names, and should you ever buy one for a premium? The simple answer is that if you want to be found on the Web, and have consistent naming for your company and website, the perfect domain name can be well worth a few thousand dollars, but don't pay a fortune for one.

The market for domain investors has been in the doldrums for the last few years, since the **Internet Corporation for Assigned Names and Numbers** (ICANN) has rolled out top-level domains for every country, such as .us and .me, as well as allowing companies to set up their own top-level domains. For instance, Cisco has applied to use URLs that end in .cisco.

Gone are the days when people like Frank Schilling (`http://domainnamewire.com/2012/12/14/2012-impact-stories-frank-schilling-becomes-a-service-provider/`) and Kevin Ham (`http://money.cnn.com/magazines/business2/business2_archive/2007/06/01/100050989/`) built $300 million empires by speculating on premium domain names, since the possibilities are now endless.

Only one sold for seven figures in 2012 (`www.investing.com` sold for $2.5 million), and the average is now down to below $5,000. The current record (`http://www.domaining.com/topsales/`) was set in 2010, when `www.sex.com` sold for $13 million. Remember that just because the domain name is very expensive, that doesn't mean it will be successful. Most expensive names are not worth the money.

So how do you decide whether you should be looking at the low end or the high end of these ranges? I suggest that you follow these steps to get the name you need for your business:

> ➤ **First, pick the right company and the matching domain name**: The names don't have to match, but it sure makes branding and recognition easier if they are at least similar. Starting and naming a company today is a world-wide decision. Make sure the names don't have negative connotations in another language. Google Translate can help you on this one.

> ➤ **Register the name and its related suffixes, if available**: Registration of the domain name is easy and simple through most hosting sites, if nobody already owns it. It's a good idea to also buy between three and twenty names with spellings and suffixes that are close to your primary address, or that could be confused with it.

> ➤ **Rename your company to match an available domain name**: With today's pervasive Internet searching and shopping, the domain name may well be more important than your company name. As a startup, the cost to rename your company and change existing collateral may be less than dealing with unmatched names or premium domain pricing.

> ➤ **Otherwise, find the owner**: With 150 million names already in use, chances are someone else may have already snagged your favorite. First, you have to find the current owner, using Domain Tools or other lookup functions available on the net. Then ask them whether the domain name is for sale, but don't tip your hand by making a specific offer.

➤ **Negotiate for the name**: Contemplate your available budget, the potential value of the name to you, and the range of possible prices mentioned above. Then, decide whether you are game to complete the negotiation yourself, or whether you should consider an intermediary, such as www.moniker.com, and expect to pay a fee ranging from $250 to $500. Every price listed should be assumed negotiable, so I would start by offering half the listed number. Only you can decide the ultimate value of the ideal domain name you want.

➤ **Consider leasing or lease-to-own**: If the price is too high, work with the domain name's owner to agree on a "lease-to-own" deal for the domain name. This will allow your company to build some assets before committing the capital. Prices may continue to go down, or in the worst case, you won't need the name for the long term. Of course, the opposite is also true, so the price may well go up as you show some success.

➤ **Get the agreement in writing as quickly as possible**: Once you have a deal, immediately open up an escrow account, such as www.escrow.com. The faster you fund the account, the better chances you have of the seller not being able to back out. Remember that many domain moguls don't have a sterling reputation, so no handshake deals.

Whether by crafting a great new name or wresting one from a previous owner, every new business needs to master the domain game early, and it need not break the bank. Spending big money up-front or changing domains down the line are both painful and costly. Do your homework up-front to save you lots of recovery work and money later.

The official start date of your business is an important milestone

In any case, the official start date for your technical startup is the date you incorporate the business. This is obviously important for tax purposes, but this may also dramatically influence how potential investors, customers, and competitors look at you.

My rule of thumb expectation is that it should take two months to set up the legal entity, six months to finalize the business plan, and by the end of the first year, you should have a prototype product ready for customers. At this point, every potential investor will listen. Timelines that vary dramatically from these will be questioned, and they need to have good explanations. Taking too much time may be seen by potential investors as a lack of commitment, or just plain poor management.

For time and effort considerations, I tell clients that a sole proprietorship or partnership is the simplest setup because it basically requires no legal forms. Incorporation as an LLC, a C-Corp, or an S-Corp is more complex, but has the great legal advantage of limiting liability to the entity, away from personal assets.

A C-Corp is the most complex, as explained at the beginning of this chapter, and is recommended when you need multiple classes of stock, expect venture investments, or have over 100 shareholders. But even this one can be done in a month in most states.

For more specific considerations, you should consult your attorney, or at least visit one of the many sites (http://www.limitedliabilitycompanycenter.com/llc_vs_corp.html) that focus on this process. Many startups defer the incorporation decision until they have an investor lined up, but that can raise significant tax issues and add an additional delay to the receipt of funding, as I will outline in the following section on protecting your founder's stock.

Apart from the tax considerations, there is nothing wrong with tinkering and honing an idea for years (on your own funding) before you incorporate a company and take it to the market. But once you incorporate the company, all measurements start and you need to keep the process moving.

Consequently, if you approach investors for funding, and they find out that your company was formed five years ago but has gone nowhere due to your other activities or false starts, they will likely assume that you are a procrastinator, or worse yet, that you have failed to make progress despite your best efforts. No investment will be forthcoming, and competitors have likely closed in.

On the other end of the spectrum, remember that you only get one chance for "first impressions" with investors, so don't rush it by trying to sell your "idea" to investors with only a verbal spiel, before you even have a company or an investment pitch. Save these discussions for friends, family, and trusted business advisors.

In conjunction with the timings above, here are my recommendations on the sequence of events:

1. Focus and solidify your product idea and company name before incorporating.
2. Incorporate before spending big money on development or assets to limit liability.
3. Assemble the core team for development using personal friends or family funding.
4. Move quickly to prepare the case for external funding, if angel investors are required.
5. Build a minimum product, add sales, and test the market quickly, then iterate.
6. Scale the business, getting venture capital funding as required.

Obviously, timings can vary dramatically when technology or regulatory constraints are involved. The key is to show everyone a record of continuing momentum. If investors or customers lose confidence in you, or you run out of cash, the momentum can stop on your startup as quickly as it starts.

Tip

Your timeline and momentum is the message you scratch in the sand for investors. Don't let the passage of too much time blow it away.

Protecting your startup founder's stock shares

Part of the incorporation process is the creation of a few stock shares (ten million is a common starting point), known initially as Founder's shares. You sell a portion of these, meaning a portion of your equity ownership, to investors when and if they provide funding, and you may give a portion to partners and key employees as part of their compensation and commitment to your startup. Try to keep at least 51 percent for yourself to retain control of your company.

In reality, so-called "founder's" shares are simply common stock, issued at the time of startup incorporation, for a very low price, and normally allocated to the multiple initial players commensurate with their investment or role. However, that's only the beginning of the story.

These shares are allocated and committed, but not really issued and owned (vested) until later. Typically, vesting in startups occurs monthly over 4 years, starting with the first 25 percent of such shares vesting only after the employee has remained with the company for at least 12 months (one year "cliff"). Vesting always stops when an employee leaves the company. For further details on these terms and other common options, there are many good sources (such as `http://www.thedailymba.com/2009/12/20/startup-stock-options-explained/`) on the Internet.

Even though the class is common stock, founders can negotiate special vesting and other terms as part of their stock restriction agreement upon venture investment. Here are some typical special terms and considerations for founder's stock. If these make no sense to you, or you have others, I recommend that you schedule some time with an attorney for further details and legal recommendations:

> ➤ **Negligible real value**: Since founder's shares are usually issued at the time the company is incorporated, they essentially have no real value. As the company builds its value, shares allocated later for employees or partners will have an appropriate price.

> ➤ **Vesting with no cliff**: Most founder vesting are not subject to the one-year cliff because partners should already know and trust each other. Thus, most founders will start vesting their shares from the date they actually started providing services to the company.

> ➤ **Right of repurchase in favor of the company**: This clause gives the founder the first right of refusal to buy shares back from a partner who decides to leave early, or otherwise makes a troublemaker out of themselves. This right usually "lifts" over time, meaning that as time goes on, fewer shares are subject to this repurchase agreement.

> ➤ **Accelerated vesting conditions**: They might also have special terms in the case of material change of control in the company, such as an acquisition, causing termination or demotion of the shares or issuance, earlier than planned (accelerated vesting). These have less to do with the type of stock and more to do with who the person is and how strategic they are to the organization.

> ➤ .**Stock dilution control**: While most employees would see their vesting suspended or stopped when the "Series A" round closes, a founder might retain some percent of their shares. Everyone wants to minimize dilution of shares (more shares issued means existing shares are worth less), so this special clause is common.

Unfortunately, founders often make the mistake of waiting until they have received a strong indication of interest from an investor before they decide that it is time to incorporate. Forming a company so close in time to raising capital can create a significant tax issue.

For example, if founders issue themselves stock for one cent per share when they form the company, and then within a short period of time, outside investors jump in at $1 or more per share, it might appear in an IRS audit that the founders issued themselves stocks at significantly below the fair market value per share.

The difference in value between what the founders paid and the fair market value of that stock based on actual sale to outside investors will be characterized as compensation income, resulting in what could be significant tax liability to the founders.

The way to avoid this risk is by filing an "83(b) election" (`http://theneighborhoodentrepreneur.com/how-to-file-an-83b-election/`) with the IRS within 30 days of the purchase of your founder's shares and paying your tax early on those shares. Failing to file the 83(b) election is a common mistake of founders that you should avoid.

There should be no tax concern for a founder investing more of their own money at any time in the process. All the tax concerns relate to "outside" investors coming in shortly after incorporation. Valuation has very little meaning until an outsider invests.

So my advice is to incorporate and allocate founder's stock as soon as you are starting real work on the company, but it should be at least six months before you anticipate any outside investors. However, don't incorporate too early, as investors will measure your growth and progress since the incorporation date. Several years of apparent inactivity since incorporation will make it look like there is a problem with you or with the company.

Of course, I have to add my caveat that I'm not a lawyer, and these comments do not constitute a legal opinion. See a qualified business attorney if you anticipate multiple investors or a complex company structure. Don't let a positive investor decision take the joy out of your future.

Minimizing the red tape and taxes of a startup

Another common question I get from technical entrepreneurs is how should I set up my company to minimize my setup costs, tax liabilities, and risk of lawsuits? The answers are different in every part of the world, but the parameters here in the U.S. should give you the considerations you need in any environment. I'll offer you a few simple rules of thumb.

If you are certain that you are building a large national corporation with more than 100 investors and multiple classes of stock, as mentioned in an earlier section, then you might as well start with a Delaware or Nevada C-Corp. If you aren't so sure, need something fast, or need to keep your costs low, then an LLC is the best legal and taxable entity to facilitate your startup. Here are the key steps:

> ➤ **Form the simplest legal entity early to cover your efforts**: Don't wait for that first investor, the first prototype, or that first lawsuit. Incorporate your startup after the business plan but before you spend a dollar on product development. The alternatives include a sole proprietorship, LLC (Limited Liability Company), S-Corp (Subchapter-S Corporation), or C-Corp (U.S. Corporation).
>
> While the sole proprietorship is the simplest, it is essentially comingling your personal and business assets. The harsh downside is that you might lose your house and other personal possessions if your business fails, or get sued. Each of the other three has a great legal advantage of limiting liability to the entity and preserving personal assets.

> ➤ **Declare a separate taxable entity to optimize taxes**: Many entrepreneurs don't realize that the tax entity election doesn't have to match the legal entity. For example, an LLC with two or more members (even a husband and wife) will revert by default to a partnership for tax purposes, and report income through Schedule K-1 (`https://turbotax.intuit.com/tax-tools/tax-tips/Small-Business-Taxes/What-is-a-Schedule-K-1-Tax-Form-/INF19204.html`). Any LLC or S-Corp can elect to be treated for tax purposes as a sole proprietorship (Schedule C) or partnership (Schedule K). Or, any LLC can use Form 2553 Election by a Small Business Corporation (`http://www.irs.gov/uac/Form-2553,-Election-by-a-Small-Business-Corporation`) to be treated for tax purposes as an S-Corp. Now would be a good time to see your lawyer or accountant if you need more details.

> ➤ **The initial paperwork defines the start date of your business**: The first step can be done online in a few minutes by filling out Form SS-4 to request an EIN (Employer Identification Number) (`http://www.irs.gov/uac/Form-SS-4,-Application-for-Employer-Identification-Number-(EIN)`). An LLC or S-Corp or C-Corp requires several more forms to create, and a publication in a newspaper. If you do it yourself, this process will likely take a couple of months and cost a few hundred dollars (much more if you use a lawyer).

> ➤ **Every startup business needs annual tax return coverage**: For corporations, the annual tax return due date is March 16th in the U.S. LLCs and sole-proprietorships become part of your personal tax-filing package, so the due date for these is April 16th. In addition, corporations have quarterly filing requirements, and even monthly ones, if you collect sales taxes and hire employees.

> ➤ **Upgrade your business entity as required**: Legal requirements and tax requirements change as a business grows, so your entity needs to be reviewed regularly. For example, you and your partner may be perfectly happy with an LLC, but venture capital or angel investors may insist on having "preferred" stock, forcing an upgrade to a C-Corp. A few states like Delaware and Nevada offer tax advantages to large companies.

If you need help, there are plenty of places you can go online, like BusinessUSA.gov. If you are totally confused by the online information, take an appointment with a local agency such as your industry association, your local SCORE (http://www.score.org/) office, or your nearest Small Business Development Center (SBDC) (http://www.sba.gov/content/small-business-development-centers-sbdcs). If all else fails, hire an attorney to guide you through the special cases.

However, don't be misled. Minimizing red tape and taxes is a necessary but insufficient effort to ensure the success of your startup. On the other hand, I've seen several innovative and substantial technical startup efforts derailed by lack of focus on legal or taxation issues. That's a painful way to die or wish you had never started.

Every technical startup needs a website

These days, if your technical startup does not have an Internet home base up and running, you are not ready for business or potential investors. Customers go there to check on the details of your offerings and verify that you are not a scam, investors look there to check out your management and sales approach, and suppliers expect to find contact information.

There should be no doubt that an Internet presence is as basic to success in business today, as brick and mortar was a hundred years ago. Yet, I am amazed to see U.S. Census Bureau data (http://www.statisticbrain.com/businesses-with-no-website-statistics/) from 2012 indicate that at least 50 percent, maybe up to 75 percent, of small businesses still have no presence at all. These are soon to be the walking dead, and the competitors you can beat today.

In fact, you need to have at least a prototype website published several weeks before you expect anyone to find yours, since it takes that amount of time for the web search engine "spiders" to find you and index your content. I still remember my disappointment the first time I published my website, did an immediate Google search on the name, and it said my company didn't exist.

There are many practical reasons for going to work early on your website. Here are a few:

➤ **Register domain name and set up hosting**: I've often said that the Internet domain name should be reserved at the same time you incorporate your company name – they need to be the same, or highly related. Yet, I still hear stories of companies being well down the road on products and collateral with a given name, only to find out that everything has to be changed because of a domain name conflict or availability problem.

➤ **Websites are a big job and take time**: I've also known startups that have worked for months on the infrastructure of their business—front office, manufacturing, product design, marketing, personnel, and sales—and then started work on a website in parallel with their "grand opening." Yet, two months later, they neither had a website nor a customer. You should allow three months for the design, building, and rollout of your first site. You can actually build it yourself these days, unless you prefer outsourcing. Either way, it should only take a few days for the first usable iteration.

> ➤ **Finalizing the website validates your product plan and sales strategy**: Many founders find that building the website forces them to commit on the product design, set a final pricing, define ordering and delivery procedures, and actually schedule and staff the marketing events that they have in mind.

> ➤ **Viral and affiliate marketing needs a website**: Everyone knows that word-of-mouth advertising is an effective and important part of any small business. However, word-of-mouth and viral marketing don't work without a website. Affiliate and other marketing programs also benefit from the visibility of a website.

> ➤ **The website can be a source of revenue**: If your business and product are as attractive as you believe, the traffic to your website will build quickly. Now, you should monetize that aspect of your business through the use of Google AdSense to display ads for related products and businesses, and get paid for the "click-throughs."

> ➤ **Your website will promote your business 24 hours a day, 7 days a week**: Like you probably do, many people search for products and services over the weekends and in the evening. They are busy business people, and often, this is the best time for them to concentrate on researching a new product or service. As a business owner, there is nothing more satisfying than having several orders and email inquiries waiting for you when you get up in the morning!

In fact, you can set up a web presence these days on social media alone, by creating a company page on Facebook, company profile on LinkedIn, or a free blog with static pages on WordPress. These may not have the globally recognized *www.companyname.com* domain name, but will certainly put you in touch with the new Internet generation.

I've heard all the excuses for not stepping up to this requirement—like I don't have the time, skills, or money. But believe me, the costs these days are trivial, compared to the benefits. For the first time, you have at your disposal the whole world market for whatever product or service you happen to provide. It's time to turn the light on and let the world know you exist.

Business blog – an alternative to a business website

Blogging has come a long way in the past few years, from a social release for narcissists to today's required vehicle for promoting your consulting business and gaining valuable online exposure. Even with product businesses, it's the ultimate way to build your brand credibility, bring in customer leads, and get feedback from your target market.

Let me be clear—a product or consulting startup today without a blog, even with a static website, risks not being competitive in cost and time to reach and hold that critical mass of online customers. If you can't justify both a website and a blog, skip the old-fashioned website and make your blog do double duty as described later.

The challenge, as with all new technologies, is to make it work effectively and avoid wasted effort and expensive mistakes. Here are some tips I've gleaned from experience:

> ➤ **Lead with your blog**: You should start blogging about your business before you have a product, to test interest and establish your credibility. Several free blog platforms, such as WordPress, are so flexible that you can configure them as a website as well as your blog, without separate hosting.

> ➤ **Add content regularly**: Every business wants its website to appear on the first page of search engine results from a relevant search , known as Search Engine Optimization (SEO). Blogs help because sites that update data frequently get higher SEO rankings. When you post to a blog multiple times each week, you content is constantly changing and growing.

> ➤ **Anchor the blog in your domain name**: If you do have a separate web domain name, such as *www.domainname.com*, then your blog name should be the domain name suffix "/blog" or "blog.domainname.com." Otherwise, your blog content will be indexed separately from your website content, resulting in a lower overall Google rank.

> ➤ **Conversational style**: Search the Internet for blogs in your industry and do a little research before you start. Studying other people's blogs will help you identify what you like and don't like, and how you want yours to look and feel. An informal writing style is generally recommended.

> ➤ **Add outgoing links**: For example, if you mention an article you read in XYZ magazine, make sure to include a hyperlink to the article. Your readers will appreciate the option to view the sites you reference, and having links that point to other sites will further improve your search engine rankings.

> ➤ **Create incoming links**: Promote your blog by including your blog link in your e-mail signature, on your website, in social networking profiles, and by providing signed comments to other blogs on a daily basis. You should also submit your blog name to directories such as *Blog Catalog* and *Technorati*.

> ➤ **Leverage blog content**: It doesn't take long to build up a sizable amount of blog content. You can repurpose your posts into articles, books, and reports. Many bloggers have found publishing success and Google ads revenue from the blog to be a substantial source of revenue to bolster their mainline business.

Finally, if you don't have the time, energy, or skills to write a blog, it may be a good investment to hire a ghost writer, or hand the job over to your marketing executive. Don't be shy. I don't know many CEOs today who write their own speeches and marketing materials. Focus on what you do best, and let professionals do the rest for you.

To be successful, you have to get your message out there, and make your company stand out above all the clutter. Use social networks such as Twitter to "pull" in the business. Be a blogger today, and trump your competitors tomorrow.

The biggest excuse most technical startup founders mention is too much to do while building a product, and mapping strategy, investors, etc. For blogging to work, you need to do it consistently and frequently, at least once a week, or the value evaporates. I know that finding time is hard, and good writing is simply not what most people do. But here are some key reasons for giving it a priority early, even before shipping a product:

> **You can validate the need and your solution before spending money**: Too many technical entrepreneurs spend big money on development, only to find out that the solution isn't quite right. Feedback from your blog will tell you quickly whether anyone agrees with your assessment, and whether you have a customer base waiting.

> **Find potential partners**: Most of the people you would want as cofounders are now cruising relevant blogs for ideas and partners. It's a great way to find like-minded people, and get a dialog going. From a networking standpoint, it's a lot more efficient than going to seminars and other industry events.

> **Populate your team**: Smart potential employees are also reading blogs to stay up-to-date in their field, and finding new leaders. More and more employees work for people they respect rather than companies. Take the initiative to put yourself out there. Of course, ultimately, you want employees who can blog for you and your company as well.

> **Cultivate early customers**: It's never too early to start a dialog with customers, as long as you don't mislead them about where you are in the cycle. Build your brand and get leads today. There's also the opportunity to do some consulting with interested customers to provide the required revenue while the product is still under development.

> **Build your credibility with investors**: A blog is an excellent vehicle to meet investors before you are ready to ask them for money. You will also learn about competitors who can't resist responding to a well-written blog. Once you gain real traction as an expert in your space through the blog, investors will put you at the top of their funding list.

> **Hone your communication skills**: Writing a blog is all about communication, and that's your number one job as a founder of a new startup. Trying to write something for someone else to understand quickly will tell you if you really understand it yourself. Even if you use a ghost writer for your blog, the briefing process will enhance your skills.

> **Your Google ranking will go up dramatically**: Whereas Google and other search engines may take two or three weeks to list your new website in search results, new blog sites and blog entries are indexed every day. From comments, you will accumulate external links both into and out of your site, and get additional ranking from Google.

Since a startup by definition is not a recognized brand, you are the brand, based on the social media culture of today. People assume your startup is real if they see real people, and they will attribute credibility to your startup based on your own credentials and the quality of information you offer through your blog. If no real person is visible, and no blog is presented to show a culture and personality, your technical startup may be relegated to the bottom of a very long list.

Kick-starting your startup with Twitter

First, I'll try to answer the most common question I still get from business people, "What is Twitter, really?". For business people, it's a way to put out "sound bites" or tiny ads on the Internet, much like you see in the mainstream media on TV, but without the cost to your prime audience.

Actually, they are "text bytes," like cell phone text messages in length, and they are broadcast to all your followers, or directed at select recipients. People can respond in the same fashion with personal requests or general comments. The important responses are real "business leads."

A lot of technical entrepreneurs are doing some very innovate things with Twitter in order to build their brand and find leads for their business. Here are some practical tips to get you started:

> ➤ **Offer something of value**: Make the relationship win-win. This means give before you expect to get—free advice, special promotions, a pointer to useful information, or sometimes just a friendly conversation. Show that you are a real, sincere, and trustworthy person.

> ➤ **Search tweets for business leads**: With Twitter Search and a host of free tools on the Internet, you can mine the universe for all tweets of people who need your product or service. Set up filters to find them and follow up diligently and politely on every lead.

> ➤ **Use free tools to improve efficiency**: Twitter's native user interface is designed primarily for personal use and not optimized for business. Use tools like TweetDeck to set up your control room, SocialOomph to spread out your responses, and WeFollow to find key players in your domain. There are many others, including the smart phone app for remote use.

> ➤ **Create a separate account for your business**: If you like Twitter for personal notes to your friends, use another account for business activity. Your business account should have a name, picture, and tone that reflect your business brand and logo.

> ➤ **Become an authority in your area**: One of the challenges of buying things on the Internet is to identify quality sources from the scammers. Use Twitter to personalize your business, knowledge, integrity, and your leadership. People still buy from people.

> ➤ **Stay top-of-mind with experts**: Seek them out, offer interesting links, respond to tweets, and post thoughts for conversation at least a few times a day. Twitter is not like e-mail, where people diligently save and respond to every message. Stand out from everything else in the stream.

> ➤ **Follow potential clients**: That's how you tell your potential clients and customers that you exist. They will see you following them, check out your profile, and if you have something they can relate to, they will follow you back. This is *pull* marketing.

> ➤ **Increase the size and quality of your following**: Never stop working to increase your following, by finding others and improving your offering. A larger following means more credibility, which iteratively attracts more followers. Don't be afraid to un-follow people who don't fit.

> ➤ **Retweet for double impact**: Adding "RT @username" in front of the original tweet forwards it to your followers, and is a double win, if used selectively. It improves your value to your followers, and increases the audience and credibility of the original sender.

> ➤ **Cross link all your web profiles**: Make sure people can find you from all directions on the Internet. Your website should have a link to your blog, your Twitter profile, LinkedIn profile, Facebook, and vice versa. This also improves your Google search ranking.

> ➤ **Use analytics tools for metrics**: Free tools such as VisibleTweets.com can be used to visually analyze how much impact your tweets have made, and help you better understand your audiences.

Twitter is merely a constant stream of absolutely current public communication. The good news is you can turn it on or off as often as you like, and mine the database at very low cost for useful information. Even big technical companies such as Dell and HP use it to find customers, and claim million dollar returns. It should be on the list of valuable resources for every technical startup.

Every business needs momentum

The overall theme of using other resources, such as a website, social media, and blogging, is to build and maintain momentum for your technical startup. Too many technical entrepreneurs confuse motion with momentum and results. We all know someone who repeatedly tells us how "busy" they are, when it's hard to see what they get done. Momentum is moving things forward (mass x velocity). Founders or employees in constant motion but with no momentum will never get off the ground.

It is true that motion in any direction is often better than no motion at all. But motion without momentum is even less productive than no motion at all. For a more complete discussion of this phenomenon, refer to the book titled *Fake Work: Why People Are Working Harder than Ever but Accomplishing Less* (http://www.amazon.com/Fake-Work-Working-Accomplishing-Problem/dp/1416948244), by Brent Petersen and Gaylan Neilson.

So how do you fight this and get real momentum going in your startup? Here are some key recommendations:

> ➤ **Measure results, not work**: Build your business plan and day-to-day operations around real results that are quantifiable and measurable. For example, a result is not forty hours of work, but a prototype complete, partner contract signed, or first customer sale.

> ➤ **Focus and prioritize**: There will always be more things to do than anyone has hours in a day. Focus means act instead of react; act on the important things. Don't allow yourself to be interrupted by "urgent" issues of the moment, which may not be important.

> ➤ **Live the 80/20 rule**: Pick 20 percent of your important tasks that will deliver 80 percent of the results. Judiciously apply 20 percent of your energy where it will achieve 80 percent of the momentum you desire. Maintain that balance of work, family, sleep, and unwind.

> ➤ **Communicate effectively**: People can't do the job you want unless you communicate effectively. So they scurry around trying to look busy, or work on random things that they hope might generate momentum. Tell people what results you expect, tell them how they measure up so far, and tell them how much you appreciate their efforts.

> ➤ **Recognize the finish line**: Don't burn yourself and everyone out by continuing a forced march after you pass the finish line or even a major milestone. Gather your thoughts and savor the small successes along the way.

During the early startup phase, most of the momentum in a new company derives from the entrepreneur's own commitment and self-sacrifice. You do almost everything by yourself, and your focus is on building enough cashflow so you can start bringing in people to help you. Watch yourself for wasted motion during this stage.

Cashflow is the element of momentum that allows you to hand over jobs to other people and do more of your core passion jobs, such as creating content or designing new products. This creates more value in your business and increasing cashflow, that is more momentum.

What you then want is for the momentum to compound with each new employee or outsourcer you hire to help, in order to give you more time to create value, and ultimately, increase profits. At this point especially, you need to watch out for fake work, which thrives in less dedicated hires, outdated cultures, and old work processes.

Recent research (http://www.forbes.com/sites/dovseidman/2012/09/20/ everything-we-think-about-employee-engagement-is-wrong/) indicates that across all business organizations, as much as 50 percent of the work that people do in that stage is just motion that is not related to their company's strategies. Think of the drag this can put on your momentum.

Starting a new business is a little like taking off for the first time as the pilot of a new airplane. You need to push that throttle all the way to the dashboard until your knuckles are white, but never forget the relationship between motion and momentum. If you don't push the right levers, you may have a product or an invention, but you won't have a business.

Summary

The goal of this chapter has been to identify those key non-technical things that you need to do to start a technical business, assuming you already know the requirements for building your product. Starting a technical business is not rocket science, but it does require an understanding of many key legal, financial, and marketing expectations. Attention to due diligence on the challenges of incorporation, stock issuance, accounting, website naming, and social media setup are just as critical to your success as getting your technical product right.

Now that these have been carefully evaluated and resolved, it's time to focus on a business plan. The next chapter will tell you what you need to know about the requirements for a business plan, as well as the specific elements that have to be addressed for potential investors and strategic partners, and just for managing your own team. Let's get started.

Does a Technical Entrepreneur Really Need a Business Plan?

The thought of preparing a business plan for the first time can be very intimidating. There are many critical elements, and it's easy to get lost in the details. Many entrepreneurs tell me that they don't know where to start or if a business plan is even required. The goal of this chapter is to clarify the considerations and guide you through the implementation you choose.

There are indeed situations where a business plan is not a high priority; these situations will be outlined in this chapter. However, I always recommend that you write a business plan, as I have found from personal experience that I don't realize what I don't know until I try to write it down. Very few entrepreneurs can keep the whole blueprint for their business in their head and communicate it effectively to all the stakeholders without a written document.

To be effective, it must also be a living document. This means that it must be updated as you learn more and things change. It should be the primary means of educating new employees, new contractors, and keeping your own personal company goals aligned.

This chapter discusses all the pros and cons of a business plan and then tells you how to build one with all the basic sections, including supporting elements such as a financial model, market research, and an elevator pitch, without a huge cost or investment in time.

When do you really need a business plan?

On a regular basis, I am approached by technical entrepreneurs who assert that business plans are a waste of time. They cite sources such as a recent BusinessWeek story, *"Real Entrepreneurs Don't Write Business Plans"* (http://www.businessweek.com/articles/2013-04-25/real-entrepreneurs-dont-write-business-plans) and "Investors Pay Business Plans Little Heed, Study Finds" (http://www.nytimes.com/2009/05/14/business/smallbusiness/14hunt.html?_r=0). From my perspective as a professional investor and long-time advisor to entrepreneurs, much of this urban legend advice is just plain wrong.

Of course there are scenarios where a written business plan is not critical, but I haven't seen one yet where a well-written 15-page document or at least a 10-slide pitch is negative. Let's look at some common scenarios and put this into perspective for technical entrepreneurs:

➤ **You don't need or want investors or a loan**: With bootstrapping, no business plan is expected by anyone. Yet I would suggest that creating a plan is still a valuable exercise, as you need the plan as the blueprint for your company, team communication, and progress metrics, unless your management style makes this a waste of time.

➤ **You have built a successful startup and plan to use the same investors**: If you have a proven track record, investors don't have to see a written plan to believe you can do the job. In fact, they are probably in such a hurry to give you money that they don't want you to waste time writing anything down and passing it along to new investors.

➤ **You need funding and plan to get it from friends and family**: Hopefully, you know your friends and family better than I do, so you decide when a business plan is required. If your rich uncle is an accountant or has his own business, I recommend a good business plan. On the other hand, your mother probably won't read one.

➤ **You need an investor and want a document to mass mail everyone**: Creating a business plan for this purpose is a waste of time. In fact, the whole process is a waste of time. Most VCs and Angel investors don't read unsolicited proposals, unless they have met you first or have a glowing recommendation from another investor or acquaintance.

➤ **You need money and plan to do crowdfunding**: Although, technically, the major crowd funding sites today including Kickstarter and Indiegogo, don't request a business plan, they do require essentially the same information in a project format. Thus, building a business plan ahead of time will improve your application and chances of success.

➤ **You need an investor and want to solicit professionals online**: Major platforms are available online to find Angel groups or VCs, including Gust and AngelList. These platforms and every investor who uses them to find entrepreneurs expect to find a good business plan posted. You won't even be considered without a business plan.

➤ **You find an interested investor and need to close the deal**: Most professional investors, even if they like your story and were properly introduced by a friend, will ask for a business plan at the due diligence stage. They want to see if you have done your homework, have reasonable expectations, and are willing to commit to something.

You might fairly conclude from these points that a business plan is only "required" if you want to close funding from professional investors who don't already know you or know your track record. As the best VCs deal primarily with known and proven entrepreneurs, it's easy for them to say that they don't read business plans.

On the other hand, don't forget Angel investors who funded 60 times as many startups as VCs to the tune of $20 billion last year. They start their search primarily from platforms such as the ones mentioned earlier. A business plan may be a small investment to get a shot at that opportunity.

For the rest of you entrepreneurs, consider the value of a business plan when it is not "required." Clemson University professor, William B. Gartner, looked at data a while back from the Panel Study of Entrepreneurial Dynamics (http://www.entrepreneur.com/article/198618), and found that writing a plan increased the chances that a person would actually go into business, by two and a half times.

Of course, building a plan is not an alternative to getting out there and doing something. There is no substitute to knowing your customers first hand and iterating on a minimum viable product to find the most marketable solution. Writing it down promotes both understanding and commitment.

Overall, I sense that not writing a business plan is more often an excuse rather than a time saver. Building a business is a long-term, complex task, like building a house. Would you give money to someone, without a plan, who had never built a house before? Hopefully, you wouldn't even build your own house without a plan. You should treat your new business with the same respect.

Valid reasons for not writing a business plan yet

If you are still intimidated by the thought of writing a business plan, it may be that you just have too many open issues on your mind for a plan to even make sense. In this case, more and more professionals suggest that an alternate strategy is to explore and fine-tune your assumptions before declaring a specific plan with financial projections based only on your dream and passion.

In the process, you can save yourself considerable rework and money or even decide that your dream needs more time to mature before you commit your limited resources or sign up with investors to a painful and unsatisfying plan.

For details on activities suggested in lieu of building a business plan, I recommend the book, *Beyond the Business Plan*, Simon Bridge and Cecilia Hegarty, Palgrave Macmillan, which outlines tradeoffs and recommends 10 principles for every new venture explorer. Here is my edited summary of their 10 principles, which I like and which might convince you that you don't need a business plan at all, or, at the very least, will help you write a better one later:

> ➤ **A new venture is a means, not an end**: A new enterprise should be pursued primarily to help you achieve your goals such as providing a better life for others, satisfying a passion of yours, or enjoying the benefits of a technology you have invented. In this context, it could be a social enterprise or even a hobby, and a business plan may not be beneficial.

➤ **Don't start by committing more than you can afford to lose**: New ventures are usually exploratory and risky in nature, so don't let any business plan process convince you to commit more than you can risk as a person, if your exploration fails. Start with an effectual approach that evaluates risk tolerance, and suggests a more affordable means to an end.

➤ **Pick a domain where you have some experience and expertise**: Don't handicap yourself by starting something for which you have to build or acquire knowledge, skills, and connections from scratch. No business plan will save you if you are just picking ideas at random or copying others just because the story sounds attractive.

➤ **Carry out reality checks and make appropriate plans**: Before a business plan has any validity, some work is required to validate that your technology works, a real market exists, and your assumptions for cost and price are reasonable. Don't be totally driven by your own passions, the emotional enthusiasm of friends, or even third-party research.

➤ **The only reliable test is a real one**: Using market research techniques to try to predict the market's response to a new venture can be costly and are often unreliable. Testing for real is the assumption behind approaches such as Lean Startup. It is also what explorers do—they go and look, instead of trying to predict from a distance what they will find.

➤ **Get started and get some momentum**: Too much hesitation will kill any new venture, as markets move quickly and difficulties mount. Getting started helps generate momentum and the sense of having done something that provides encouragement, more incentive to keep going, and can carry your startup over obstacles. Early perseverance pays off.

➤ **Accept uncertainty as the norm**: You will never remove all uncertainties, so accept them, and plan your activities in an incremental fashion. Too often, a business plan is seen as a mechanism to eliminate uncertainty, lulling the founder into complacency. Eliminate major uncertainties before the plan, and update any plan as you learn.

➤ **Look for new opportunities**: Many useful opportunities are either created by what you do early or are only revealed once you have started and can see out there. So, keep your eyes open and respond to new customers, new markets, and new partnerships. You will also find that looking hard also eliminates opportunities that are not acceptable.

➤ **Build and use social capital**: Social capital is people and connections. No entrepreneur can survive as an island. Social capital is as important as financial capital for all ventures. As with all capital, you can use only as much as you have acquired to date. If you have no social capital, no business plan will likely get you the financial capital you need.

➤ **Acquire the relevant skills**: Three basic skill sets are required for successful delivery of almost every venture. These include financial management, marketing and sales, and the appropriate production ability. If you don't have the relevant skills and knowledge, take the time to build them or find someone to partner with, before you attempt any business plan.

After exploring these principles, if you do decide to continue building a conventional business, especially with investors and employees other than yourself, I'm more than ever convinced that a business plan is a valuable exercise. You should do it yourself to make sure that you understand all the elements of the plan and facilitate communication of the specifics to your team and investors.

In essence, building a complete and credible plan is the final test of whether your venture has "legs," which means whether the opportunity matches your resources, skills, opportunity, and a level of risk you are prepared to handle. The entrepreneur lifestyle is all about doing something you enjoy, without undue stress, uncertainty, and risk. Don't let the lack of a plan bring back that stress and risk.

The difference between product plans and business plans

Once you seriously start working on your business plan, the most common shortcut I see with technical entrepreneurs, which doesn't work, is to use their product plan with a few changes as the business plan. The result is a disaster, as these may sound similar but are not even close to being the same thing. I define a product plan as a detailed description of your product or service, with a bit of business thrown in at the end. A business plan is a detailed description of your business, with a bit of product description thrown in near the front.

Don't get me wrong. It's definitely positive to have a product plan or specification. A simple differentiation is that a product plan is designed for internal use, to get the product out. A business plan is an "outward facing" document for external investors or for C-level executives within your own company.

The product plan tells your developers what to build and the marketing team what to market. As it addresses an internal audience, it can use technical jargon and assume that the reader understands the technology. Here are the key components of a good product plan:

> **Detailed features**: For software, websites, and high-tech products, this is the "meat" of what you intend to build. Enough detail is required so that someone else can build it without you (outsourcing). Equally important is that marketing and sales people should be able to identify benefits and marketing strategies, set prices, and validate a business model.

> **Market research**: This section defines the market, sizes the opportunity, and discusses the needs and requirements that will be addressed by your product and service. Establishing credibility is the key, so this data should come primarily from industry experts, with footnotes to the source, rather than from your assumption that everyone needs one.

> **Competition analysis**: There are always competitors or alternative ways to get the job done. Here is where you pick a few of these, categorize what they do, and position your own product to show your competitive advantage.

> ➤ **Development and rollout**: Show the timeline, milestones, costs, and people required to produce the product or service. Address proof of concept, performance considerations, quality certification, and support ramping.

Concurrently or later, it's necessary to build a separate business plan. As this document is "outward facing," the tone and level has to change so that it is understood by customers and investors. Here are some key components:

> ➤ **Problem statement and solution**: Skip the acronyms, write at an eighth-grade level, and talk in terms of "benefits" rather than "features." Assume that readers don't know or share your vision, knowledge, and passion, so you have to sell them on your plan at all levels.

> ➤ **Market research and competition**: Reuse the two comparable sections mentioned earlier, making sure you refocus the words for an external audience and remove the technical jargon. These are the only sections that these two plans have in common.

> ➤ **Business model, executive team, marketing and sales, financials, and funding**: These are all new and critical sections of a business plan. More details will be provided on these later in this chapter.

Actually, it's the most disconcerting when people approach me with neither—just a verbal description of their "idea," looking for a business assessment of its potential. In frustration, I usually comment to them that ideas are worthless outside the context of a realistic business plan. Even with a product pitch, I get no view of the business model and opportunity, so no business assessment is possible.

I realize that most technical entrepreneurs feel certain that an exciting product plan will highlight an exciting business opportunity. Instead, most investors will see it as a "solution looking for a problem." That's a big red flag and will usually get your plan a quick toss to the circular file.

Creating a good business plan

Every investor I know is frustrated with the poor quality of the business plans they get. This is sad, as "how to write a business plan" is a frequent topic found in every business journal, and it is a common title in the business section of every book store. Too many technical entrepreneurs still believe the urban myth that you can sketch your idea on a napkin, and investors will throw money at you. Believe me, an idea sketched on a napkin is not a good business plan, unless you are pitching to your rich uncle.

What is the definition of a good business plan? In simple terms, it is a document that describes all the *why, what, when, where, and how* of your business for you, your cohorts, and potential investors. Forcing yourself to write down a plan is actually the only way to make sure you actually understand it yourself.

Make sure your plan answers every relevant question that you could possibly imagine from your business partners, spouse, and potential investors. That means skip the jargon and include explanations and examples. A plan that generates more questions than it answers is not a good plan.

Finally, hone the result into a professional document. Remember that you only get one chance to make a great first impression. Make sure your plan has a cover page, table of contents, headings, page numbers, and is organized logically.

Notice that I didn't say anywhere that a good business plan has to be at least 20 pages, have 10 sections, or must start with an executive summary. These are good things, but I've seen great business plans that are 10 pages or have totally nonstandard formats. In fact, it should be adapted and tuned to the audience and the business stage, as different investment opportunities may have different expectations.

However, if you must ask, 10 sections is a nice round number and would include the following:

1. Executive summary
2. Problem and solution
3. Company description
4. Market opportunity
5. Business model
6. Competition analysis
7. Marketing and sales strategy
8. Management team
9. Financial projections
10. Exit strategy

You can get free downloads of sample business plans from the Internet, and there are thousands of customized samples to highlight every business area. You can buy software that walks you through the right questions and then generates a document in the right format. You can even download a free sample of my own business plan from my website (http://www.startupprofessionals.com/Startup-Professionals-Products.html) as a starter.

So, what if you know that you simply aren't a good writer or don't have the time or patience to write? No problem. That's why they invented ghost writers and came up with the concept that you can pay someone else to do it for you. A few thousand dollars is a small price to pay for a successful business or for that $1M investment you expect the plan to entice. However, you still have to own the plan and understand it.

The tougher case is where you really don't understand the business you are about to enter, so you don't know what to write. This is a recipe for failure that most investors and professionals can quickly see, so no investment will be forthcoming, and your startup will likely wither and die.

My advice here is to swallow your pride and find a partner or give it away to someone who has the "domain knowledge" and business experience to get you going. Your idea may be right, but dead right is not very satisfying to anyone.

Keep in mind that thoroughness and clarity of the plan are factors that will play key roles in successfully financing, starting, and operating your business. A great business plan is one that your team can learn from, attracts investors, and will guarantee your species a future. However, it needs to be great without reading like a doctoral thesis, and it should not be the size of the book *War and Peace*.

Make it a simple but effective business plan

The most effective business plans keep the wording and formatting straightforward and the plan short. The overriding principle is that your business plan must be easy to read. This means writing at the level of an average newspaper story. Understand that people will skim your plan and even try to read it while talking on the phone or going through their e-mail.

However, don't confuse simple wording and formats with simple thinking. You're keeping it simple so that you can get your point across quickly and effectively to team members and investors. With this in mind, here are some specifics that bear repeating, updated from an old article on simple plans by Tim Berry (http://www.entrepreneur. com/startingabusiness/businessplans/businessplancoachtimberry/ article76478.html):

> ➤ **Keep the plan short**: You can cover everything you need to convey in 20 pages of text. If necessary, create a separate white paper for other details and reports. The one-page plan, popularized on www.oprah.com, is a good executive summary, but it's not enough to get the investment.

> ➤ **Polish the overall look and feel**: Aside from the wording, you also want the physical look of your text to be inviting. Stick to two fonts in a standard text editor such as Microsoft Word. The fonts you use should be common sans-serif fonts, such as Arial, Tahoma, or Verdana, 10 to 12 points.

> ➤ **Don't use long complicated sentences**: Short sentences are the best, because they read faster, and reader comprehension will then be higher in all audiences.

> ➤ **Avoid buzzwords, jargon, and acronyms**: You may know that NIH means "not invented here" and KISS stands for "keep it simple, stupid," but don't assume anybody else does.

> ➤ **Simple, straightforward language**: Stick with the simpler words and phrases such as "use" instead of "utilize" and "then" instead of "at that point in time."

> ➤ **Bullet points are good**: They help organize and prioritize multiple elements of a concept or plan. However, avoid cryptic bullet points. Flesh them out with brief explanations where they are needed. Unexplained bullet points usually result in questions.

> ➤ **Don't overwhelm the plan with too many graphics and flashy colors**: Pictures and diagrams can effectively illustrate a point, but too many come across as

clutter. Good infographics can be a powerful and eye-catching tool, especially to convey essential information to skimmers, if not used to excess.

> ➤ **Use page breaks**: We can use page breaks to separate sections, separate charts from text, and highlight tables. When in doubt, go to the next page. Nobody worries about having to turn to the next page.

> ➤ **Use white space liberally, use spell-checker, and proofread**: Include 1-inch margins all around. Always use your spell-checker. Then, proofread your text carefully to be sure that you're not using a properly spelled incorrect word.

> ➤ **Include table of contents**: No investor likes searching every page for key data such as executive credentials or exit strategy. Most word processors these days can automatically generate a table of contents from your section headings. Use it.

Investors hear from too many entrepreneurs who envision a great business opportunity but don't have any written business plan at all. They think they can talk their way to a deal. It won't work. On the other end of this spectrum are entrepreneurs who present long product specifications with a few financials at the end. This is a failing strategy as well.

If you're not the type who can connect with people based on a simple message, which is told succinctly, then hire someone who can. In fact, simplicity and readability are two of the most effective strategies to sell even the most complex proposal. A business plan that is easily understood and looks professional is already half sold. Simple is not stupid.

Focusing on investors' questions

If you expect your plan to attract Angel investors or Venture Capital investors (VCs), you need to hit all their concerns as well as yours, including exit strategy, return-on-investment, and your executive credentials. The result is an investment-grade business plan. Things that make it investment-grade for outside investors will also benefit you, as you are the ultimate investor, so this really isn't extra work.

First of all, any good business plan should demonstrate that you have done the homework to be an expert in your industry and in what it takes to build a successful business from your idea. I'll skip the basics in the following sections here and highlight only the key elements that investors focus on.

Define the problem

Every plan must start with the problem you are solving, not a description of your company and product. Explain in terms that your mother could understand, and quantify the "cost of pain" in dollars or time. Terms such as "every customer needs this" and "next generation platform" are far too soft and should be avoided. Test your problem statement on friends and family to see if they get it quickly.

Many entrepreneurs scare away potential investors by claiming that their technology represents "truly disruptive technology." What this may mean is that you haven't yet figured out what problem it solves, and it may take many years for people to get it. No investor wants to wait that long for their payback or fund the years of waiting.

Solution and benefits

This is not the place for a detailed product specification, but an explanation of how and why it works, including a customer-centric quantification of the benefits. Skip the technical jargon and hyperbole. Do describe your intellectual property and "secret sauce".

Focus is the keyword here. Pick a specific solution that you have built or prototyped rather than rambling about all the possible things that could be done with your idea. Clearly define the customer, channel, and revenue model associated with this solution. Which products and services do you offer that help your customer get either a functional, social, or emotional job done, or help them satisfy their basic needs?

Industry and market sizing

Start with the evolution of the overall industry, market segmentation, market dynamics, and customer landscape. Remember that investors like industries that have a billion dollar opportunity, and a double-digit growth rate. Data from accredited market research groups such as Forrester or Gartner is required for credibility, usually couched in terms such as Total Addressable Market (TAM).

It always amazes me how an entrepreneur can define their market opportunity so broadly, and then assess their competition so narrowly in the next breath. You won't impress investors by claiming that everyone in China needs one, and nobody else has exactly the right features to compete with you.

Explain the business model

This business model is the formula that describes how you will make money, who pays you, and must include the gross margin and other parameters. In this section, you need to be passionate about revenue, profit, and volume growth. Many people seem to use the social network advertising model for revenue but forget that it assumes at least 100M users and $50M investment.

Avoid any statements like "All we have to do is get 1 percent of the market." There are two problems with this assertion: first, no investor is interested in a company that is only looking to get 1 percent of a market, and second, the first 1 percent is the toughest of any market, so you look naïve by implying that it's easy to get.

Competition and sustainable advantage

List and describe your competition, direct and indirect, including customer alternatives. Asserting that you have no competition is not credible. Then, detail your sustainable competitive advantage, and highlight barriers to entry; this will keep your competitors at bay.

Often, I see statements like "Microsoft is too big/slow to be a threat." Usually, the reason the big companies are no threat is because the market is too small. However, investors know that sleeping giants do wake up the moment your company shows some traction. Competing with IBM, Microsoft, and other large companies should never be underestimated.

What's your "sustainable competitive advantage"? How can you not be easily copied? For a software company, if another company stole your source code, is there anything unique that keeps you in business?

Marketing, sales, and partners

Describe your market penetration strategy, sales channels, pricing, and strategic partnerships. Here is also a good place for a rollout timeline with key milestones. Convince investors that you have lined up sales channels, strategic partners, and a viable marketing strategy.

Be careful with assertions like "We have strong interest from a major customer." The mention of unsigned contracts normally takes away more credibility than it adds. You can bolster this position by including a Letter of Intent (LOI), contract summaries, or even testimonials.

Executive team

Investors invest in people—not just ideas. Convince investors that your team is experienced in starting a new business and have great expertise in the selected business domain. Include Advisory Board members and key industry connections.

Sometimes, I see statements such as "A world-class CEO will be joining us after funding." Rest assured that potential investors will ask for names and place some calls. Soft responses from your candidates will definitely kill your credibility.

Funding requirements

Explain how you calculated the funding requirements, and show details on planned use of funds. Quantify existing skin-in-the-game, by insiders and outsiders, including sweat equity and capital. Include a current valuation estimate.

The most credible sizing approach is to do your financial model first with the volume, cost, and pricing parameters that you want. See where your cashflow bottoms out. If it bottoms out at minus $400K the first year, add a 25 percent buffer, and ask for $500K funding.

Financial forecast and metrics

Project both revenues and expense totals for the next 5 years and past 3 years, if relevant. Show break even and growth assumptions. Details should be available in a separate financial model, but should not be included here.

Remember that investors are looking for large, scalable, high-growth opportunities. Attractive deals show double-digit positive growth per year and revenues that are projected to $20M or more within 5 years.

If you do not have these financial projections, don't force it. Go back and look at your market and market need, and re-evaluate. Alternatively, be accepting that this is a lifestyle business and see how you can bootstrap it.

Exit strategy

This section is only required when you expect outside investors. These investors want to know that you are thinking about a liquidity event—when and how they will get their money out, with ROI. For a family business, don't project an exit.

Otherwise, identify your preferred exit strategy, including specific candidates for merger or sale, and timeframe. "Going public" (IPO) is another alternative, but it is not common. Show how your rate of return would be attractive to investors.

In summary, an investment-grade business plan is a professionally prepared document, preferably about 20 pages, to satisfy both Angel investors and Venture Capitalists. In preparing your plan, try to look at your project through the investors' eyes. If your plan is missing one or more of the elements mentioned earlier, it will likely be deemed not "fundable", and rejected. Investment-grade plans attempt to answer every question an investor could possibly ask, except maybe, "Where do I sign"?

How to do market research on a startup budget

Most technical entrepreneurs know exactly what they want to design and sell, and they are personally convinced that everyone will buy their gadget or software, for example. Yet, they often fail to realize that their view is likely biased and will be instantly discounted by potential investors. Business plans with no "industry expert" data on your target opportunity size and growth are routinely rejected.

As mentioned in an earlier section, your business plan must have an "Opportunity" section, where industry market size and growth projections are included. Within this section, investors look for footnotes that reference external sources, or quotes from notable domain experts. Absence of these raises a big red flag.

Yet, most startup teams have no idea where to start and what kinds of data to look for in building this key section of their business plan. Is it possible to get this information with minimal cost? Let me offer a few suggestions that should allow you to do the work yourself:

> **Use Internet search engines**: The Internet today, is like the Library of Congress at your fingertips. Search for any product name for census data, online research reports, trade association publications, and online newspapers with relevant statistics. Look for growth and opportunity tables than can be copied and footnoted in your plan. However, vet your sources carefully, and do not just copy data that fulfills your assumptions.

> **Visit your local university library**: On or off the Internet, there are dozens of reputable market research reports available for purchase. To give you a look first and often get the data you need, visit a university library where many of these are stocked for free access.

> **Check local economic development offices**: Almost every county and municipality has an economic development office that features market research on popular market segments in your area. Also, this is a good place to ask for pointers to other sources.

> **Visit the local bookstore**: Browsing in the business section of your local bookstore is a great way to do market research while enjoying a cup of coffee. Information here is more current than your local library, and you might even buy a book for later research.

> **Purchase online reports for a fee**: After exhausting all the free sources, go back to the Internet and order any additional report or association journal that you need, for a fee. Credible sites include Gartner Group, Market Research Reports, Frost & Sullivan, and industry trade organizations. Many trade shows and conferences also keep relevant and up–to-date industry statistics, available for a fee.

> **Informal focus groups**: In conjunction with some outside expert data, it is acceptable to add your own research, such as setting up a small focus group and documenting results. Variations include online forums, telephone surveys, direct-mail surveys, and online surveys such as SurveyMonkey or AskYourTargetMarket (www.aytm.com).

There are two types of research you'll want to collect. The big-picture market opportunity data is often considered secondary in nature. It consists of previously collected data such as demographic information, industry trends, and census information. Next, you need data as specific as possible to your product and market. This is called primary research and might include information that you generate yourself.

The information you discover will help you build a profile of your market and the industry. For instance, if you're developing a product for vehicle owners, you'd want to find out the number of vehicle owners, broken down by gender, age, and geography. Then, you would also want to know how much this market spends on vehicles, spending growth or shrinkage in the past 10 years, and industry projections.

Having no data to back up your opportunity and financial forecast is the kiss of death for any startup funding request. We all know that you can use statistics to prove any point you want, so just quoting data doesn't mean your plan is sound. Certainly, paying more for the data doesn't make it any more sound either, so check the low budget alternatives first.

What is your business model?

Every business, and every business plan, needs to have a clearly defined business model. In simple terms, this is how you plan to make money, or how your revenues will exceed your costs, including all direct and indirect costs. Even non-profits have to do this to cover overhead costs, unless they rely totally on donations. Yet I continue to see business plans, or even talk to founders, and can't find the specifics of the business model anywhere.

As Guy Kawasaki says in his book, *The Art of the Start*, if you can't describe your business model in 10 words or less, you don't have a business model. Avoid whatever business jargon is currently hip, such as strategic, mission-critical, world-class, synergistic, first-mover, or scalable. Try something like "the product costs $X, and we sell it for $Y."

Guy also says, and I agree, that the smart approach is to copy somebody else. You can innovate in technology, markets, and customers, but inventing a new business model is a bad bet. Try to relate your business model to one that's already successful and understood. Here is a summary of a half-dozen of the most common models:

➤ **Facebook model**: This is the most often attempted and failed business model today on the Internet—all the services are free, and you make money off the online advertising. This model only works once you have exceeded about 1 million pageviews per month and spent maybe $50 million to get there.

➤ **E-commerce model**: This was one of the first Internet business models à la Amazon.com and is still a popular one today. It's the electronic version of a catalog and shopping cart, and today, it rarely involves any stock of product. Products are usually drop-shipped directly by the manufacturer.

➤ **Shopkeeper model**: This is the most traditional and successful approach in use for centuries. It implies setting up a store in a location where potential customers are likely to be, with products and services on display, being sold at some multiple of cost to cover the overhead and realize a profit.

➤ **Bricks-and-clicks model**: This is a hybrid of the shopkeeper and e-commerce models, in which a company integrates both offline (bricks) and online (clicks) presences. It is also known as "click and mortar" as well as "bricks, clicks, and flips," with flips referring to catalogs. It's great for big companies such as Wal-Mart, but I don't recommend it for startups.

➤ **Razor-and-blades model**: This one has been around for many years now, and is sometimes called the "bait and hook model" or the "tied products model". The premise is offering a basic product at a very low cost, often at a loss (the "bait"). It then charges compensatory recurring amounts for refills or associated products or services (the "hook"). I'm sure you can think of many examples.

➤ **Subscription or licensing model**: Here, a customer must pay a contracted price to have access to the product or service on a periodic basis (monthly, yearly, or seasonal). The model works online, offline, through magazines, newspapers, and television. The advantage is recurring revenue without finding new customers.

There are many more models, with descriptive names such as the auction model, direct sales model, value-added reseller model, multi-level marketing model, and the freemium model. There are many sources (http://money.howstuffworks.com/5-influential-business-models.htm#page=0) on the Internet if you want more details.

The point I am making is this: pick one and provide specifics in your business plan. Define clearly who your customer is, what the customer will pay for, how much they will pay, and how much do you expect it to cost for that revenue.

Then, as investors, we can argue other equally important parts of the model, such as how big the opportunity is, how fast it's growing, and who the competitors are. Don't let your business plan get tossed before you are in the game.

You can't succeed in business without an operational model that delivers value to customers at a reasonable price, with an underlying cost that allows you to make a profit. There are no higher-level conditions that supersede this requirement—for example, businesses don't thrive just because they offer the latest technology, because everyone wants to be "green", or because their goal is to reduce world hunger.

I expect that should seem intuitive to all entrepreneurs, but every investor I know has many stories about startup funding requests with major business model elements missing. The most common failures are solutions looking for a problem, lack of a defined market, and giving away the product.

There are dozens of sources to help you construct your business model, and a good example is a recent book by venture capital investor Elizabeth Edwards, simply named *Startup* (http://elizabethedwards.com/). It is really designed as a handbook to launch a company for less. I support her assertion that a business model consists of at least the first seven of the following 10 basic elements:

➤ **Value proposition**: What is the need you fill or problem you solve? The value proposition must clearly define the target customer, the customer's problem and pain, your unique solution, and the net benefit of this solution from the customer's perspective.

➤ **Target market**: Who are you selling to? A target market is the group of customers that the startup plans to attract by marketing and selling their product or service. This segment should have specific demographics and the means to buy your product.

➤ **Sales/marketing**: How will you reach your customers? Word of mouth and viral marketing are popular terms these days but are rarely adequate to initiate a new business. Be specific on sales channels and marketing initiatives.

➤ **Production**: How do you produce your product or service? Common choices include manufacturing in-house, outsourcing, and off-the-shelf parts. The key issues here are time to market and cost.

➤ **Distribution**: How do you distribute your product or service? Some products and services can be sold and distributed online; others require multilevel distributors, partners, or value-added resellers. Decide whether the product is local or international.

> **Revenue model**: How do you make money? The key here is to explain to yourself and investors how your pricing and revenue stream will cover all costs, including overhead and support, and still leave a good return.

> **Cost structure**: What are your costs? New entrepreneurs tend to focus only on product direct costs and underestimate marketing and sales costs, overhead costs, and support costs. Test your projections against actual published reports from similar companies.

> **Competition**: How many competitors do you have? If there are no competitors, it probably means there is no market. If there are more than 10 competitors, it indicates a saturated market. Think broadly here, like planes versus trains. Customers always have alternatives.

> **Unique selling proposition**: How will you differentiate your product or service? Investors look for a sustainable competitive advantage. Short-term discounts or promotions are not a unique selling proposition.

> **Market size, growth, and share**: How big is your market in dollars, is it growing or shrinking, and what percent can you capture? Venture Capitalists look for a market with double-digit growth, greater than a billion dollars, and a double-digit penetration plan.

Investors will want to understand your business model very well and very early. They don't want to hear your customer sales pitch, which naturally avoids any discussion of how much money you intend to make and how many customers you expect to convince. Giving that pitch to investors will only frustrate both you and them. Investors are looking for profit, and you should be doing the same for long-term viability. A business model tells them how you are going to make a profit for them and for yourself.

A viable and investable business model is one of the first things you need to highlight in your business plan. In fact, without a business model, your technical startup is just a dream.

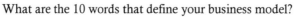

Action Point

What are the 10 words that define your business model?

Take a moment to reflect on how you would explain to your team and your investors who your customer is, how and when you collect money for value, and how your revenues relate to costs, all in 10 words or less. A simple example is, "We sell consumers $10 per month subscriptions, with costs under $5."

Financial forecasts – a key element of every business plan

Many technical entrepreneurs actually refuse to do financial projections beyond the first year, insisting that no one can predict the future. They need to realize that investors ask for projections not merely as predictions but more as commitments from the founder and their team. If you are not willing to commit, don't expect anyone to back you.

In reality, you need to set these projections as goals for your own use, to convince employees as well as investors that you have a business that is challenging but achievable. Projecting the financials should be the last step of your business plan preparation, as it assumes that you already know the opportunity size, customer buying habits, pricing, costs, and competition.

Using your data, here are the basic elements of the projection process. They are measurable by milestones and can be tracked to show when a reforecast is required:

> ➤ **Start with sizing per-unit profitability**: Gross margin, the difference between product cost to you and price to your customer, is everything. Unless your volumes are in the millions or higher, the difference between manufacturing cost and customer price better be 50 percent or greater. This should be true even if your customer is really a distributor. Otherwise, sales, marketing, and operational costs will kill you.

> ➤ **Next comes sales volume by channel**: Here is where you need a "bottom-up" estimate from the people in your organization who have to deliver. This forecast is really their commitment. It's tempting here to simply calculate one percent market share and assume anyone can do at least that much. It's not credible and won't happen.

> ➤ **Don't forget that pesky overhead**: Even with a slow economy, it's amazing how fast office space costs add up, in conjunction with insurance, utilities, and administrative help. Then, there are computer costs, trade shows, inventory, and a thousand other things. Check industry average statistics to make sure you are in the right range.

> ➤ **Cash flow is king**: Your "burn rate" or net cash flow out is usually the single most important survival parameter to a startup. The Holy Grail is to break even, which is when revenues first catch up with the outflow. Projecting, tracking, and controlling cash flow is the single most important job of the CEO and all other startup officers.

Beyond these basics, here are some common-sense strategy elements. They will maintain your credibility with investors and minimize your chances of failing:

> ➤ **Add a buffer to your required investment**: Calculate what you need based on the cash flow calculations mentioned earlier. See where your cash flow bottoms out. If the bottom is minus $400K, add a 25 percent buffer and ask for $500K funding. The request size must correlate to your projections to be credible.

> ➤ **Plan to reforecast every quarter**: Everyone understands the reality that startups have to adjust to market fluctuations, and financial projections are an art and a science. Cost projections should never be missed, unless you suffer an emergency or get caught in a tsunami.

> ➤ **Target aggressive but rational projections**: Initial forecasts should be aggressive for credibility, but don't shoot for the moon. Most investors have never seen a startup achieve its initial projection, so here is your chance to be a hero.

Just the process of doing financial projections allows you to see areas of strength and weakness in your proposed business model, thus enabling you to make critical adjustments sooner. For even more value, you should develop a financial model. With a few variables such as volume growth rate and number of salesmen, a what-if analysis is possible on cash flow, break even point, and revenue growth.

Financial projections can be intimidating. However, a solid financial forecast is a required cornerstone for any business plan. Without it, you will likely prove the old proverb, "He who fails to plan, plans to fail."

Benefits of using a financial model

Most technical entrepreneurs tend to avoid this area of the business, and as a result, they are badly surprised by cost realities and investor expectations. They seem to think that financial projections are simply invented numbers for investors and not useful. In reality, it's like jumping in your car for a long hard drive with no destination in mind. Chances are, you won't enjoy success from the trip.

Here are the key questions you need to understand before you start any modeling efforts:

> **What is a business financial model, really?**: In most cases, it is merely a Microsoft Excel spreadsheet loaded with your cost and revenue projections for your startup, starting now in time and extending five years into the future. For more value, a few variables can be added, such as product volume growth rate and number of sales people for what-if analyses.

> **Why do I need it?**: For you to make decisions and manage the business—because we are all mere mortals and can't possibly keep all these numbers and calculations in our head—you need to decide whether and when the business is going to be profitable given rational projections of costs and income (these assumptions are referred to as your business model). Second, it will be required by potential investors to validate how much money you need to get started and how much return they can expect on their investment.

> **When should the modeling work begin?**: The financial model should be running even before you incorporate the business and build prototype products (would you start driving your car on a long trip before you knew where you were going?). If you can't make that objective, then at least don't approach potential investors until your model is working—investors who are part of my Angel group have little tolerance for startups with no financial plan.

> **How do you produce a model efficiently?**: Start with a "sample" business model, available in generic form or customized for specific industries, from many sources on the Internet. Another alternative is to download from my website a free sample model (http://www.startupprofessionals.com/Startup-Professionals-Products.html) that I built for a specific startup, with elements suggested by Angel investors and venture capitalists. It is ready to be customized to your business.

If you are not computer literate in Microsoft Excel, your first task is to find someone who has the time and expertise to convert your base set of costs and revenues into projection formulas, cash flow summaries, and a profit-and-loss statement.

Do your own, if you can, because you know the numbers. In fact, this is the easy part. More challenging is *defining* the business model (assembling all the real variables of your projected business, pricing assumptions, staffing requirements, marketing costs, sales costs, and revenue flows).

This business model can then be used for many purposes, such as risk and profit assessment, projecting the values of assumptions that are made based on the existing market conditions, calculating the margins that are needed to avoid adverse situations, and various forms of sensitivity analysis. These are necessary to estimate capital investment requirements, plan capital allocation, and measure financial performance.

Creating financial projections allows you to see areas of strength and weakness in your proposed business model, enabling you to make critical changes that will allow your business to run more successfully.

While people start businesses for many reasons, making money is usually important. Even a nonprofit can't afford to lose money. You won't know if you can meet these expectations until you build a financial model with reasonable financial projections.

It's a great learning experience, and you can do it yourself, but don't hesitate to ask for help from a professional if you need it. You will be amazed at how clear the relationship becomes between pricing, cost, and volume. When you lose money on every item, it's hard to make it up in volume.

Summary

The goal of this chapter has been to clarify the rationale and need for a business plan, and provide specific guidance to create specific elements. In summary, I would like to emphasize some of the key points by looking at what can go wrong if you don't get it right or don't use it correctly with investors once it's done.

After struggling to create your business plan for months, every technical entrepreneur likes to think that their document is inspirational and will reach someone who is smart enough to see the brilliance of the idea, intuitive enough to recognize their business acumen, and enthusiastic enough to offer the money required to make it happen.

Every serious investor, on the other hand, has a stack of these in their in-basket (e-mail or real plastic), awaiting review. They are looking for the flaw or less-capable entrepreneur in each that predicts failure, allowing them to discard it like another piece of junk mail. Many VC firms and investment banks receive as many as 10 plans per day, so it's hard to get them salivating.

Thus, I think it's helpful to know some of the most common turnoffs that investors encounter in plowing through this stack of requests for money. This is what investors say you shouldn't do, and I can attest to this from my own meager efforts:

> ➤ **Tease or spam the investor**: Every investor is annoyed by persistent messages that say, "Give me a call to hear about the most disruptive technology since the wheel." You can bet that if they ever see a real business plan from you, it will go to the bottom of the pile. Asking them to check out your website first and then comment is equally bad.

> ➤ **Send the plan without a summary**: An Executive Summary is a one-page elevator pitch of the whole plan (may be separate from the plan), which gives an investor a net perspective on the key business parameters. Too many plans don't have a summary section, or the summary is all you get. You lose in either case.

> ➤ **No plan in the business plan**: Many business plans that investors see are really modified product specifications. These tell investors more about the internals of the product than they want to know. However, this type of plan tells investors nothing about the business, meaning nothing about how and when you plan to sell the product and make money.

> ➤ **Embarrass your English teacher**: Obvious draft markings and handwritten or unprofessional results such as misspellings and grammatical errors in the plan will only convince investors that your business will be run the same unprofessional way. Remember, investors invest in people before ideas.

> ➤ **Fill the text with acronyms**: Remember that the people reading your plan are smart but not intimately steeped in the acronyms of your technology. They assume a heavy use of acronyms to be inconsiderate, lazy, or maybe an intentional obfuscation of facts. Stick to layman's terms.

> ➤ **The base plan is a book**: Avoid being excessively wordy or redundant in your plan. The base plan should be in the 20-page range. Stick to the facts, state them clearly, and do not repeat them unnecessarily. At best, long plans make your business seem complex and more risky.

> ➤ **It's all in an appendix**: Investors don't mind supporting documents with the base plan, but the base should make sense and be complete without jumping to an appendix. Making the total plan heavier, with 10 appendices or 100 pages is not impressive.

> ➤ **Trash your competitors**: Don't say things about your competitors or customers that you wouldn't be able to defend if they were in the room with you. I see lots of statements about poor usability, poor quality, fat and slow, all with nothing but anecdotal data. Investors read these as unprofessional and even unethical, unless supported by third-party data.

> ➤ **Prototypes and demos attached**: Remember that early prototypes and demos usually break or don't work for unfamiliar users, and we can't see all the work and love you have already put into them. Pictures and words leave a much better impression at this stage.

> ➤ **Letters from your friends**: Introduction letters from friends of the investor are always appreciated, but letters of praise from your friends don't carry the same weight. Customer testimonials and vendor contracts are much more impressive.

When you present a business plan to an investor, remember that the purpose is not to sell your product or service, but to sell you and your business model. You are looking for scarce investor financial resources, and your competition at this stage is your peers who may have more convincing and credible proposals.

When you review the business plan for your own use or use it to communicate expectations to key members of your team, it should be a clear roadmap for their actions and your success. Remember that a good business plan is always a working document and should be updated at least once a month as you learn more about your product, your customers, and your competition. Don't let the plan become a historical artifact of your company, or your passion and dream may also become a historical artifact.

Let me reiterate that a business plan should always be a *living* document. It must be continually re-evaluated as your plan changes so that it continues to be an effective means of educating new employees, new contractors, and keeping your own personal company goals aligned.

With a well-rounded and up-to-date business plan, you are also ready to take on what many technical entrepreneurs believe to be the toughest and most mysterious challenge of building a company—closing with investors. I think that from the next chapter, you will find that it's not all that mysterious and challenging if you have done the right job of preparation here. Let's take a look.

> 5

When and How Do You Find Funding for a Technical Business?

Money to build the business is the number one challenge for most technical entrepreneurs. However, it's not easy. Don't believe the urban myth that you can sketch your idea on a napkin, and professional investors will throw money at you. In reality, only 3 out of 100 companies that seek funding are successful with Angel investors (http://en.wikipedia. org/wiki/Angel_investor), and the success rate with venture capital investors (VCs) (http://en.wikipedia.org/wiki/Venture_capital) is even lower. A large percentage of startups never apply to either, simply because they aren't ready for the associated work.

This chapter explores the most common and most productive approaches for getting your startup funded as early as possible. Of course, every approach has its pros and cons. For example, with any outside investment, you give up some ownership and control, and with bootstrapping, your growth curve will likely be longer and more organic.

If you are new to the entrepreneurial world of startups, you are likely to get confused by the terminology of seed-stage, lean startups, micro-VCs, Super Angels, and Venture Capitalists (VCs). Don't be embarrassed, as even professional investors are often confused these days by the new terms as well as old terms used with new meanings. In any case, this chapter looks at the options you realistically have, and how to make them happen.

Finding cash sources to start a technical business

I find that technical entrepreneurs often fixate on one or two funding sources, often to the detriment of their business and personal objectives. In reality, there are at least ten sources of funding for startups that every entrepreneur should evaluate. Your funding strategy is a key part of every business plan, so don't hesitate to check out all the alternatives before you start.

The following is my prioritized larger list of the major sources, with some **rules of thumb**, which may save you a lot of time and energy:

> ➤ **Bootstrapping**: Bootstrapping means using only your own resources. Self-funding is the preferred source of cash for your startup – if you can do it. The advantage is you don't need to spend time and effort in searching and preparing for the other alternatives, and you don't have to encumber yourself or give up control of your company. Just don't quit your day job before your new company starts producing revenue. Surprisingly, over 90 percent of startups use this approach. Entrepreneurs who fund their own business may allocate an amount as low as $5K, or as high as their life's savings.

> ➤ **Friends and family**: After bootstrapping, friends and family are the most common funding sources for early-stage startups. Use this approach before you have a real valuation, a real product, or any real customers. As a rule of thumb, it is a required first step, as outside investors will not normally consider providing any funding until they see **skin in the game** from one of these first two sources. Funding levels from these sources start with a few thousand dollars, but rarely go higher than $100K.

> ➤ **Small business grants**: This source, which includes Small Business Innovation Research (SBIR) grants, often gets overlooked, since grants are more often associated with universities than entrepreneurs. It's not a quick solution, but state and federal funding agencies do not want ownership or interest payments from your company. Related sources include local business development agencies. You have to be relentless in this pursuit to win. Grants can vary in size from $100K to over $1 million.

> ➤ **Loans or line-of-credit**: If your company needs only a temporary or small infusion of cash, you should try for an SBA loan, or a bank line of credit. Many people are afraid to tap into debt sources because they don't want to be burdened with the debt if the startup fails. However, if you don't believe in the company enough to place your own credit behind it, why should anyone else? Of course, startups are always very risky, so be careful. An initial loan might be $100K, and a line of credit could be much higher.

> ➤ **Startup incubators**: A startup incubator is a company, university, or an organization that provides resources for equity to nurture young companies, helping them survive and grow during the startup period when they are most vulnerable. These resources would likely include office space, consulting, and even a cash investment. Y-Combinator (http://en.wikipedia.org/wiki/Y_Combinator(company)) in Silicon Valley is probably the most visible and successful one out there. Cash investments from incubators will likely be $50K or less, and you will retain full control of your startup.

> ➤ **Angel investors**: If you are looking for $250,000 to $1 million, the next step is to tap into a local Angel network. If you don't know any high-net-worth individuals, use your advisors to find them. Networking is the key here, and you need to find an Angel who understands your industry and shares your passion. Angels will normally ask for less control than Venture Capital managers.

➤ **Venture capital**: As a rule of thumb, don't try this one in the earlier stages, and don't try it unless you need more than $2 million. An investment from a venture capital firm is usually expensive in equity and control. If you go for venture capital, don't expect a quick fix, so prepare to spend at least six months searching for and closing the deal.

➤ **Bartering services for equity**: Bartering technically means exchanging goods or services as a substitute for money. An example would be getting free office space by agreeing to be the property manager for the owner. Exchanging equity for services is worth negotiating with legal counsel, accountants, engineers, and even sales people.

➤ **Partner with a distributor or beneficiary**: A related company may see the value of your product as complementary to theirs, and be willing to advance funding, which can be repaid when you develop your revenue stream. Consider licensing and white labeling. White labeling means you provide your service or product under someone else's brand with only minimal attribution.

➤ **Commit to a major customer**: Find a customer who would benefit greatly from getting your product first, and be willing to advance you the cost of development. The advantage to the customer is that they will have enough control to make sure it meets their requirements and will get dedicated support.

Just remember that you don't get "something for nothing" in any of these cases. All funding decisions represent complex tradeoffs between near-term and long-term costs, ownership, control, and time and effort, and all funding sources expect some return. For example, the SBA wants their loan to be repaid, an Angel investor may be happy to receive a few times their investment, and most VCs expect to get at least 10 times on their $MM investment, so carefully consider your total addressable market and a realistic growth plan.

As you look at the alternatives that involve an outside investor, you need to know how they see you. Different types of investors look for startups at different levels of maturity. If your startup is at the wrong stage for the investor you are approaching, fishing for money is a waste of time for both of you.

For instance, if your company is only a few weeks old and you have zero customers and your product offering is still in the design stage, don't expect someone to hand over $10 million to fund your efforts. It wouldn't work anyway, since your valuation at that stage would be less than the funding, meaning you would have to give away all ownership for the money.

You will also find that the stage your startup is in dictates where you go to seek funding. Funding sources specialize in certain growth stages. Angel investors typically provide early-stage funding, while venture capital firms typically come in at later stages.

Of course, growth and development are really a continuum. Yet, most investors will tend to categorize your progress into one of the following five stages:

1. **Idea stage**: This is the initial excitement period, the time when you dream of riches and fantasize about having the life of a business owner, but you have no real plan. At this stage, no professional investor will touch you unless you have a beautiful track record of success with previous startups. Funding will only come from you, or friends, family, and fools.

2. **Early or embryonic stage**: Investments at this stage are typically called seed investments. As mentioned earlier, funding of $250,000-$1 million is available from Angels if you have credentials and have done the homework of a good business plan, financial model, and executive presentation. Anything less than $250,000 or any amount at this stage with no credentials still has to come from friends and families, loans, or federal grant sources.

3. **Funding or rollout stage**: This is the realm of venture capital professional investors, with funding amounts of $2-10 million, often referred to as the **A-round**, or first institutional funding. At this stage, your startup better be selling a commercial offering, have price and cost validated, with significant customer sales and a real revenue stream. Lesser amounts remain in the Angel realm.

4. **Growth stage**: Additional funding rounds for growth are often called the **B-round** through **G-round**, with each being in the range of $5 million to more than $50 million from venture capital and other sources. Companies at this stage must have a large market, good traction, and be focused on scaling infrastructure and market adoption. This normally means more than 30 employees and more than $1 million in revenue.

5. **Exit stage**: This is the final stage of investment in venture opportunities, and is the point where investors expect to see the returns and gains from the original investment. At this stage, you need investment bankers to negotiate a merger or acquisition (M&A), go private, or help you go public with an **Initial Public Offering (IPO)**.

As startups pass through each stage, they must attract appropriate financial partners that can provide the increasing credibility, capital, and industry networks to support movement to the next stage. Otherwise, they will never get to roll out or exit. Typically, they must also change and tune their executive team to keep up with the increasing demands of a growing company on process discipline and sustainable success.

Another important thing to remember when selecting investors is that not all money is the same. VC money, for example, usually comes with high expectations of milestones met, board seats, and dominant control. Angels may be less demanding, but typically add less value. Friends and family hopefully believe fully in you, and just want you to show them success.

Obviously, if you bootstrap your business, you can avoid all these stages and the investment implications. Otherwise, not paying attention to the expectations associated with each stage will most likely jeopardize your one chance to make a great first impression on potential investors, and land the big one.

A while back, I heard a talk by Dave McClure, a long-time Angel investor, who also proclaims to be one of the **new breed** of venture capitalists in Silicon Valley, as the CEO of 500Startups, which is either a micro-VC seed fund or a startup incubator, or both. He is going gangbusters, and is now targeting a $50M second round of funding. The good news is that he is all about helping early-stage startups. The hard part for technical entrepreneurs is figuring out what it takes to play.

Here is just a sampling of the latest terminology and lingo that I gleaned from Dave, and from some additional research on the Internet, which I think every technical entrepreneur should know, who may be looking for funding now, or down the road:

➤ **Micro-VCs**: These are emerging groups of professional venture capital investors who are investing from a fund of other people's money, with a particular focus on seed-stage startup opportunities. Seed-stage means promising companies that don't yet have a revenue stream, and may not yet have a proof of concept.

➤ **Super Angels**: These are Angel counterparts to VCs, who traditionally only invested their own money, but now have begun raising funds from outside investors, to do more than a few deals per year. Like most Angels and micro-VCs, however, they still start with relatively small sums of money, often investing only $10,000 to $50,000 in the first increment.

➤ **Series-seed round**: Since the economic downturn started, neither Angels nor VCs have given much attention to startups without a product and a revenue stream. That was left to the realm of friends and family. In the last year, there has been a resurgence of interest, some say a bubble, by both Angels and VCs, in a pre-Series A kicker to identify promising startups with seed funding before a major portion of the equity has been given away.

➤ **Early-stage startup**: Every startup is early-stage to someone. For a startup founder, this stage is when the *big idea* has become a passion for them, but they haven't written anything down yet. For Angel investors, early-stage means there is a good business plan and maybe a prototype, but no customer revenue. For VCs, early-stage indicates that the customer revenue is less than $10M. Thus, the more precise term these days for early startups is **seed stage**.

➤ **Business accelerator**: This term is replacing **startup incubator**, which is a facility provided by an individual, university, or local community for any new startups to congregate for almost no cost, with the hope of learning from each other. Well-known examples of the business accelerator model include Y Combinator and TechStars, who select only the best applicants, have a demanding process, and provide experienced coaching/mentoring and some seed funding, with a required exit from the program in about six months. Incremental investment may follow. There are many others in every major city in the USA and elsewhere.

➤ **Lean startup**: This was a concept coined (and trademarked) by Eric Ries a few years ago, primarily for software and web applications. Lean startups operate on minimal money, an open source environment, and assume multiple iterations, with customer feedback, to get it right. A popular phrase heard in this environment is *rinse and repeat*. Today, if you do well in this mode, you will get funded if and when you need it.

> ➤ **Crowdfunding**: The recently passed JOBS bill now allows even non-accredited investors to contribute small amounts to new startups through **crowdsourcing** sites such as Kickstarter, IndieGoGo, and Crowdtilt. While the exact rules are still being set, suggested limits for a given startup will likely be a maximum of $1M, with each investor limited to an amount equal to either $10K or 10 percent of their annual income, whichever is the lower amount.

Overall, the trend for investors, including micro-VCs and Super Angels, is to place **lots of little bets**, ($10K to $50K) with milestones applied, which can then lead to incremental and larger funding checks.

Pundits call this the **spray and pray** approach to funding. Even though significant deal vetting and filtering is performed by the investor teams that run these seed programs, in effect, they spray little bits of capital onto as many good ideas as possible, help them along, and pray some eventually strike it big.

Despite these pundits, I sense a fundamental change in the early-stage financing ecosystem. With the Internet and other powerful but inexpensive business tools, the cost of development and rollout of new startups is lower than ever before, so the **big bang** theory of funding no longer makes sense.

Crowdfunding basics for technical entrepreneurs

The new hot topic for technical entrepreneurs in the last couple of years is crowdfunding, or appealing to average people for help with your startup on the Internet. This is anticipated by many entrepreneurs to be the hot new source of cash, which will replace all the alternatives outlined earlier, especially the slow and mysterious process of current Angel and venture capital investors.

The challenge is that crowdfunding means something different to everyone, and I too have been confused by the different ways the term gets used. So, I have set out here to outline and offer some practical advice on the many different models currently used with the term **crowdfunding** and **crowdsourcing.**

The latest equity version of the crowdfunding model was passed into law in early 2012 via the JOBS Act (`http://en.wikipedia.org/wiki/Jumpstart_Our_Business_Startups_Act`), and still has no scheduled date for availability in the USA, which is waiting for the rules for equity crowdfunding to be defined by the SEC:

> ➤ **Startup equity crowdfunding**: This new model (now only legal in the UK) will allow large numbers of *regular* people to each invest small amounts online to get an ownership position in early startups. This is not a get-rich-quick vehicle for consumers. As a current Angel investor, I can attest that any investments in startups are more risky than the commodity markets, and you shouldn't expect to see any return for many years.

> ➤ **Good-cause crowdfunding**: This model is a good thing, and has been around for years. Example sites include StartSomeGood and the Facebook Cause page (`https://www.facebook.com/causes`). People can invest (donate) money to a project that has good moral/ethical values. No financial return should be anticipated, but contributors should enjoy the feeling of a good deed or charity.

> ➤ **Pre-order crowdfunding**: Here, people make online pledges with their credit cards during a campaign in order to pre-buy the product for later delivery, if it is ever built. Kickstarter is a big player in this space. It has had some notable successes for entrepreneurs (over $1M in funding), as well as many non-starters. There is no concept of ROI other than an early delivery of product.

> ➤ **Reward-based crowdfunding**: This is a variation on the two previous ones, where investors get the satisfaction of helping, and immediately get a pre-determined reward or perk of value, such as a t-shirt, or other recognition, but no equity or finished products. A good example site, and one of the earliest in this category, is IndieGoGo.

> ➤ **Debt-based crowdfunding**: In this model, which is sometimes called micro-financing or peer-to-peer (P2P) lending, you borrow money from a number of people online and pay them back after the project is finished. This has been popular in many countries for years via sites such as LendingClub and Kiva. The allure is fat returns, but they come with a huge risk.

> ➤ **Ideas crowdsourcing**: Technically, this model is not involved with funding at all, but **crowdsourcing** and **crowdfunding** are often used interchangeably. Sites such as IdeaBounty get your ideas off the shelf and give you the wisdom of the crowds. Of course, this might also lead to investors, partners, and licensing opportunities.

> ➤ **Software crowdsourcing**: This is basically the open source concept (`http://en.wikipedia.org/wiki/Open-source_software`), where sites such as IdeaScale (`http://ideascale.com/crowdsourcing-software.html`) facilitate the outsourcing of application development to the Internet community in the form of an open call. Sometimes, contributors may get compensated later, but usually, the rewards are just kudos and intellectual satisfaction.

Don't confuse any of the models with other popular funding sites for startups, such as Funding Universe and Startups.co. These are primarily matchmaking sites between entrepreneurs and professional investors or banks. Often, they do sponsor pitch contests with small cash prizes for funding, as well as other valuable services to support entrepreneurs.

So, it's easy to note that irrespective of whether you are a new technical entrepreneur or a new potential investor, the Internet has opened several new options for the crowd to help you. These also unfold new concerns about lost intellectual property, Internet scams, and long-term return on investment. Crowdfunding is an exciting new territory, but I don't see it replacing Angel and venture capital investors any time soon.

Most professionals maintain that there is plenty of money for equity in qualified startups, and funding marginal startups via any source will only make more people unhappy. Startups should pay more attention to their business plan, business model, products, and market.

Certainly, crowdfunding offers the technical entrepreneur some big positives, including the following:

➤ Access to a major new source of funding

➤ Quick and free consumer feedback on the idea

➤ Opportunity to test and improve your marketing pitch

➤ Potential introductions and exposure to many new funding sources

However, from my perspective in really helping entrepreneurs, a crowdfunding strategy often falls short on several counts:

➤ **Focuses too much on the product, and not enough on the business model**: When pitching to consumers, online or offline, the feedback will likely be on features and design. The key success factors of the business model (how a business survives and grows), management expertise, and financial projections will likely get overlooked.

➤ **Amount of funding provided is usually not enough**: The amount of time and money required for the publicity and promotion of any crowd-funding activities may be more than the return. In reality, a few thousand dollars to a few winners is tantalizing but probably not a return on the investment required.

➤ **Multiple micro-investments are not manageable**: Investors know how tough it is to get a set of terms accepted by even two investors, much less hundreds. The administration of legal conditions, signatures, disclosures, and distributions is a nightmare. In my opinion, that's why micro-finance has rarely worked, even for loans.

➤ **Proposal content is too short to be meaningful**: In all cases, to keep non-professionals' attention, the content of the offer online, or the pitch presented, is very limited. No one contemplates including a business plan, investor presentation, or even the equivalent of an executive summary.

➤ **Crowd sample size and makeup not representative of market**: If the pitch is offline, the audience will most likely constitute small and mostly budding entrepreneurs. Even online, the type of people who respond to social media requests may bear very little relationship to the intended market.

➤ **Investors are not prepared for the high risk of startups**: Crowd-funding investors are not constrained to be accredited professional investors. They may not understand that nine out of ten startup investments provide no return, and the risk of securities law violations is very high.

➤ **Intellectual property is jeopardized**: Non-disclosure agreements can't be done in these environments. In an environment populated by technical entrepreneurs rather than investors, when you are new to the game, you are exposing your plan to your biggest potential competitors.

Overall, there is no doubt that crowd-funding makes sense for non-profits that solicit donations, artists that seek support from fans, and many small technical entrepreneurial efforts that need a single funding boost. However, in the competitive world of the **next big thing**, with millions of dollars at stake, counting on these mechanisms in lieu of professional investors may be ignoring the real problem.

Tips on how much money to ask for from investors

If you do decide to seek investors or even crowdfunding, the next question is "*How much money should I ask for?*". The simple answer is the amount you need to make your plan work. Some technical entrepreneurs try to start with a huge number, hoping they can negotiate and close on a smaller one, while others understate their requirements, in the hope of getting their foot in the door with an investor.

Neither of these strategies is a good one, as both are likely to damage your credibility with potential investors even before they look hard at your plan. Here are the parameters you should use to size your request, and be able to justify your request to investors:

- ➤ **Consider implied ownership costs**: If your company is in its early stage and has a valuation under $1M, don't ask for a $5M investment. The investor would be buying your company five times over, and he doesn't want it. If your valuation is around $1M, you can validly ask for $200K-$300K, and offer 20 percent-30 percent of your company in exchange.

- ➤ **Type of investor**: Angel investment groups usually won't consider a request over $1M, while venture capitalists won't look at anything under $2M. Amounts of $100K or less are usually relegated to **friends and family**. Approaching any one of these groups with a funding request outside their range is a waste of your time and theirs.

- ➤ **Company stage**: If your company is still in the **idea** stage, you have no valuation, so size your investment request on the basis of **goodwill** that you have with your rich uncle, and your business track record. Angels might be interested during the **early stage** if you have a prototype, but VCs won't bite until you have a product, customers, and revenue.

- ➤ **Calculate what you need, and add a buffer**: Do your financial model first with the volume, cost, and pricing parameters you want. See where your cashflow bottoms out. If it bottoms out at minus $400K, add a 25 percent buffer and ask for $500K funding. The request size must tie into your financials to be credible. For more details, there are many sources available on the Internet as well as whole books on this subject (http://www.amazon.com/Building-Financial-Models-Microsoft-Excel/dp/0471661031).

- ➤ **Investment terms**: The most common case is an equity investment, but there are many terms that can impact what request size is credible. I'm talking about things such as anti-dilution clauses, preferred versus common stock, valuation tied to later round, warrants, and bridge loan options. More restrictive terms reduce the credible investment amount.

- ➤ **Single or staged delivery**: In many cases, a single investment request may be scheduled for delivery in stages, or tranches (often misspelled as traunchs or traunches), based on milestone achievement. Obviously, this reduces investor risk and allows a larger commitment, since they can limit their loss if you fail to meet key objectives.

> **Use of funds**: Investors expect to see a **use of funds** list, and they expect the uses to apply only to your core mission. In other words, don't tell investors that you intend to buy a fancy office building or executive cars with your funding. Even executive salaries should be minimal at this stage.

> **Projected return on investment**: Most technical entrepreneurs skip this step, but it helps your credibility to include it. Estimate a return on investment (ROI) by projecting company valuation at exit, to show the investor having 20 percent ownership what he will get back for that initial investment. He's looking for a 10 times return on his investment, since he assumes only one in ten survive.

Make a note

Obviously, determining the proper size of your investment request is a complex exercise, but it's one of the most critical factors for investors in making a decision to invest or not to invest in your company. You need to get it definitively right the first time, because changing your request under pressure will definitely kill your credibility.

Honing your elevator pitch and executive summary

An **elevator pitch** is a concise, well-practiced description of your startup and your plan, delivered with conviction and enthusiasm that your mother should be able to understand in the time it would take to ride up an elevator. Everybody knows about these, but few people seem to deliver a good one.

A good elevator pitch is not just for an elevator discussion with potential investors. Use it in every networking situation and business conference introduction. The elevator pitch should be the first few paragraphs of your business plan, your executive summary, your investor presentation, and the first page of your website. A different message everywhere is no message.

An elevator pitch should always contain the following key elements:

> **Problem-solution attention grabber**: Open your pitch by getting the investor's attention with a marketing hook. This is a statement or question that piques their interest to want to hear more. Good hooks succinctly define a real problem, and suggest the solution. For example, "*I just patented a new cell-phone technology that will double battery life for half the cost. I need your help in getting it to the market.*"

> **About 150-225 words**: Your pitch should be about 30-60 seconds (average elevator ride). Don't think that you can just talk fast to cram 500 words into that time. It won't work.

> **Obvious passion**: Investors expect energy, conviction, and commitment from technical entrepreneurs. How do you expect them to get excited, if your startup sounds like a dull subject to you?

> **A request**: At the end of your pitch, you must ask for something. Ask for time to give a full presentation, or ask for a referral to someone who can help.

My friend and fellow Angel investor, Dave Bittner, offers a simple template to get started that will work for most products and services: "*We sell [product/service deliverable] to [market niche] who want [unmet market need]. Unlike [competition], we [differentiation].*". All you have to do is fill in the brackets and you have the essence of an elevator pitch.

Here are some additional recommendations to increase the impact:

> **Describe your product or service**: Provide a one-paragraph description of what you sell. Focus on customer benefits rather than features, indicating real pain, rather than just nice to have.

> **Quantify the market**: Make sure you clarify how large the market is, how much money they have to spend, and a positive level of growth. A product may be great, but it won't make a business if you don't hit customers with money to spend.

> **Outline the revenue model**: Giving the product away or selling below cost may make it attractive to customers, but your business won't be attractive.

> **Highlight people strengths**: *Bet on the jockey, not the horse* is a familiar saying among investors. Tell them the high points about you and your team's background and achievements. The team credentials are often viewed as more important than the idea.

> **Present a sustainable competitive advantage**: You need to effectively communicate how your company is different and why you have an advantage over the competition. This could be a patent, key partners, domain expertise, or a better distribution channel.

More importantly, avoid the most common mistake of turning this into a sales pitch for your product or service. The investor is buying the business, not the product. Tell them why and how you will run a winning business.

Consistency and redundancy are the keys to communicating any message. Another key to effective communication is practice, practice, practice early. Remember, you only have one chance to make a great first impression.

Use the elevator pitch, not only as your opening spoken gambit with an investor, but also as the first sentence of an executive summary document that you can hand to a potential investor.

Modern investors love to see a two-page executive summary of your proposal, formatted like a glossy marketing collateral sheet, with text well laid out in columns and sidebars, and a couple of relevant graphics, before they tackle the whole business plan or even your investor presentation. This summary had better grab their attention, or they won't look or listen further.

You may have already found several articles, web pages, or books about writing the perfect executive summary. They all offer a list of requirements that might take 50 pages to address, but of course, they ask you to write concisely. Take a look at my website for the Sample Executive Summary (`http://www.startupprofessionals.com/Startup-Professionals-Products.html`), which shows what can be done on one page (both sides).

Before you start, remember that the goal of the executive summary is to provide a printed version of your best elevator pitch, followed by a net of your entire business plan, to provide a positive first impression to the reader. Think of it as a selling effort, not an attempt to fully describe your startup. Here are the key components:

> ➤ **The problem and your solution**: These are your hooks, and they better be covered in the first paragraph. State your value proposition, and specify what you are offering to whom. Skip the acronyms, history of the company, and the disruptive technology behind your solution.

> ➤ **Market size and growth opportunity**: Investors are looking for a large and growing market. Spend a few sentences providing the basic market segmentation, size, growth, and dynamics - how many people or companies, how many dollars, how fast the growth is, and what is driving the segment. Skip the comment that you are conservatively estimating your penetration at 1 percent.

> ➤ **Your competitive advantage**: Identify your sustainable competitive advantage, such as unique benefits, cost savings, or industry ties. Don't kill your credibility by saying you have no competition. At minimum, you compete with the way things get done currently. The investor has most likely already seen multiple plans with similar solutions.

> ➤ **Business model**: Who is your customer, what is the price, and how much does it cost you to build one? Do you now have real customers, or are you just starting development? Outline your sales and marketing strategy (direct marketing, sales channel, viral marketing, and lead generation). Identify key quantities, such as customers, licenses, units, and margin.

> ➤ **Executive team**: Remember that investors fund people more than ideas. Why is your team uniquely qualified to win, and what has it done before? Explain why the background of each team member fits, by naming roles and names of relevant companies. Include outside advisors if they have relevant experience.

> ➤ **Financial projections and funding**: You need to show your summary revenue and expense projections for three to five years. Investors need to know the amount of funding you are asking for now, and what they get. The request should generally be the minimum amount of cash you need to reach the next major milestone in your plan.

This outline need not be applied rigidly or religiously. There is no magic that fits all startups, but make sure you touch on each key issue. You need to think through what points are most important in your particular case, and capitalize on your strengths. Key points skipped are red flags, and investor first impressions will go negative.

A final important element that is not even in the executive summary is the paragraph you use in the email that introduces your company and has the executive summary attached. Less is more here, so include the grabber, show your passion and commitment, and be sure and ask for something (like a follow-on meeting or specific feedback). That's your metric to see if you have their attention.

Structuring your investor presentation

As a member of the local Angel group selection committee, I have seen a lot of technical entrepreneur presentations to investors that are too long, but I've never seen one that was too short—maybe short on content, but not short on pages! A perfect round number is 10 slides, with the right content, which can be covered in 10 minutes. Even if you have an hour booked, the advice is the same.

Remember that the goal is an overview presentation that will pique the investor's interest enough to ask for the business plan and a follow-on meeting, but not close the deal on the spot. If you can't get the message across in ten minutes, more time and more charts won't help.

Every startup needs both a business plan and an investor presentation completed before you formally approach any investors. The approach I recommend is to build the investor presentation first, by iterating on the bullets with your team, and then fleshing out the points into a full-blown text-based business plan document. Here are the 10 slides you need:

➤ **Problem and market need**: Give the **elevator pitch** for your startup. Explain in analogies that your mother could understand, and quantify the **cost-of-pain** in dollars or time. Fuzzy terms such as **not user-oriented** or **too expensive** are not helpful.

➤ **Solution product and technology**: Here, you show how and why it works, including a customer-centric quantification of the benefits. Make sure to communicate the relevance of your product / services to market needs. Describe your technology patents and **secret sauce**.

➤ **Opportunity sizing**: Define the characteristics of the overall industry, market forces, market dynamics, and customer landscape. Investors such as $1B markets with double-digit growth rates. You need data from industry experts such as Forrester or Gartner for credibility.

➤ **Business model**: Explain how you will make money and who pays you (real customer). In this section, you need to be passionate about recurring revenue, profit margin, and volume growth. Implicit in this is the go-to-market strategy.

➤ **Competition and sustainable advantage**: List and position your competition or alternatives available to the customer. Highlight your sustainable competitive advantages and barriers to entry.

➤ **Marketing, sales, and partners**: Describe the marketing strategy, sales plan, licensing, and partnership plans. This is also a good place for a rollout timeline with key milestones. Make sure your marketing budget matches the scope of your plan.

> ➤ **Executive team**: Qualifications and roles of the top three executives and top three on your Board of Advisors. They need domain knowledge and startup experience. Highlight their level of involvement, and quantify their skin in the game.

> ➤ **Financial projections**: Project both revenues and expense totals for the next five years and past three years. What is the current valuation of the company? Show breakeven point, burn rate, and growth assumptions.

> ➤ **Funding requirements and use of funds**: What is the level of capital funding sought during this stage? What equity is the company willing to give in return for the investment? Show a breakdown of the intended uses of these funds.

> ➤ **Exit strategy**: What is the timeframe of the return on investment? What is the planned exit strategy (IPO, merger, sale, including likely candidates)? What is the timeframe for the exit? What is the rate of return expected for the investor?

Hand out copies of the slides before the presentation for note taking, with a proper cover sheet, with brochures, product samples, or other marketing material you may have. Offer to do a demo later, but don't try to squeeze it in the presentation.

My last recommendation is practice, practice, practice. The CEO should give the pitch, and prepare by asking your team to be the opponents, asking critical questions, and checking you on timing. Investors hate long rambling presentations. Show some energy and enthusiasm, and remember that if you lose their attention, you have lost the deal.

Guidelines for pitching to professional investors

The biggest complaint I hear from investors is that technical entrepreneurs often talk way too long, and neglect to cover the most relevant points, or they get sidetracked by a technical glitch due to poor preparation.

If you start by pitching your extended life story, that's the wrong point. Equally bad is an extended pitch on your new disruptive technology. Investors are more interested in your solution and your business rather than your technology. Here are some guidelines on the right approach and the right points to hit:

> ➤ **Match your material to the time allotted**: If you have 10 minutes, this means no more than 10 slides. Then, set your pace to cover all the material. I've seen several presentations that never moved past the first slide before running out of time. An obvious effort to keep talking after the time limit won't save your day with investors.

> ➤ **Remember you are pitching to investors, not customers**: Some entrepreneurs seem to think that their product pitch is also their investor pitch. I outlined what investors expect to see in the preceding section. These comments are tuned to the 10-minute limit, but are just as adequate if the investor gives you an hour.

> ➤ **Check the setup and set the stage**: If the projector doesn't work or won't connect to your laptop, it's your loss. Have at least one backup plan, such as copies of your slides to hand out and discuss, in case all else fails. The first words out of your mouth should be *"Can everyone hear me and see the screen?"*

> ➤ **Research your audience before presenting**: The most respected presenters are the ones who have done the research beforehand to know who is in the audience, and have tailored their message to these interests. If you know only a few people in the audience, acknowledge them, and convince the others that this is not a random cold call for you.

> ➤ **Dress appropriately and professionally**: It's always better to be over-dressed rather than under-dressed. Business casual is the standard. Remember that most investors are from a generation where faded and torn jeans were on the wrong side of success in business.

> ➤ **Let the top person do all the talking**: Tag team shows don't work in short venues. More importantly, investors want to see and hear the top guy—typically the founder or the CEO. They will be judging aptitude, character, and passion. Others can be present for effect, but repeated deferrals to team members for answers are a sign of weakness.

> ➤ **First, get their attention with your elevator pitch**: Start with the problem and your solution. These are your hooks, and they better be covered in the first 30 seconds. State your value proposition, and specify what you are offering to whom. Skip the acronyms, history of the company, and the colorful autobiography.

> ➤ **Lead with facts, but skip the details**: Skip the generic marketing phrases such as more user friendly, massive opportunity, and paradigm shifting. *"According to Gartner, the opportunity is 100 million by 2015, with 12 percent compounded growth."* Investors don't need to know the implementation details of your patent or customer support plan.

> ➤ **Don't forget to ask for the order**: How much money do you need, and what percent of your company are you willing to give up for that amount? If you want investor interest, the business parameters of a deal should be presented as clearly as the product parameters.

> ➤ **Close by asking for questions and promising a follow-up**: Acknowledging feedback and actually listening for ways to improve will always lead to a positive impression. You should answer questions with data if you have it, but avoid defensive responses in favor of a promise to follow up after the meeting.

Just because you have given a thousand pitches in your life, don't assume you can finesse this one by reading the bullet points in real time from the slides that your team put together for you. You need to be totally familiar and comfortable with your pitch to render it effectively.

Forget the theory that you can *rise to the occasion* and impress everyone with your dynamic speaking ability. If you are pitching the wrong point in the wrong way, the occasion will be more the demise than the rise of your dream.

Rules of thumb for startup investment valuation

Once you have a potential investor excited about your team, your product, and your company, the investor will inevitably ask *"What is your company's valuation?"* Many technical entrepreneurs stumble at this point, losing the deal or most of their ownership, by having no answer, saying *"make me an offer"*, or quoting an exorbitant number.

In a previous section, I discussed how to calculate how much money you need. This section will help you determine how much of your company the investors will expect to get for that amount of money. That's what the valuation discussion is all about.

It is a complex and mysterious subject, and I don't plan to cover the theory or any academic approaches here. I'll be offering you a **rules of thumb** common sense approach, and I'll use a hypothetical health-care website company named NewCo as an example to illustrate the points.

Two founders have spent $200K of personal and family funds over a one-year period to start the company and get a prototype site up and running, and they have already generated some buzz in the Internet community. The founders now need a $1M Angel investment to do the marketing for a national NewCo rollout, build a team to manage the rollout, and maybe even pay themselves a salary.

How much is NewCo worth to investors at this point (pre-money valuation)? What percentage of NewCo does the investor own after the $1M infusion (post-money ownership percentage)? Well, if the parties agree to a pre-money valuation of $1M, then the post-money investor ownership is 50 percent (founders give up half interest, and lose control). On the other hand, if the pre-money valuation is $4M, the founders' ownership remains at a healthy 80 percent level.

So what magic can the founders use to justify a $4M valuation (or even the $1M valuation) at this early stage? Here are the components that I recommend to every technical entrepreneur:

> ➤ **Place a fair market value on all physical assets (asset approach)**: This is the most concrete valuation element, usually called the asset approach. New businesses normally have fewer assets, but it pays to look hard and count everything you have. NewCo might be able to pick up an initial $50K valuation on this item.

➤ **Assign real value to intellectual property**: The value of patents and trademarks is not certifiable, especially if you are only at the provisional stage. NewCo has filed a patent on one of their software tool algorithms, which is very positive, and puts them several steps ahead of others who may be venturing into the same area. A **rule of thumb** often used by investors is that each patent filed can justify a $1M increase in valuation, so they should claim that here.

➤ **All principals and employees add value**: Assign a value to all paid professionals, as their skills, training, and knowledge of your business technology is very valuable. Back in the heyday of the dot.com startups, it was not uncommon to see a valuation incremented by $1M or every paid full-time professional programmer, engineer, or designer. NewCo doesn't have any of these yet.

➤ **Early customers and contracts in progress add value**: Every customer contract and relationship needs to be monetized, even ones still in negotiation. Assign probabilities to active customer sales efforts, just as sales managers do in quantifying a salesman's forecast. Particularly valuable are recurring revenues, such as subscription amounts that don't have to be resold every period. This one doesn't help NewCo just yet.

➤ **Discounted Cash Flow (DCF) on projections (income approach)**: In finance, Discounted Cash Flow is the income approach that describes a method of valuing a company using the concepts of the time value of money. The discount rate typically applied to startups may vary anywhere from 30 percent to 60 percent, depending on maturity and the level of credibility you can garner for the financial estimates. NewCo is projecting revenues of $25M in five years; even with a 40 percent discount rate, the NPV or current valuation comes out to about $3M.

➤ **Discretionary earnings multiple (earnings multiple approach)**: If you are still losing money, skip ahead to the cost approach. Otherwise, multiply earnings before interest, taxes, depreciation, and amortization (EBITDA) by some multiple. A target multiple can be taken from industry average tables, or derived from scoring key factors of the business. If you have no better info, use 5x as the multiple.

➤ **Calculate replacement cost for key assets (cost approach)**: The cost approach attempts to measure the net value of the business today by calculating how much it could cost for a new effort to replace key assets. Since NewCo has developed 10 online tools and a fabulous website over the past year, how much would it cost another company to create similar quality tools and web interfaces with a conventional software team? $500K might be a low estimate.

➤ **Look at the size of the market and the growth projections for your sector**: The bigger the market and the higher the growth projections are from analysts, the more your startup is worth. For this to be a premium factor for you, your target market should be at least $500 million in potential sales if the company is asset-light, and $1 billion if it requires plenty of property, plants, and equipment. Let's not take any credit here for NewCo.

> ➤ **Assess the number of direct competitors and barriers to entry**: Competitive market forces can also have a large impact on what valuation this company will garner from investors. If you can show a big lead on competitors, you should claim the **first mover** advantage. In the investment community, this premium factor is called **goodwill** (also applied for a premium management team, few competitors, high barriers to entry, and so on). Goodwill can easily account for a couple of million in valuation. For NewCo, the market is not new, but the management team is new, so I wouldn't argue for much goodwill.

> ➤ **Find comparable companies who have received financing (market approach)**: Another popular method to establish valuation for any company is to search for similar companies that have recently received funding. This is often called the market approach, and is similar to the common real estate appraisal concept that values your house for sale by comparing it to similar homes recently sold in your area.

Remember that all the components, except the last one, are cumulative. Even if a given investor excludes some of the components from consideration in your case, your credibility will be bolstered by the fact that you understand their interests as well as yours. In any case, the analysis will prepare you for the heavy negotiation that follows.

Precision is not the issue here – the task for the entrepreneur is to build a company that is worth at least $50M before thinking about an exit—no investor wants to spend more than five minutes arguing the finer points of the last valuation dollar.

So what is a reasonable valuation for a company like NewCo? The national average for all Angel investments is about $2.5M, so my advice for early-stage companies like this one is to target their valuation somewhere between $1.5M and $5M, justified by the elements we just mentioned. A lower number suggests that the founders are giving away the company, while a much higher number may suggest hubris or lack of reality on the part of the owners.

Of course, we have all read about that *new* company with a $100M valuation, but I haven't met one yet.

Every technical entrepreneur needs a startup exit strategy

Somewhere near the end of your investor pitch and business plan, you must include an exit strategy. I usually get pushback on this element for the following reason. If your startup is your dream, why would you want to think about an exit? It's going to be so successful and so much fun that you don't need to think about what comes after. Wrong. There are two very real and practical reasons why you need to plan an exit:

> ➤ **Outside investors want to collect their return**: Remember that equity investments are not like loans with interest. The investor sees no return until they cash out, or the company is sold. Even three years is a long time to wait for any pay check.

> ➤ **Entrepreneurs love the art of the start**: Assuming your startup takes off, you will probably find that the fun is gone by the time you reach 50 employees, or a few million in revenue. The job changes from creating a **work of art** to operating a **cookie cutter**.

In three to five years, you will be anxious to start a new entity, with new ideas and spinoffs that have built up in your mind, and certainty that you can avoid all those potholes you hit the first time around. If your startup was less than a success, you'll definitely want to erase it from memory and start over.

I recommend that every technical entrepreneur pick a preferred exit strategy, no more than two, and focus on these in their pitch. Here are the most common exit strategies and considerations these days for planning purposes:

> ➤ **Merger & Acquisition (M&A)**: This normally means merging with a similar company, or being bought by a larger company. This is a win-win situation when bordering companies have complementary skills, and can save resources by combining. For bigger companies, it's a more efficient and quicker way to grow their revenue than creating new products organically.

> ➤ **Initial Public Offering (IPO)**: This was the one preferred mode, and is a quick way to riches; take your company from private to public, issue a stock, and sell it to anyone. However, since the Internet bubble burst in the year 2000, the IPO rate has declined every year until 2010, and is now at about 15 percent. I don't recommend this approach to startups these days. Shareholders are demanding, and liability concerns are high.

> ➤ **Sell to a friendly individual**: This is not an M&A, since it is not combining two entities into one. Yet it's a great way to *cash out* so you can pay investors, pay yourself, take some time off, and get ready to have some fun all over again. The ideal buyer is someone who has more skills and interest on the operational side of the business and can scale it.

> ➤ **Make it your cash cow**: If you are in a stable, secure marketplace with a business that has a steady revenue stream, pay off investors, find someone you trust to run it for you, while you use the remaining cash to develop your next great idea. You retain ownership and enjoy the annuity. But cash cows seem to need constant feeding to stay healthy.

> ➤ **Liquidation and close**: Even lifetime technical entrepreneurs can decide that enough is enough. One often-overlooked exit strategy is simply to shut down, close the business doors, and liquidate. There may be a natural catastrophe, like 9/11, or the market you counted on could implode. Make rules up front so you don't end up going down with the ship.

To some, an exit strategy sounds negative. Actually, the best reason for an exit strategy is to plan how to optimize a good situation, rather than get out of a bad one. This allows you to run your startup and focus your efforts on things that make it more appealing and compelling to the short list of acquirers or buyers you target.

The type of business you choose should depend on your goals, and the way you grow it should be aligned with your exit strategy. Don't wait till you are in trouble to think about an exit, rather think of it as a succession plan, or a successful transition.

Getting ready for the dreaded due diligence

After you have successfully attracted Angels or venture capital with your business case and your million dollar product idea, and you have a signed term sheet, there is still one more hurdle to overcome before investors write the check. This is the dreaded **due diligence** process. This is the last step of the process, where surprises in the evaluation of the management team, documentation, and personnel problems can derail the investment.

For no good reason, this process seems shrouded in mystery, when in fact it is nothing more than a final integrity check on all aspects of your business model, team, product, customers, and plan. In my view, understanding due diligence can only improve information flow, and leads to a better long-term partnership with your investor(s).

Remember that up to this point, the investor has primarily seen and talked to the technical entrepreneur and CEO, and studied written documents. Before smart investors write a check, they, or a trusted consultant, will want to meet and talk to your key team members and several customers, and evaluate the real product. If the results don't match with what they have been told, all bets are off.

This is where they find out if your team is all behind you, your customers are truly excited, your product is ready to ship, and there aren't any skeletons in the closet. All investors and private equity groups go about due diligence in their own way, but there are a few key areas of focus that technical entrepreneurs should always expect:

> ➤ **Team strength and health**: For small teams, every team member will likely be interviewed. Investors are looking for your depth of talent, loyalty and commitment, strengths and weaknesses, teamwork, and management style. A dysfunctional team or even one naysayer in a critical position can stall your investment.

> ➤ **Product or service design and readiness**: Technical due diligence typically starts with a full one- or two-day review with the engineering and product marketing staff. Investors are evaluating your process as well as your product. The goal is to feel 100 percent confident that the product has the features and quality you assert, and the team and process to keep it true in the future. Finally, they need to validate intellectual property protections and status.

> ➤ **Market need and size validation**: A good investor can do a lot to help a company, but can't make customers buy products. Investors will likely talk to dozens of potential customers, starting with your reference list (undoubtedly well-prepped). They will also speak to technical leaders and industry contacts where they have prior relationships. No validated pain, no deal.

> **Sustainable competitive advantage**: The kiss of death is for investors to find unanticipated competition you neglected to mention. They try to confirm from industry analysts that your differentiators are indeed unique, and that there are no future competitors or big gorillas in stealth mode just around the corner.

> **Business and financial status**: How well have you met previous financial and business milestones? Investors will validate pre-existing investments and stock ownership to create an accurate market capitalization sheet for your company. Founders with bad credit, active lawsuits, or recent bankruptcies dramatically increase the risk.

Smart entrepreneurs understand that due diligence will be a part of their funding, follow up on funding, and their eventual IPO/acquisition/exit, so they should bake good habits and organization into their companies from the first day. For example, by keeping all of your corporate governance, IP, and finances in good shape and in a Dropbox folder, you are much closer to being able to share this info with advisors and also prospective investors.

As you go through the due diligence process, there are some practical tips to keep in mind. First, be proactive in asking if you have answered all the key questions, and ask how you compare to others. Get to the truth early. Waste no time. Use the feedback to strengthen your presentation and your company.

Secondly, conduct your own due diligence of the investor. This process is the foundation for long term partnerships, so both sides need the same level of comfort and trust. The investor relationship is akin to marriage. It's nice to have a little mystery in your marriage, but you better understand each other on the fundamentals.

Some startups do nothing to prepare for the due diligence process, assuming the people and business plan documents will speak for themselves. Others stage elaborate *training* sessions to *assure* that everyone tells the same story. The right answer is somewhere in between.

I believe that proactive preparation for due diligence is a bigger job than the work for investor meetings, because your whole team is involved, not just you as the CEO. If there are financial anomalies, or someone in the team doesn't know the current strategy, or is unhappy with you or the company, the investment will be jeopardized.

Even if you feel that all is well, here are some thoughts and actions I would strongly recommend:

> **The whole team must know the plan**: Make sure the business plan and all related documents are current, synchronized, and in the hands of every key employee. If everyone gives a different story, you have no story.

> **Personnel situation is stable**: Ask everyone to update their resume, and personally call probable references, so there are no surprises. You need to brief the investor ahead of time if there are career anomalies or personnel situations that could be a problem.

> **Don't surprise the team**: Call a company meeting to communicate what is happening and why. This is a good time for the CEO to present the final investor charts, and answer any questions from employees. All need to know who will be there and what you expect.

> ➤ **Contact key vendors and existing customers**: Explain that they may be called, and use the opportunity to check their satisfaction with your company and your product. Again, if you find problems you can't fix, be up front with the investor to avoid a surprise.

Depending on the availability of staff and information needed, the due diligence process generally takes 2–6 weeks to perform. Here is a quick summary of the priorities normally covered by the due diligence process:

> ➤ **Evaluation of key players**: This is the highest priority item. As a starting point, an investor will ask for resumes of the *key players*, and will then follow up to verify that executives are experienced, honest, and committed. This means questioning each of these key players, and calling references or prior associates.

> ➤ **Validation of the product**: This will cover the technology, the current state of development, and customer satisfaction. Is the product something consumers need or simply want, does it work, and is it ready to ship? What are the kinks or certifications that need to be resolved? If the product is in the customer's hands, expect some customers to be interviewed.

> ➤ **Size of the market**: Having a great product or service is not enough. One of the criteria for a good investment is a large and fast growing **potential market**. Investors will talk to their own experts on the size of the potential market and the expected growth rate. They will also assess trends in the market and how current economic, political, and demographic conditions relate.

> ➤ **Sales and marketing strategy**: This will involve an analysis of the company's distribution channels, advertising, and pricing strategy. An investor will try to get an independent reading on competition, barriers to entry, price sensitivity, and what percentage of the market your company can expect to capture.

Remember, once investors contribute money to a company, a long-term relationship is created. Unlike a marriage, however, it may be very difficult, if not impossible, to get a divorce. Your objective is not only to survive, but also to make it an enjoyable win-win relationship.

Also, the technical entrepreneur needs to remember that due diligence should always be a two-way street. We just covered what investors do to validate your startup before they invest. There is also the inverse, sometimes called **reverse due diligence**, which describes what you should do to validate your investor before signing up for an equity partnership. Every entrepreneur should talk to people from companies that were previously supported by this investor, and get their perspective on the working relationship, value provided, trustworthiness, and expectations of this investor.

I've had startup founders tell me that it's only about the color of the money, but I disagree. Particularly if you are desperate, keep in mind the person who finds a good-looking partner to take home from the bar at closing time, but then wakes up in the morning wondering *"What did I just do?"* Taking on an investor is like getting married—the relationship has to work on all levels.

The vast majority of accredited investors are totally trustworthy, but a few may have slipped or fallen from their lofty perch, so entrepreneurs must take great care to validate the character and reputation of every prospective investor. The technical entrepreneur's tendency to be in a huge hurry to obtain the funding can end up being disastrous, and play into the hands of these less scrupulous investors.

If you think of investors as Angels, most Angels are pure, but there are some exceptions that may cost you more than an investment:

> **Shark Angels**: These are the ultimate bad guys whose sole interest in early-stage investing is to take advantage of what they believe is the technical entrepreneur's lack of financial and deal-making experience. If the term sheet process turns to pure torture, it may be time to respectfully bow out. Not all shark Angels are on the Shark Tank TV show.

> **Litigious Angels**: The litigious investor will look for almost any excuse to take you to court. This type of investor never really focuses on the returns your company can deliver, but instead tries to make money by intimidation, threats, and lawsuits. They know you won't have the resources to fight them, so they count on you *caving*. Keep your attorney close by your side.

> **Superior Angels**: A number of successful business people, some of whom become Angels, develop the belief that they are destined for greatness because of their clear superiority over everyone else. These are usually overbearing, negative people who are hypercritical of every decision you make. Don't be intimidated into bad decisions.

> **Control freak Angels**: This Angel starts out looking like your new best friend. Once you are funded, he waits until you hit your first pothole and then points out *gotcha* clauses in your agreement that give him more control. This escalates into a requirement that he must step in to run your company himself. Only your Board of Directors can save you here.

> **Tutorial Angels:** The tutorial investor is not after control, but wants to hold your hand on every issue. The mentoring offer always sounds good up front. But after they write the check, it soon becomes apparent that their desire to be helpful 24 hours a day is a nuisance at best. Initially, your gratitude for their investment may prompt tolerance, but eventually the burden wears you down. Keeping your distance from them is the best solution.

> **Has-been Angels:** These tend to appear with every perturbation in the economy. They are usually high-flyers with a liquidity problem. They are still at the country club every day, but are now running up a tab. They will meet with you, and ask a thousand questions, but never get around to closing the deal. Learn to ask the closing questions.

> **Dumb Angels:** Wealth is not synonymous with business savvy. You can spot dumb Angels by the questions they ask (or don't ask). If they ask superficial questions or don't understand business, a successful long-term relationship is not likely. But don't forget that people with wealth usually have some savvy friends to meet.

➤ **Brokers posing as Angels**: These people are all over the place, often posing as lawyers and accountants. They have little intent to invest in your company, and will eventually solicit you to sign a fee agreement to pay them to introduce you to actual investors. Brokers are often worth the fee, but don't be misled about who is the Angel.

How do you avoid most of these undesirable types of Angels? Whenever possible, only accept investments from individuals in credible, professional Angel investing organizations—not people who solicit you. Even then, do your own due diligence in the business community. Ask what other companies they've invested in, and talk to the CEOs of those companies to find out what kind of investor they've been.

Also, make sure your lawyer writes the initial investment document or term sheet and not the investor. This document should be standard for all your investors and not negotiated on a one-on-one basis. Watch out for any attempts to add clauses that can come back to bite you. Not all Angels these days are even trying to earn their wings.

To re-iterate, due diligence on an investor is where you validate the track record, operating style, and motivation of your new potential partner. Maybe more importantly, you need to confirm that the investor *chemistry* matches yours. Here are some techniques for making the assessment:

➤ **Talk to other investors**: The investment community in any geographic area is not that large, and most investors have relationships or knowledge of most of the others. Of course, you need to listen for biases, but local Angel group leaders can quickly tell you who the bad Angels and good Angels are, and what kind of terms they typically demand.

➤ **Network with other entrepreneurs**: Contact peers you have met through networking, both ones who have used this investor and ones who haven't. Ask the investor for *references*, meaning contacts at companies where previous investments were made. Don't just call, but personally visit these contacts.

➤ **Check track records on the Internet and social networks**: Do a simple Google search like you would on any company or individual before signing a contract. Look for positive or negative news articles, any controversial relationships, and involvement in community organizations. Check the profile of principals on LinkedIn and Facebook.

➤ **Spend time with investors in a non-work environment**: As with any relationship, don't just close the deal in a heated rush. Invite the investment principal to a sports event, or join them in helping at a non-profit cause. Here is where you will really learn if there is a chemistry match that will likely lead to a good mentoring and business relationship.

➤ **Validate business and financial status**: Visit the firm's website and read it carefully. Look for a background and experience in your industry as well as quality and style. Conduct a routine credit and criminal check, using commercial services such as HireRight. Be wary of individuals or funds sourced from offshore.

If you think all this sounds a bit sinister and unnecessary, go back and read some of the articles about Bernie Madoff and the most common investment scams (http://www.bankrate.com/brm/news/investing/20020829a.asp). Remember, if it sounds too good to be true, it probably isn't true. Entrepreneurs are optimists by nature, so I definitely recommend the involvement of your favorite attorney (usually a pessimist).

I recognize that it has been tough to raise capital these last couple of years, but don't be tempted to take money from any source. This can be a big mistake, with common complaints running the gamut from unreasonable terms, constant pressure, to company takeovers. Be vigilant and ask questions.

A successful technical entrepreneur-investor agreement better be the beginning of a long-term relationship. If you don't feel excited and energized by your initial discussions with an investor, give it some time and do your homework. If the feeling doesn't grow, it may be time to move on. As with any other relationship, it's better to be alone than to wish you were alone.

Rejection, and how you learn from it

Almost every early-stage startup who has approached investors for funding has heard the innocuous-sounding rejection "*I love your idea, but come back when you have more traction*". What does traction really mean to investors, and how much is enough? Let me try to clarify the rules, and what it takes to win at this game.

First of all, let's start with the definition. **Traction** is evidence that your product or service has started that **hockey-stick** adoption rate, which implies a large market, a valid business model, and sustainable growth. Investors want evidence that the *dogs are eating the dog food*, and your financial projections are not just a dream.

Obviously, this definition is generic, so my first recommendation is that you take the lead in defining traction metrics for your startup, and then selling your results convincingly to investors. A graph that shows a hockey-stick **up and to the right** curve with at least three data points per key indicator is a great visual assist.

One or more of the following parameters are viewed by most investors as traction indicators, but good technical entrepreneurs are often creative and define their own to supplement these:

> **Start with sales to-date for a priced offering**: As an investor, I would like to see one month of sales, and see how that compares to your projections. One customer is not traction, and beta tests with a thousand customers at no cost don't count. Your graph should show that sales have **turned upward** per projection, beyond friends and family.

> **Free and freemium products need a solid base**: If your product is free, with advertising revenue from click-throughs, you need a sign-up rate and page-view rate that approaches one million page views per month. I like to see at least 10,000 active users, or a user base, page-views, or mobile downloads that double every three months. Great marketing and promotions are usually required.

> ➤ **Market penetration**: Percentages may be difficult at this early stage, but you need to get creative about slicing and dicing the market, sector, demographic, and subcategories. For example, if your value-add is with first-time parents, show me a graph of how many 20- to 30-year-old moms have signed up each week the first month.

> ➤ **Average transaction size and revenue per customer**: Often, enterprise customers, or even consumers, test a new channel by signing up for a few small transactions or trial products. If your average transaction size, number per customer, or margins, have been turning up dramatically, it should mean you have gained real traction in the market.

> ➤ **Customer acquisition cost**: In an inverse fashion, real traction usually means that your cost to acquire a new customer is coming down rapidly, as your marketing kicks in, and your offering is known and accepted by the mass market. You need to position these numbers to investors as positive, based on your domain experience, before being asked.

> ➤ **Show acceptance by major customers and key distributors**: Sometimes, it is not the numbers that indicate traction, but who you have signed up. Signed contracts with big name customers such as IBM, AT&T, or Wal-Mart, is a strong indication of traction. The same is true if your offering has been accepted by major distributors in your industry.

> ➤ **Public statements from industry experts and groups**: In the enterprise world, if your offering is even included as a new contender by respected industry groups, such as Gartner Research, you should claim traction. In the consumer world, groups such as Consumer Reports will give you similar credibility, if positive. Start early to work these relationships.

You need to take the lead when choosing the key metrics that accurately and positively express (both quantitatively and graphically) that your startup has broken through the traction barrier. Don't ask investors if you have traction—if you have to ask, you probably won't like the answer.

However, never forget that traction is necessary, but may not be sufficient, to lower the risk perception of investors and assure an investment. The quality of the team and the overall financial health are equally important, as well as how your offering compares to competitors.

Overall, you should think of traction as an indicator or indicators that demonstrate that your offering has shifted from being an *idea* to being a profit-making *business*. As such, it should be just as important to you as to potential investors. Make sure you understand what it means to you, and communicate where you stand. If investors have to raise the subject first, you don't have enough traction to win.

Investors fund solutions rather than technology

Perhaps the most common reason for technical entrepreneur funding failure is that they will develop a new technology, because they love it, without regards to the market demand. They will then build an entire strategy based on creating a need, rather than acting on an existing market need. Investors characterize this approach as a *solution looking for a problem*. These don't get funded because they usually fail as a business.

The best technical startups find a way to drive the market with their technology, rather than push their new technology-driven "solution" on the marketplace. An example of market-driven technology is the basic automobile, but combining a car with an airplane is technology looking for a market.

New technology really doesn't have any value until it is integrated into a market-driven solution. Here are a few thoughts on a process that will keep you on the right track:

> **Get real customer input first**: Temper your product with actual market and customer feedback. Everyone's personal perspectives and interests are different, so the key is starting from market problems, and going from there to technology—not vice versa. Show your prototype to real customers, and listen.

> **Quantify the pain points**: Measure the major pain points in time or dollars, based on feedback from intended users of your product or service. Users that "like" your product, but have no pain, will not pay real money or endure change for your product (even early adopters won't make a market).

> **Keep it simple and easy to use**: Have you solved the user problems in the simplest possible way, with the fewest possible features? Or have many features been thrown in, just because the technology can deliver them? "Easy to use" and "lots of features" are usually contradictory statements.

> **Analyze how competition will react**: If you are tempted to respond with "*We have no competition*", then you almost certainly have a solution looking for a problem. Think about how your customers have survived all these years without your product, and how many will pay your price to change. Will your competitors quickly copy you, or undermine your price?

> **Experience the pain first-hand**: The best entrepreneurs solve problems that they and their team have personally experienced. This will keep you laser-focused on the solution, and make you more effective and credible in selling the solution.

I'm sure that some of you are thinking by now that if all technical entrepreneurs followed these guidelines, the world would have missed many great leaps in technology, like the laser, television, and the Internet. These are usually called "disruptive" technologies.

Disruptive technologies and grand new solutions can ultimately change the world and create a large opportunity, but they are not exciting to early-stage investors for the following reasons:

> ➤ **Fundamental changes take a long time to happen**: According to the **Gartner Hype Cycle** (http://en.wikipedia.org/wiki/Hype_cycle), every major new technology goes through four stages before reaching general acceptance, and that can take as long as 20 years. Investors are looking for a big return in five years. Only people and organizations with their own big resources will survive.

> ➤ **Creating a need is much more costly than marketing to an existing need**: To build a new market, you have to educate people on the concept, create the *need* in their mind, and solidify it by constant repetition. This means building a brand, viral marketing, and multiple expensive promotions. Early-stage investors won't risk this much.

So, if you have a new technology that you believe can change the world, you need to team up with someone who has really deep pockets. Angel investors can't help you, and most venture capitalists won't be interested in contributing the first several million.

Often, a better alternative is to focus on existing problems with real pain points, and customers that have money to spend on a better solution today. You will get help from investors, feel the near-term satisfaction of success, and build your skills and your bank account for that earth-shaking new technology the next time around.

Differentiating startup viability from fundability

In other cases, new technical entrepreneurs also seem to confuse viability with fundability. Certainly, a non-viable business should be non-fundable, but many viable businesses are also non-fundable. Thus, when an investor declines your funding request, you need to curb your anger and understand the real reason for this outcome.

In my experience, here are the most common issues that cause funding requests for potentially viable businesses to be rejected, in priority order:

1. **An inadequate business plan**: Some investors say half the ideas pitched to them don't have any plan at all, even though some have great potential. Other entrepreneurs skip just a couple of the elements outlined in an earlier chapter on business plans. Investors know that technical entrepreneurs who start a business without a good written plan almost always fail.

2. **An inexperienced team**: Investors bet on the team more than the business plan. Your business model may be very attractive, but if you are new to this, you may not be fundable. If you can find a partner who has deep domain knowledge and a track record of building businesses, I can assure you that your luck will improve.

3. **The business domain is high risk or not squeaky clean**: Certain business sectors have historical high failure rates and are routinely avoided by investors. These include food service, retail, consulting, work at home, and telemarketing. Also, don't expect investor enthusiasm for your gambling site, porn site, gaming, or debt-collection business.

4. **Opportunities are not large or growing**: Investors are looking for a large and growing market to offset the huge risk of funding a startup. Rules of thumb include an opportunity projection that exceeds a billion dollars, with at least double-digit growth. Smaller numbers may easily make a viable business, but won't attract investors.

5. **No sustainable competitive advantage**: The market may be large and growing, but you need some *secret sauce* or intellectual property to keep the big guys from jumping in, once they get the picture. Sleeping giants do wake up, and investors hate to see their money used to build a market for Microsoft, IBM, or Procter & Gamble.

6. **Financial projections are too conservative or too optimistic**: Investors won't fund people who won't push the limits, or inversely won't recognize business realities. More rules of thumb. Your five-year revenue projections better reach at least $20M, but should not exceed Google's actual revenues of $3B in the fifth year.

Make a note

Don't expect a straight answer on your rejection reason from most Angels or venture capitalists. They will probably tell you all looks good, but come back later, after you have finished the product, signed up a few customers, or reached some other future milestone. This is called *not burning any bridges*, in case you start to show traction and they want back in the deal.

Thus, you need an experienced advisor who can do their own analysis of your plan, and follow up informally with all investors to give you the real reason for your rejection, so you can fix it. I find it completely disheartening to see technical entrepreneurs banging their head against the same wall over and over again with every investor, without even realizing their problem.

There were at least half a million startups last year, and only a few thousand received investor funding. In fact, most of the others avoided all these rejections by simply using their own money (bootstrapping), or using the old standby funding source of friends, family, and fools.

Even if you don't intend to run the gauntlet of external investors, it will be worth your while to navigate your startup into a category that is both viable and fundable. Isn't your personal risk just as important as investor risk?

Summary

The goal of this chapter was to clarify the startup funding process for technical entrepreneurs, especially as it relates to external investors, and provide specific recommendations to improve your odds of success.

Most importantly, every investor expects to see some business traction, both before and after a funding request. If you have been working 20 hours a day, and spent your last dollar, but have no results to show, investors will be sympathetic, but will probably tell you that your dream doesn't have wheels. Traction means forward progress.

I hear a lot of technical entrepreneurs contemplating their great idea for several years with little discernable progress, and looking for money to start. Talk and time are cheap, but they need to understand that investors judge past results as a good indicator of future expectations. Here is my summary of the key milestones to complete, which will signal traction and fundability to investors, as well as to your team:

> **Document your business plan**: It's hard to build a business without a plan, just like it's hard to build a house without a blueprint. If you have a product description, that's necessary, but not sufficient. If you have neither, and choose to approach an investor, you will get no attention, and probably never again get a shot at funding with that investor. Make sure your plan answers every relevant question that you could possibly imagine from your business partners, spouse, and potential investors.

> **Set realistic implementation milestones and achieve some**: You can't measure results if you don't have a yardstick. On the other hand, if your objectives are off the chart, you look bad when you set them, and you look even worse when you miss them. Only written milestones are credible. Traction means that you have achieved one or more significant milestones, which will give you credibility with investors. Don't expect them to believe your $100M revenue projection, if you are still waiting for the first revenue dollar. Only real results count.

> **Put together a well-rounded team**: A great business often starts with one person, but it doesn't end there. If you are strong enough to surround yourself with a strong team, that's great progress towards success. A CEO who has *been there and done that* is traction, especially if teamed with a financial lead (CFO) and a product lead (CTO). A team of friends and family that work for free on weekends is not likely to impress investors, unless they are your investors.

> **Build a qualified advisory board**: If you can convince a couple of domain experts or a couple of experienced executives to join your board and be your advocate, that's traction. Investors love to have smart and experienced people in the boat. Investors are likely to make a few phone calls, so make sure these people really have taken the time and commitment to work with you, and know your business. Ideally, they will have links to distributors you need, or even be investors in your company as well.

➤ **Ship a minimum product now**: For a true scientist, the product is never good enough, so it's never done. For a business, you must define the absolute minimum features you need to satisfy the customer problem, and test it in the market. It will be wrong, so count on iterating, but you learn something each time, and that is traction. By using a laser-focused approach for the first iteration, you may actually produce something and get a customer without funding. Now, investors will pay attention, since scale-up funding is less risky and has a timeframe.

➤ **Get a real customer and real revenue**: If you give away your product or service to the first 10 customers, that's a good learning experience, but it's not real traction. It doesn't prove your business model of pricing, distribution, and support. Sell one. Real customers give you real feedback, rather than just telling you what you want to hear. Funding for pre-revenue startups used to be the domain of Angel investors, but they have moved upstage. Without revenue, your investors are largely limited to friends and family.

➤ **Register some intellectual property**: File a provisional patent, register a trademark, and reserve your company domain names. These are things that can cost very little money, but go a long way in convincing someone that you are making progress. Intellectual property is a large element of most early-stage company valuations, and this value determines what percent of the company an investor will expect to get for their money. It's also the keystone to convincing investors that you have a *sustainable competitive advantage*.

➤ **Letters of intent or endorsement**: If it's too early for real customers, a **Letter of Intent** (LOI) or a written endorsement from a potential big customer is good traction to show potential investors. These indicate that you have the ability to make the connections you need. Of course, a real contract or purchase order from a big customer is even better. If you have neither, you better have a prospect pipeline and connections to distributors, or partner relationships with a known company to bolster your credibility.

➤ **Show personal investment**: Investors like to see that you have committed personal funds as well as unpaid personal time (*sweat equity*), and they like to see real progress at this level. If you haven't risked anything or used funds effectively, investors won't let you risk theirs. A related issue is your apparent commitment to the project. If your startup is an evening hobby for you and some friends, and they all have a full-time day job elsewhere, don't expect investors to get excited.

➤ **Become a visible expert**: If your business is a new job site for boomers, you need to establish yourself as the expert on this subject in the press or on social networks, and join related organizations. This is traction that will impress investors and get you customers. Other ways to be visible include writing a blog, speaking at local groups, and issuing press releases that are related to the market need rather than the product you are producing. These efforts should be started well before you are ready for funding.

Your funding journey will be easy if you demonstrate that you are building a technical business that is marching with power and purpose past its goals and objectives. Both your team and potential investors are watching, and if all they see and feel is words and work without progress, it's easy to conclude that your startup is still a dream and a prayer.

In the next chapter, the focus will be on how to make progress and build momentum—to satisfy yourself and your investors. You will find that it's all about taking the right risks, and surviving the bad ones. Remember, you never get anywhere unless you take a chance. Let's go for it!

>6

After the Funding, How Do You Survive the Execution Risks?

Once you have validated the concept and solidified the funding, it's all about the execution. Every new technical startup is fraught with risks, but that's what makes it exciting and makes the opportunity large. Yet, every entrepreneur needs to understand that there are smart risks that everyone should take and stupid risks that should be avoided at all costs.

In the context of startups, I would define new technology as the making, modification, and usage of new hardware, software, systems, and methods of organization in order to solve a customer's problem. Launching any new technology is risky—it might not work exactly as you envisioned. There might be quality problems or unintended side effects. However, if you wait until someone else works out all the bugs and proves its value, you will be too late for the business opportunity. It's smart to take that risk.

On the other hand, if you invent something new and great but don't patent it before you make it public, you run the risk that someone else will copy what you do and take away your competitive advantage. This is a stupid risk you shouldn't take, even though it clearly takes valuable time and money to do the patent work before you ship, and might cost money later to defend your position.

In fact, a large portion of every startup's competitive advantage and potential value to investors is the size of their intellectual property portfolio. When someone says Intellectual Property (IP), most entrepreneurs think only of patents. In reality, patents are only one of many items that should be in your IP portfolio.

This chapter explores the range of startup execution risk issues and helps you understand the pros and cons of each, cost considerations, as well as value to investors, founders, and customers. Specific recommendations are given for each based on my own experience and the feedback of many other technical entrepreneurs before you.

Risks to be avoided

The first rule for survival is to avoid all the risks that have nothing to do with the new technology you are developing, and defy the rules of common business sense. Examples that will be discussed in this section include ignoring or violating commonly accepted accounting principles, legal standards, and confidentiality disclosure norms. The pros and cons of several other important issues for investors, such as intellectual property, are also covered.

Learn the laws of the jungle for technical startups

Some technical entrepreneurs think that creating the product is the hard part and building a business around it should be easy. In fact, many experts will tell you that it's the other way around. It's a jungle out there in business, and you need to learn the rules for survival in the jungle.

In 2012, total entrepreneurial activity in the United States hit its highest level since their survey started in 1999, according to Babson College (http://www.babson.edu/Academics/centers/blank-center/global-research/gem/Pages/home.aspx). This is the good news and the bad news. The opportunities for change are many, with everyone taking a new look at the world after the recession, but the competition is also huge, as the cost of entry is at an all-time low.

In this context, it's time for every business, not only startups, to take a fresh look at the basics of business success. Jamie Gerdsen, in his book of lessons on business change, creatively titled **Squirrels, Boats, and Thoroughbreds** (http://www.amazon.com/Squirrels-Boats-Thoroughbreds-Jamie-Gerdsen/dp/1938416309), aims primarily at existing businesses, but I believe that most of his points, like his laws of the jungle, can be rewritten for startups as follows:

1. **If you want to eat**: I don't believe in greed, but we all need to make enough money to eat. This means building a revenue stream and tuning your business model to produce margins in the 50 percent range or above. I support being socially and environmentally conscious, but you can't help anyone else if you can't eat.

2. **If you want to survive**: Survival means growth and scaling. Once you have a proven business model, you need to scale the business up quickly to stay ahead of competitors. These days, doubling your business volumes every year is the *norm* that investors and potential acquirers are looking for.

3. **If you want to be feared**: Every startup needs a sustainable competitive advantage. In the jungle, it might be the strongest jaws, but in startups, it's more likely the strongest intellectual property. With no competitive advantage, startups with new ideas that gain traction are never feared and are usually eaten for lunch as sleeping giants wake up.

4. **If you want to mate**: In the business world, we call this finding the right strategic alliances. This means you have to stand out above the crowd and aggressively pursue those candidates who can help you breed even more presence and power in the marketplace. Sitting quietly on the sidelines, waiting to be found, is lonely.

Every startup in the business jungle begins with a limited amount of three precious commodities: **time**, **talent**, and **treasures**. The smart ones have a plan for how they intend to spend these resources, and measure themselves against that plan. Otherwise, they will likely look back later and find that one or more of the laws of the jungle have been compromised:

➤   **Time**: Start with a timeline of how much runway you have, with objectives and milestones mapped against the timeline. Time management is an art. Don't waste precious time on the *crisis of the day* in favor of strategically critical tasks. The best entrepreneurs work on making better time management a top objective.

➤   **Talent**: Every startup needs talents to give the company value. In the beginning, the entrepreneur has to cover all talents, which is made more possible these days by the wealth of information available on the Internet, as well as through books and online courses. Talent can also be outsourced, but surviving in the business jungle without talent is unlikely.

➤   **Treasure**: Most entrepreneurs assume that treasure means funding. In reality, more important treasures often include intellectual property, the ability to innovate, and well-defined processes that can deliver great products and reach new customers more efficiently and effectively than the competitors. Money is no substitute for these other treasures.

In summary, whether you are running a technical startup, a family business, or a famous brand such as IBM, you are all part of the jungle. You can be a small tiger with big teeth or an aging dinosaur. The laws of the jungle apply to all. It really is a world of survival of the fittest.

The jungle framework is a great one to set the right perspective. Startups that prosper and succeed learn the rules of the jungle early, don't make excuses, and don't look for any entitlements. Your goal is to be the king of the jungle with your technology.

Every technical startup needs business accounting and records

As a result of their love for technology, I've noticed a great tendency among technical entrepreneurs to ignore the essentials of business accounting in the early stages of their startup. Just because you are not profitable yet doesn't mean you can skip the record keeping. This might seem obvious to many of you, but I see it so often that it's worth some special emphasis.

In fact, keeping records is even more important before profitability. When you anticipate losses for the first year or two, it is more important to properly document all expenses, including tricky ones such as business travel, business meals, and your home office. Sloppy documentation and reporting of these expenses is an open invitation to an IRS audit, which is the last thing you need or can afford during the busy startup period. This information will also be needed for due diligence on investment and potential strategic partnerships and acquisitions.

Expense accounting is just one of the key record-keeping requirements for a successful business:

> **Expenses and income.** You'll need a check register, a cash receipt system, and a record of bills. Also, you should include tax records, bank statements, cancelled checks, bank reconciliations, notices from and to your bank, deposit slips, and any loan-related documents. Keep good backups of all computer files.

> **Corporate records.** These include articles of incorporation, bylaws, shareholder minutes, board minutes, state filings, a stock ledger, copies of stock certificates, options and warrants, and copies of all securities law filings. In all cases, don't forget permits, licenses, or registration forms required to operate the business under federal, state, or local laws.

> **Contracts.** All the contracts you have, even expired ones, should be saved indefinitely. These would include equipment leases, joint venture agreements, real estate leases, and work-for-hire agreements. It is also good to keep correspondence sent and received by mail, faxes, and important e-mails that you might want in hard copy.

> **Employee records.** These include completed employment applications, employee offer letters, employee handbooks or policies, employment agreements, performance appraisals, employee attendance records, employee termination letters, W-2s, and any settlement agreements with terminated employees.

> **Intellectual property records.** This is an especially important category. Make sure you file a copy of all trademark applications, copyright filings, patent filings and patents, licenses, and confidentiality or nondisclosure agreements.

Of course, these days, you need a personal computer or laptop dedicated to your business with some basic software tools. You should investigate the wide variety of software systems that are on the market and pick one that makes you comfortable, as you will probably be doing the basic data entry yourself. This will not only save you money, but it will also keep you intimately aware of all expenses and the condition of your overall business. In my experience, the most common small business accounting system I see in startups is QuickBooks Pro by Intuit.

Even if you have the money to hire an accountant, you should keep a grip on your business' financial affairs. You should be able to explain to yourself how much money you owe out to others, how much others owe you, and how much cash you have in hand. Don't be shy about investigating local classes such as adult education or even a seminar with the SBA on bookkeeping.

An accountant might not be necessary, but you still can't skip the tools. You can't walk in with a bag full of receipts. The more organized you are, the more organized you will be when presenting this material to an accountant. This translates to reduced bills from the accountant and a reduced tax bill from the IRS. You will save time and money, and be more confident about your status.

Good record-keeping practices are required to comply with tax laws and to operate your business properly. When you incorporate your business, it is the right time to establish the records system. Don't let your dream get killed by ignoring business basics.

Think carefully before taking legal risks and shortcuts

Although every technical startup is unique, there are certain common avoidable mistakes that can lead to legal complications, which jeopardize the long-term success of the business. I'm not suggesting that every startup needs a lawyer, but you should definitely pay attention and not be afraid to consult legal counsel if any of these raise qualms for you.

Like other environments, most legal issues don't result from fraud, but from ignorance of specific requirements or simply never getting around to doing the things that common sense would tell you to do. Here are five of the most common examples:

> **Failure to document a founder agreement at the beginning**: This oversight can lead to the so-called *forgotten founder* problem. Early partners or cofounders often drop out of the picture early due to disagreements, and you forget about them, but they don't forget about the verbal or e-mail promises you made.
>
> Later, when your venture is trying to close on financing or even going public, that forgotten partner surfaces, demanding their original share. This problem can be avoided by immediate implementation after early discussions and issuing shares to the founders, with normal vesting and other participation rules.

> **Trouble with the IRS over a founder's stock value**: Many startups delay incorporation until the first formal round of financing, which is too late. At this point, your entity might already have several million in valuation, so the IRS will tax your shares at that value immediately as income, just when your cash flow is at its lowest.
>
> The solution, again, is to incorporate early, when founders' shares clearly have trivial value, and file an 83(b) election with the IRS within 30 days of the agreement. Then, you will only have to pay tax on the increasing value of your shares when they are sold.

> **Disclosing inventions before the patent application is filed**: Entrepreneurs often put off the hassle and the cost of filing a patent until the first funding. Then, they realize that they have talked to many people without signing nondisclosure statements and precluding a patent, or someone else has now beat them to the filing docket.

The US Patent System is now consistent with the rest of the world in enforcing the *first to file* rule. Filing a provisional patent, essentially a short form that you must follow with a full patent application within a year, is the best way to grab your place at the head of the line as the first to file on an innovative new idea.

Thus, there is no excuse for not filing at least a provisional patent early. This will hold your place in the patent line for a year, and the costs and time for this filing are much less. Even trade secrets need to be documented, and reasonable steps should be taken to keep them secret. Business plans and other documents should always be labeled as confidential.

➤ **Founders ignore noncompete clauses from former employers**: If your new business is even remotely similar to that of your current or former employer, think hard about any written or implied noncompete agreements you might have. Do the same for every business partner or employee you might hire.

The best way to short-circuit this problem is to have a frank and open discussion with former employers, perhaps under the guise of asking them to invest in your venture. This is a smooth way to end the relationship and get some money, or get their lack of interest documented in a note back to them. If a lawsuit is inevitable, better sooner than later.

➤ **Taking money from unknown or nonprofessional investors**: Investment fraud continues to be a common subject, even though Bernie Madoff has long been safely behind bars. It's not a good idea to take money from anyone, even friends and family, without an experienced investment attorney drafting or reviewing the agreement to make sure it complies with federal and state securities laws.

This works to protect you from unscrupulous investors as well as nonprofessional investors who might later say that your business plan was misleading. The best advice is to only take investment funds from people who can financially afford to lose and who qualify as accredited investors.

Overall, the biggest legal mistake that a startup can make is to assume that any legal problems can be resolved later. Finding a lawyer early is easy these days, through local networking or even online services such as LegalZoom. In reality, it will cost you much less to get it right the first time, when the stakes are still low, compared to the heartache and cost of correcting it later.

Register all your intellectual property

A large portion of your competitive advantage in the marketplace and your potential value to investors is the size of your intellectual property portfolio. When someone says **Intellectual Property (IP)**, most entrepreneurs think only of patents. In reality, patents are only one of the eight items that should be in your IP portfolio. You need all these before you start looking for funding and success.

In fact, some of the other items might cost a lot less than patents and might be worth far more in the long run. Here are the specifics:

➤ **Company name**: The company name becomes your intellectual property the moment you incorporate your startup as an LLC or a corporation. Sole proprietorships need to trademark the name to protect it. Select it well— marketers will tell you that you will be selling your name more than your products. Actual incorporation fees in many states are below $100 if you do it yourself. Don't pick a company name until you are certain that you can get the comparable domain name, so Internet brokers won't hold you hostage.

➤ **Internet domain name**: This name (www.**domainname**.com) is just as critical as the company name, and the two should match as closely as possible. Significant differences will confuse your customers and open the door to imitators and scam artists. Internet domain names can be acquired from most hosting providers or network solutions for as little as $10/year each.

➤ **Social media accounts**: Immediately, go to relevant social media sites and grab the same name, even if you never plan to use the accounts. Many companies such as Sears, Coca-Cola, and Twitter have already been hurt by people using company names they don't own on social sites. These days, every business needs a blog, so sign up your domain names' accounts on TypePad, Wordpress, and Blogger, or all of the three, before someone starts blogging in your name.

➤ **Patents**: Remember that ideas cannot be patented, only novel implementations can. However, the application or provisional application has to be registered before you disclose the details to investors or consumers, or the implementation will be deemed un-patentable. Patent attorney fees start at around $5K.

➤ **Trademarks**: A trademark is a name, phrase, or logo that tells the consumer about the origin of the goods and distinguishes your goods from those of your competitor. Trademarks require a federal trademark registration from the United States Patent and Trademark Office in the U.S. The cost for a single trademark is around $300. Similar procedures apply in other countries.

➤ **Copyrights**: No registration and cost is required to secure a copyright on written, audio, or video material that you create to be attributed to your company. Still, it is recommended that you add the familiar ©Copyright 2010 symbol at the beginning or end of each media and document segment.

➤ **Trade secrets with employment agreement**: Companies often use non-patentable but important trade secrets to run their business. These trade secrets need to be documented and coupled with an employment agreement, to keep them from migrating to your competitors when employees move on.

➤ **Business plan**: Your business plan holds the keys to your kingdom, so you don't want it in the hands of competitors. If you need early reviews or assistance by people you don't know well, get them to sign a non-disclosure agreement first. A sample agreement (`http://www.startupprofessionals.com/Startup-Professionals-Products.html`) is available for free download from my website.

In cost, all of these elements of intellectual property might be acquired for a few hundred dollars (or a few thousand with an attorney) if you act early and quickly. Later, good intellectual property can be worth millions when your company valuation is set for investment purposes, or when the company is acquired or sold. In between, you need all the intellectual property you can muster to survive.

Know the value and risks of patents

I always advise technical entrepreneurs to file patents to protect their *secret sauce* from competitors and to increase their valuation. The good news is that a patent can scare off or at least delay competitors, and as a *rule of thumb*, during investment and acquisition valuations, patents can add up to $1M to your startup valuation.

The bad news is that patent trolls (non-practicing companies that make their money from licensing patents) can squeeze the lifeblood out of unsuspecting entrepreneurs, as exemplified by the continuing mess around Lodsys (http://www.applepatent. com/2011/05/lodsys-targets-small-ios-developers.html) suing small Apple iOS developers. This patent holding company has charged infringement and demanded royalties from every app developer for iPhone and Android, for a feature most agree has been in apps for many years.

Yes, the patent process, especially for software, is a mess. I say this with conviction even after I survived the process and have a software patent pending. Consider this list of commonly recognized software patent flaws, as summarized from my research, Paul Graham's **Are Software Patents Evil?** (http://paulgraham.com/softwarepatents.html) essay, and the original Lodsys article **Enough is Enough** (http://www.avc.com/a_ vc/2011/06/enough-is-enough.html) by VC Fred Wilson.

> ➤ **The process is onerous, expensive, and time consuming**: Count on spending $10K to $20K per patent just for a USA application today, unless you do most of the work. Even after your application is accepted, the issuing process takes a lifetime in today's technology (4-5 years). Then, you need to repeat the process for every country of interest.

> ➤ **Patents have become a tax on innovation**: A lot of companies, such as Lodsys mentioned earlier, buy up software patents that are overbroad and hold startups hostage, after the fact, through royalties and litigation. They know that these entrepreneurs don't have the skill or resources to defend themselves. Patents only help the big guys who want no change.

> ➤ **Software technology changes rapidly**: Software changes fast and the government moves slowly. The United States Patent and Trademark Office (USPTO) has been overwhelmed by both the volume and novelty of applications for software patents, and they can't maintain a qualified staff. Patents currently last 20 years, which is way too long in the software business.

> ➤ **Patents granted that don't meet the criteria**: To be patentable, an invention has to be more than new. It also has to be *novel* and not obvious. Moreover, patent law in most countries says that software *algorithms* aren't patentable. So, lawyers routinely frame a software algorithm as a *system and method* to meet the criteria.

> ➤ **Valid patent can be overturned by unpatented prior art**: The USPTO used to operate on the doctrine of *first to invent* rather than first to patent. This is ugly, as it means that a valid patent can be overturned by another inventor with a preponderance of evidence of prior art. This happened to RIM (Research In Motion), http://en.wikipedia.org/wiki/NTP,_Inc.#RIM_patent_ infringement_litigation, and cost them nearly $650M to recover. If you are licensing or purchasing an old patent, this can still be a serious issue.

> ➤ **Applying for a patent is a negotiation**: As a result, lawyers always apply for a broader patent than they think will be granted, and the examiners reply by throwing out some of the claims and granting others. They don't insist on something very narrow, with proper technical content.

> ➤ **Different rules around the world**: What I have described so far is the situation in the U.S. In Europe, software is already deemed not patentable, and other parts of the world are somewhere in between. In some countries, software patents are not recognized, and in others, they are not enforced. We need a global solution.

So, what's the answer? I would argue to simply eliminate the software patent, as software is an implementation and is already covered by trademark and copyright law anyway. Others are putting their hopes in a new patent reform bill (http://www.techdirt. com/articles/20120801/00181919902/new-patent-reform-bill-defines- software-patents-targets-trolls.shtml), which tightens the definition of software, hardware, and process patents and targets trolls.

Either way, new computational technology algorithms would still be patentable as long as the algorithm meets the defined requirements for novelty, usefulness, and inventiveness. I'm a big supporter of building and protecting a portfolio of real intellectual property and maximizing your startup's valuation, but it shouldn't be just a legal game.

When to use non-disclosure agreements

Technical entrepreneurs often get advice from their lawyers and friends to always get a non-disclosure agreement (NDA) or confidential disclosure agreement (CDA) signed before disclosing anything about their new technology or their new venture. Most investors and startup advisors I know hate them and refuse to sign them. Who is right?

Let me try to put this question in perspective. If you are totally risk averse, then push to always get signed NDAs. You won't last long as an entrepreneur in this category, as a startup is all about taking risks. On the other hand, if you intend to patent an idea, you need a signed confidentiality agreement from everyone who knows the details, or you will legally lose patent rights.

The format of an NDA is simple, and you can download a sample from my website (http://www.startupprofessionals.com/Startup-Professionals-Products.html). Here are some rule-of-thumb considerations that should help you decide when an NDA is really required or when it actually has a negative value:

> ➤ **Trusted professional**: If you want advice or funding and the person you are about to pitch to is a certified investor or a senior business advisor, skip the NDA. These people value their professional integrity, such as your doctor or lawyer, and they are not competitors. Asking for an NDA is an insult and will jeopardize your case before you start.

> ➤ **Unknown interested party**: If you meet someone through Internet networking or if someone with no visible professional standing contacts you with interest in your plan, an NDA is the least you should do to protect yourself. Verifying credentials through multiple sources is even better.

> ➤ **Strategic partner**: The line between competitor and partner is a fine one these days. An NDA is highly recommended before you talk to a similar company about a joint venture, white labeling, or any investment options. I recommend a mutual non-disclosure, with a non-compete clause, for protection in both directions. In addition, a good practice after a meeting with a strategic partner where you have both signed an NDA is to send an e-mail that summarizes and documents what was discussed at that meeting. It's not only a good record of the meeting for both parties, but also useful in case of future due diligence or litigation.

> ➤ **Prior to patent application**: As I mentioned earlier, you should never disclose the details of a potential patent to anyone without getting a signed and dated NDA. That doesn't mean you can't talk in general terms about your idea and even pitch to investors. Investors don't need to hear the details anyway, until, at least, the due diligence phase.

> ➤ **Trade secrets**: A trade secret is a formula, practice, process, design, instrument, pattern, or compilation of information that is not patentable, but gives you an economic advantage over competitors or customers. When someone needs to know the details, get an NDA, even with your own employees.

> ➤ **Period covered**: Typically, NDAs have terms of 2-5 years. In today's fast moving world, a longer term makes no sense and is viewed by the signor as an unreasonable restriction on future activities. You can always renew the NDA before it expires, if it is still relevant.

Venture capitalists and Angel investors won't sign NDAs for two reasons:

> ➤ They don't want the constraints or litigation a few have faced from rogue entrepreneurs

> ➤ They feel that if by simply describing the problem you solve, you give away your business, then there is almost no chance you will be able to create a defensible position in the market

They see the same good ideas so often that if they signed a non-disclosure on just a few, they would not be able to talk to new entrepreneurs. It's the people that count anyway, not the idea. Besides, one of the reasons for talking to investors is that they will spread the word to other good investors, so you really want them to talk about you to others to improve your funding odds.

Nevertheless, I would never imply that you can trust every VC and Angel investor. Most of them are good, but there are still some bad ones that want to steal your businesses. There is no substitute for your own due diligence on the background of every potential investor. Getting an NDA signed is not a potential substitute for due diligence.

There will be some companies that, for perfectly valid business reasons, do not wish to sign an NDA. This doesn't mean that they are dishonest, but simply that they might not wish to manage the risks involved. As an example, they want to avoid any future conflict with products they might already be working on.

Sharing original work that you intend to commercialize with a startup requires a high degree of mutual trust. Remember that without an NDA, you can still explain what your idea does, but not how it functions or how it's made. This should be enough to excite interest at a first meeting, and the feedback is worth more than the risk.

Risk factors that scare investors most

If you are seeking external investors for your technical startup, you need to know what investors consider as high risk factors. In addition to the normal business risks, which you might know better than the investors for your own business area, they look to avoid certain *macro* risks or technical startups that have characteristics which have a history of causing investment failures.

Of course, every investor has their own *rules of thumb* on what makes a specific startup too high a risk for their investment taste. You need to know these guidelines to set your expectations on funding or know when it's time to stop courting a specific investor. Here is a summary of the *big picture* high-risk considerations:

> **Inexperienced team**: I've said many times that investors fund people, not ideas. They look for people with real experience in the business domain of the startup and people with real experience in running a startup. An expert in software is considered high risk in manufacturing, and a Fortune 100 executive running a startup is high risk. The best way for new technical entrepreneurs to address this issue is to find a cofounder who has previous experience with a startup in the same business domain. Not all members of the team need to have prior experience.

> **Historically high failure rate category**: Certain business sectors have historical high failure rates and are routinely avoided by investors. These include many nontechnical areas such as food service, retail, consulting, work at home, and telemarketing. On the Internet technical side, I would add new social networking sites and new matchmaking sites.

> ➤ **Dependent on government regulations**: If your technical business model is dependent on government approvals, it can take a long time or require political connections. All new medicines, for example, require expensive and extensive testing for side effects before FDA approval. Of course, successful approvals might also mean high returns.

> ➤ **Large initial investment required**: If your startup involves new electronic chips, it might require a huge investment (more than $1B) to ramp-up manufacturing. By definition, all but the largest investors will pass, and it becomes a high risk to all investors. New drugs often fall in this category due to long clinical trials and FDA approvals required.

> ➤ **Businesses with small return potential**: Businesses with a low growth rate or a small opportunity (less than $1B) are considered high risk by investors who get measured on portfolio return over time. This eliminates from consideration family businesses, small niches, and business areas with declining growth.

> ➤ **Poor public image businesses**: Most investors like to maintain a squeaky clean image, so they would consider it high risk to invest in businesses on the margin of legality or social acceptability. Don't expect investor enthusiasm for your gambling site, porn site, gaming, or debt collection business, no matter how much technology you claim.

> ➤ **Operations in another country**: Investors in one country are generally reluctant to invest in a company outside their realm of operational knowledge. We all know that the success *rules* in Russia are different from the USA, so cross-boundary technical investments are considered high risk, even if you have operating experience there.

These rules of thumb should not be viewed as barriers, but just another factor that needs to be addressed specifically in your business case and investor presentation. It's better to be proactive on these rather than hope your investor is too naïve to notice. Your challenge, if your interest is in one of these areas, is to point out quickly why the high risk is mitigated in your case.

In summary, it pays to have some insight into how investors will likely see you, as this allows you to prepare the best case, both for your own decisions and to approach an investor. It's never smart to switch your plans to a *less risky* business that you know nothing about, because your lack of experience there simply moves that alternative to the high risk category.

Other common startup risks to avoid

I've been advising and mentoring technical entrepreneurs and growth companies for years, and find myself always pushing them to take a risk with something new for the sake of growth and survival. When you try new things, you make mistakes, and I've seen many. Smart startups do all they can to avoid these mistakes, learn from them, and profit from the mistakes of other entrepreneurs before them.

In the spirit of saving you a few lifetimes of pain, here are some common specific and risky mistakes that seem to happen routinely:

➤ **Wait until your company is up and growing before you formalize it**: Some technical entrepreneurs can't decide if they want to be a Limited Liability Corporation (LLC) or a C-corporation, or they don't have the money, so they put off doing anything until the first venture capital round or until the first lawsuit occurs.

The simple answer is to do something and start simple. In almost every state, you can incorporate as an LLC with minimal effort and a cost in the hundred-dollar range. This step shows everyone you are serious and limits your liability on any mistakes. It also forces you to pick a name for your company and put other intellectual property stakes in the ground. It's not that hard to change later to a C-Corp.

Company and product naming might also seem simple, but should be a key early effort, because mistakes can be very costly. You might recall the Chevy Nova, a compact car from GM. Pundits in Latino countries quickly pointed out that the name, 'no va' means 'does not go' in Spanish. Professional advice in this area is highly advised. Cultural and religious implications must be very carefully considered.

➤ **Rely on informal agreements with partners**: You might all be friends or spouses today, but things do change quickly in the stress of a growing company. The same principles apply to strategic partners. Early cofounders often drop out of the picture due to disagreements and you forget about them, but they don't forget about the verbal promises you made.

Later, when your venture is trying to close on financing or even going public, this forgotten partner surfaces, demanding their original share. This problem can be avoided by incorporating the business immediately after early discussions and issuing shares to all founders. I know two former friends who are still killing each other financially years later over an unwritten agreement, remembered differently by each.

➤ **Be quick to hire and slow to fire**: If you are growing quickly and desperate for help, you might skip on the homework of a proper job description, or validating applicant credentials are a fit before you proceed to interview. The message here is that if you don't know exactly what help you need, you probably won't get it. Hiring after one interview is like hopping a red-eye to Vegas to get married after one date.

Equally bad, you might know what you want, but you are trying to force-fit the candidate into the position. Maybe they are related to the boss, or you are confident that the candidate will be a good helper and can learn a lot from you. Helpers are expensive, as it often takes longer to jointly do a job than it would take one qualified person to do it alone.

At the other end of the process, don't hesitate to pull the trigger fast when a new hire isn't working, but don't forget to be human and follow all the steps. Carrying a non-performing employee probably triples the costs, as you are paying two people to do the job, and at least one other is demotivated by the inequity.

> **Only hire people who like you or think like you**: Flattery feels good, but it doesn't pay the bills. Look for a thoughtful challenge to your ideas and practice active listening when you are selling your vision. High three-digit intelligence (IQ well above 100) has value.

Some executives think they can mix business with pleasure with interoffice relationships. We all have our favorite story on this one. Make it a rule to not fraternize with your employees, and choose your partners wisely.

> **Be super-conservative on your funding requests**: Double-check both the money you need before funding and the size of investor funding requests. You will be amazed at how many items you forgot to cover and how fast the cash disappears. You should buffer the first by 50 percent, and the second by 25 percent. Severe cash flow problems are a big mistake and might not be recoverable.

When you have people and their families depending on you for their paychecks and you are strapped for money, there certainly won't be any money for growth. Even if you can find someone willing to help, it might be a very expensive proposition. Cash is more important than profit.

> **Let your accountants manage the expenses**: Too many founders think it's more important to work on products and customers. In reality, the most important task of every small company CEO is to review every expense with a miserly hand before the money flows out. Do not delegate this task.

A variation on this theme is promising a burn rate to investors than you can't deliver. This means managing a bottoms-up budget process and living within the budget. The result of budget and expense overruns is not only lost growth opportunities, but lost credibility and lost support from investors and vendors.

> **Make all the decisions yourself**: One person making all the decisions doesn't mean better decisions, and certainly not faster ones. For a company to grow, the team has to grow and decisions must be delegated. Smart growth companies hire decision makers, not more helpers.

Even early in the startup process, you need someone like-minded but complementary in skills to help you with the startup plans. It's always good to have someone to test your ideas, keep your spirits up, and hone your business skills.

Lastly, make good use of your board members. One or two *experts* who have *been there and done that* can head off many mistakes and suggest a calm recovery plan for the ones you make. Resist the ego urge to *go it alone* or to convince yourself that you are smarter than your competitors.

> **Assume defining the strategy is a one-time process**: Your initial strategy will be wrong, no matter how carefully you think it out. Most startups I know have *refined* their target market and *pivoted* their operation several times during their rollout and growth phases. So, be alert and flexible.

Plan for strategy changes by scheduling an adjustment review every month. Watch out for the unknown, such as an economic recession you hadn't counted on, a new competitor with deep pockets, or the changing trends in the industry. Be sure to communicate changes to the team effectively and often so that it doesn't look like you are making random changes.

➤ **Let the daily crisis keep you from the** *most important* **issues**: It takes practice and effort to focus on the most important things first. In business, *most important* means time to market, customer service, low cost, and beating your competitors. It also means knowing when to delegate, when to rest, and reserving time for effective communication with your team.

If you allow yourself to be driven by the crisis of the moment, you will lose the ability to set priorities and focus on goals. Personal discipline is the key word here. Working in isolation and handling all the issues is fine during the creative phase of the startup, where the founder is often the designer and architect, as well as the builder. Now, this same individual has to graduate from short-term thinking to long-term thinking.

➤ **Ignore the mistakes of others**: The biggest mistake of growing companies is failing to learn from the mistakes of others or even from your own mistakes. You can only learn from your mistake after you admit you've made it. Wise people admit their mistakes easily and move the focus away from blame management and towards learning.

The list goes on and on. However, the reality is that making mistakes is part of every successful growth effort. Therefore, mistakes should be celebrated and learned from. However, the one unforgivable mistake you should never make is to repeat a previous mistake.

In the end, ask yourself this question: Is it better to try and fail, or never have tried at all? To grow in the business world, never trying is not an option.

Taking smart risks

Another rule for survival is to be willing to take some smart, calculated risks and make them work for you. These include responding to trends and getting there first, and finding an under-served niche and exploiting your competitor's weaknesses. The challenge is recognizing these opportunities before others and providing solutions first. This section will discuss many of these smart risks, how to build a team that can be most responsive, and how to achieve the leverage you need for ultimate success.

Entrepreneurship success is recognizing smart risks

Much of the early part of this chapter has focused primarily on bad risks and ways to avoid or contain losses. Here is the other side of the picture. If you want growth and sustainability, you need to create and capitalize on smart risks; this means you intentionally take a risk to grow your business or gain competitive advantage.

In fact, winning technical entrepreneurship is all about taking calculated risks while minimizing non-calculated risks. Here are some simple examples of *smart* calculated risk actions that you should be working on:

> ➤ **Deliver an innovative solution to a painful customer problem**: This can be high risk if your solution doesn't work or your price is more painful than the problem. A bad risk is assuming that because you like the solution, everyone will buy it, or that you can build an existing solution cheaper than anyone else.

> ➤ **Plan to replace your product with a better and cheaper one**: Probably, more companies fail by avoiding this strategic risk than any other. If the current product is making money, it seems like a bad risk to make it obsolete. Yet, new technology can quickly blindside you and market dynamics change, plus you need to broaden your opportunity.

> ➤ **Build a dynamic product line rather than a single product**: Every new product you add stretches your ability to deliver a winning function and quality. Yet, a great initial product with no follow-on will not keep you ahead of competitors. Take the strategic risk.

> ➤ **Implement a new business model**: Software as a service (SaaS) has now pretty much replaced the old licensing model, but offering it was a strategic risk for salesforce.com. Proactively implementing new business models, such as subscriptions and *freemium* pricing, are good risks, while linearly lowering old product prices is a bad risk.

> ➤ **Partner with a competitor**: Use *coopetition* for cost sharing, economies of scale, and open access to new markets. Once you have established your credibility and value, a strategic partnership might lead to other business relationships or a funding source.

> ➤ **Plan to spend money on marketing**: It's a bad risk to count only on word of mouth and viral social network buzz for marketing, as I see in many business plans today. These days, you have to spend money to make money. Of course, there is work involved to find the right media and balance the investment against the return.

> ➤ **Build your team from the best and brightest**: Good people are expensive, and they are hard to find; this adds risk to your startup, but it's a strategic risk. Lowering the risk by hiring the cheapest or counting on family members is a bad risk.

> ➤ **Count on less funding rather than more**: It's a well-known oxymoron that startups that are over-funded to reduce risk fail more often than under-funded ones. Strategically, the more you can do for less, the stronger you grow. It's a bad risk to solve problems with money.

> ➤ **Be aggressive in your forecasts**: Every investor has heard from the *conservative* founder who reduces his forecast to lower the risk. These companies don't get funded, or they under-perform anyway. On the other hand, I'm not suggesting that you portray yourself as a starry-eyed founder who offers up forecasts that are so aggressive as to be unobtainable. A healthy dose of realism is good, without appearing conservative. Forecasts should be strategic, based on the opportunity and pain level.

> ➤ **Lead rather than follow**: In the old days, the leaders always caught the arrows, so following was less risky. Entrepreneurs who try to reduce risk by following winners, like building another Facebook or another Google, will find that they don't catch arrows or customers.

The challenge with all risks is that they must be proactive, measured, and managed. If not, they automatically become bad risks. If you have a startup today, you need to take a regular self-assessment of how much of your time is spent on containing the bad risks versus initiating forward-thinking ones. If it's over 50 percent, your whole startup is probably a bad risk.

Using imitation with innovation to limit risk

If you are a technical entrepreneur starting a business for the first time, I recommend that you find a product concept that is already accepted and improve on it rather than tackling that ultimate disruptive technology. Notice that I'm not suggesting that you steal someone else's idea, but simply limit your risk by adding innovation to a proven entity.

Evidence of success using this approach is all around us. Look how the Japanese entered the auto industry, how McDonalds imitated White Castle, or how Wal-Mart *perfected* the low-price high-volume approach. Once you have experience in running a successful startup this way, you might decide that the disruptive technology of your dreams was a bad idea in the first place.

It seems to me that in the startup world, imitation gets a bad rap. People tend to look down on *me too* entrants as inferior or forced to copy because they have nothing original to offer. I can see many advantages to the imitation-with-innovation approach, beyond just limiting the risk to changing just one variable rather than many:

> ➤ **Avoid initial major R&D cost**: Statistically, the costs to the first inventor of a new technology are at least one-third higher than to follow-on innovators in the same technology (http://hbr.org/2010/04/defend-your-research-imitation-is-more-valuable-than-innovation/sb1). Of course, the first one gets the patent. However, patent disclosure requirements often make imitation easier, and smart technologists can work around most patents anyway.

> **Learn from competitors and early adopters**: Market research is more meaningful if there is already a market and real customers. Don't just copy successful formats and strategies, but learn from what has worked and not worked for your competitors. Hopefully, you can skip some of the costly pivots made by them.

> **Easier to find investors**: Even banks, as well as equity investors, look more favorably at a proven business model than a new and unproven one. This is probably why banks will often support a franchise purchase for up to 70 percent, while they rarely, if ever, support any investment in startups.

> **Imitation drives progress**: If a product or process has already proven its value, has more people working on it, and is determined to be more competitive, it will find more and quicker ways to improve the base than the company that maintains a monopoly. Good imitators often disrupt the original innovator.

> **Try a new country or market**: Good imitators actively look for a new country or market as the innovation rather than a new technology. Even though the world is getting smaller and smaller, very few startups can yet afford to patent or even sell their product in all the relevant countries at once. If that's your home country, jump in first.

Of course, you still have to do your homework and market research. Just because something works in Silicon Valley doesn't mean it will work in Peoria, Illinois. Also, imitations done without the normal operational discipline and strategic planning will fail, just like any other poorly run startup. Don't assume that imitation is reserved for children, animals, and dummies.

Thus, the place to start for new technical entrepreneurs is to look for a successful business (not a failing business) in your domain and think about how you could do it better. Your innovation might be simply a better location, better service, or a better price, or it could be a technology innovation. At minimum, it can give you the money and experience to take your dream step later with less risk. In fact, your imitation with innovation might be the *next big thing*.

Follow strategies of other successful risk takers

Even though risk is an integral part of life, as well as every business, few people learn to manage it properly or even want to think about it. I suggest that one of the best ways to learn is to understand better how successful technical entrepreneurs approach risk, and look at a summary of the strategies they use to turn it into success.

Here, I've extracted a great summary of key strategies used, with life stories, in **The Risk Takers** (http://www.amazon.com/Renee-Martin-MartinsThe-Risk-Takers/ dp/B004FZJC9Q), by Renee and Don Martin. Here is their list, with some prioritizing and comments of my own:

> **Spot a new trend and pounce**: Often, a shift in cultural or economic trends will create new entrepreneurial opportunities. The challenge is to recognize the shift early and then act on it, despite the risk. This is the origin of the *first movers* competitive advantage.

➤ **Go on a treasure hunt and find an under-served niche**: Even a huge multibillion-dollar company can't offer everything for everyone. There is nothing more exciting than finding a lucrative market that everyone else has failed to spot or target.

➤ **Exploit your competitor's weakness and make it your strength**: The sharpest entrepreneurs have a knack for viewing the world from the perspective of their customers. This quality can help you capitalize on competitor vulnerabilities and shortcomings.

➤ **Hit 'em where they ain't**: Whenever possible, set your sights on areas that your competitors have neglected or ignored. It's easier than dislodging well-recognized existing products and waiting for customer change, even if your solution is better.

➤ **Buck the conventional wisdom**: Many entrepreneurs profiled in the book succeeded in large part because they veered away from established formulas and ways of thinking. Challenging convention can open the door to competitive advantage.

➤ **Save your bucks and get notice without expensive advertising**: If your startup business is on a tight budget, there are creative ways today to get customers' attention without traditional advertising. Start with social media, blogging, and word of mouth.

➤ **Never let adversity or failure defeat you**: The ranks of successful entrepreneurs are filled with men and women who refused to stop believing in themselves, despite the derision of others or heartbreaking failures. Persistence and resiliency lead to success.

➤ **Trust your gut**: An expanding body of research confirms that intuition is a real form of knowledge. It's a skill you can develop and strengthen—one that's particularly valuable in the most chaotic and fluid business environment. At such times, intuition often beats rational analysis.

➤ **Never stop reinventing your company**: Top-performing entrepreneurs make it a point to give their business a major overhaul now and then to keep pace with changes in the marketplace. Complacency in business is like a slow leak in a tire. By the time you notice it, the damage is done.

➤ **Just start**: The *perfect* time for a business launch will never present itself. More often than not, waiting just gives would-be competitors the opportunity to beat you to the punch. If you truly believe your idea will succeed, then take the risk and just get started.

Being a risk taker in business is not the same as being reckless. Nevertheless, the word *risk* has a negative connotation to most of us, implying danger and possible loss. For the best entrepreneurs, risk is viewed as positive, with its implied challenge to overcome the unknown and opportunity of hitting the big return. You need to love risk, but know how to manage it to your advantage.

Summary

The goal of this chapter has been to outline the major risk factors for technical entrepreneurs and provide specific recommendations to improve your odds of success. These recommendations center on how to avoid the *bad* risks, and how to recognize and capitalize on the *good* ones.

Recognizing and handling risks well in business, like everything else, is really a function of the leadership team that runs the show. Thus, the next chapter will focus on what it takes to form and manage a strong leadership team. Luckily, leadership is a set of skills that can be learned, so let's take a look at how that works.

Are You Ready for All the Leadership and Team Challenges?

This chapter explores the fact that creating and building a business is not a one-man show, even when it springs from the mind and determination of a single technical entrepreneur. Turning a technical idea or technology into a business success requires many people to work together effectively, and this requires leadership, team building, communication, and continuous motivation.

Leadership is not a skill anyone is born with, but it can be learned and honed from mentoring, experience, and failures. Startups also require many different leadership skills, from technical to financial, so a technical entrepreneur needs to understand how to build the right team, be a role model, and work with all kinds of people.

In business as in life, the smartest people are the ones who know they don't know it all. However, smart people learn quickly. Not far down the road, you will be ready to mentor entrepreneurs who are where you were only a year or two ago. You then become a contributor to business leadership in the same way your mentor was to you. That's value squared.

How to be an entrepreneur role model to lead your technical startup

In the beginning, all businesses are simply people playing out an idea. It's never the other way around—there is no technical idea so big that it doesn't need people to make it succeed. Investors know this, hence the saying, *Bet on the jockey (founder), not the horse (technical idea)*. A great jockey is a great entrepreneur role model.

Like it or not, everyone looks to the entrepreneur to be the jockey role model in their new business. Typically, this energizes new startup founders, but some struggle trying to live up to their own as well as everyone else's expectations. In reality, nobody really expects anyone to be superhuman, but it can feel like that.

We certainly wouldn't expect superhuman behavior from the people looking to us for guidance, nor would we want them to expect flawless behavior from us. If not flawless behavior, what characteristics and actions do they look for? Here are some frequently mentioned ones:

> **Demonstrate confidence and leadership**: A good role model is someone who is always positive, calm, and confident in themselves. You don't want someone who is down or tries to bring you down. Everyone likes a person who is happy with how far they have come, but continues to strive for bigger and better objectives.

> **Not afraid of being unique**: Whatever you choose to do with your life, be proud of the person you've become, even if this means accepting some ridicule. You want role models who won't pretend to be someone they are not and won't be fake just to suit other people.

> **Communicate consistently with everyone**: Good communication means listening as well as talking. People are energized by leaders who explain why and where they are going. Great role models know they have to have a consistent message, and repeat it over and over again until everyone understands.

> **Show respect and concern for others**: You might be driven, successful, and smart, but whether you choose to show respect or not speaks volumes about how other people see you. Everyone notices if you are taking people for granted, not showing gratitude, or stepping on others to get ahead.

> **Be knowledgeable and well rounded**: Great role models aren't just *teachers*. They are constant learners, challenge themselves to get out of their comfort zones, and surround themselves with smarter people. When team members see that their role model can be many things, they will learn to stretch themselves in order to be successful.

> **Have humility and willingness to admit mistakes**: Nobody's perfect. When you make a bad choice, let those who are watching and learning from you know that you made a mistake and how you plan to correct it. By apologizing, admitting your mistake, and accepting accountability, you will be demonstrating an often overlooked part of being a role model.

> **Do good things outside the job**: People who do the work, yet find time for good causes outside of work, such as raising money for charity, saving lives, and helping people in need, get extra credit. Commitment to a good cause implies a strong commitment to the business.

True role models, such as Jeff Bezos of Amazon.com and Michael Dell before him, are those who possess the qualities that we would like to have and those who have changed the way we live. They help us advocate for ourselves and take a leadership position on the issues that we believe in.

We often don't recognize true role models until we have noticed our own personal growth and progress. This really implies that it takes one to know one. Thus, if you are asking the question, this might mean you are well along the road to being that role model already. Keep going, and you should find some help in the rest of this chapter in filling your own leadership gaps.

Traits of a great technical startup founder

Everyone can recognize a great business and technical leader a mile away, so why is it so hard to find one? We all remember a few that are *legends in their own mind*, but this doesn't do it. In fact, the clue here is that the view in your mind is the only one that matters rather than the other way around.

Almost every one of us in business can remember that one special leader or executive in their career who exemplified the norm, who commanded our respect, and treated us like a friend, even in the toughest of personal or business crises.

I've asked many peers for the traits or attributes they saw in that person, and most will list the following positive functional traits of a good startup founder. Notice that only one of them (domain expert) is about their technical prowess. Thus, being a leader on the technical side is necessary, but not sufficient to be a technical leader:

> ➤ **Leadership**: A good startup founder shows outstanding skills in guiding team members towards the attainment of the organization's goals and the right decisions at the right point of time. As Drucker said, "*Management is doing things right; leadership is doing the right things.*"

> ➤ **Plan and delegate**: They possess foresight and skills to understand the relevant capabilities of team members, and then schedule tasks and delegate them to the right people, to get them done within deadlines. You are a guide, not a commander.

> ➤ **Domain expert**: They demonstrate complete knowledge of their field and are confident about that knowledge, with the common sense to make quick productive decisions and the ability to think outside the box. Also, this person is able to maintain respectful relationships with other technical employees in this domain.

> ➤ **Set clear expectations**: Employees should always know what is expected of them. One of the easiest ways to do this is to set deliverable milestones for each employee over a set period of time. Then, you can review the performance versus the roadmap or deliverable at least 6 months prior to a performance review and discuss ways to improve.

> ➤ **Positive recognition**: Immediately recognize team members, publicly or privately, when they complete something successfully or show initiative. Congratulate them on a job well done. Most employees are not motivated by money alone. Good managers know that employees want regular recognition that their job is being done well.

In my view, these are all the *necessary* attributes, but are not *sufficient* to put you in that 'great' category. Most people recognize that it takes more to be *great*, but the attributes are a bit more esoteric and harder to quantify. Here are a few:

> **Active listener**: This person shows traits such as listening with feedback, an optimistic attitude, motivating ability, and a concern for people. Listening to what is said as well as what is not said is of utmost importance. It is demoralizing to an employee to be speaking to a supervisor and be interrupted for a phone call. All interruptions should be avoided.

> **Shows empathy**: This refers to the ability to *walk in another person's shoes*, and to have insight into the thoughts and the emotional reactions of individuals faced with change. Empathy requires that you suspend judgment of another's actions or reactions, while you try to understand them and treat them with sensitivity, respect, and kindness.

> **Always honest**: Simply put, today's managers live in glass houses. Everything that a manager does is seen by his employees. If a manager says one thing and does another, employees see it. Managers must be straightforward in all words and actions. A manager must *walk the talk*. This also means recognizing weaknesses and admitting mistakes.

> **Sense of humor**: People of all ages and cultures respond to humor. The majority of people are able to be amused at something funny and see an irony. One of the most frequently cited attractions in great personal relationships is a sense of humor.

> **Keep your cool**: A great manager is an effective communicator and a composed individual, with a proven tolerance for ambiguity. They never lose their cool and are able to correct the team members without emotional body language or statements.

Whole books are written on this subject, but hopefully, you get the picture. Great entrepreneurs and leaders must do the technical job well—and they also must do the people job very well. Are you ready to be one of these for your startup?

Finding the right top executive for your technical startup

There comes a time in every technical entrepreneur's life when you have to decide if you are capable or even interested in running the leadership side of your startup as the Chief Executive Officer (CEO). To help you with this decision, I suggest you look hard for the best candidate with the techniques described in this section, always including yourself in the list of candidates.

If you don't measure up or are not interested, there is no shame in taking the role that you are best suited for, such as the CTO, and let someone else run the business. You will have more fun, and the business will more likely succeed. As the founder and majority owner, it's better to own a large share of a successful business rather than all of a failing one.

To find the best CEO candidates, it makes logical sense to scour the job boards, engage an executive recruiter, or scan networking sites such as LinkedIn for a good array of candidates, and then interview the ones with the best resumes.

However, in fact, this is just the beginning. To complement local face-to-face networking, you can always use one of the many online matchmaking sites that have sprung up in the last few years, such as CoFoundersLab (https://www.cofounderslab.com/) and Founder2be (http://www.founder2be.com/) (think eHarmony™ for entrepreneurs, or Match.com meets LinkedIn).

On such sites, you can connect with thousands of potential executives and partners, or find a planned meetup in a city near you. Also, trusted advisors and experienced investors should be polled for good candidates. Sure, some executives are found from resumes, and relationships can be built online, but trust and executive chemistry are hard to deduce from a resume or quick meeting.

From the candidate's perspective, the ideal executive for a technical startup is much more likely to sign up for your job if they know and trust you, versus just meeting you online or through the interview process. In all cases, never lose focus on finding someone who can meet the following top objectives, adapted from some old advice by Jeff Richards to startup CEOs:

> **Build the team**: The CEO must focus on key management team hires and assume a few mistakes that need to get fixed. A great hire can make a company, but a single bad one can break it. As one company chairman says, "*The common elements I see in first time CEO's: a) they don't hire fast enough, b) they don't fire fast enough, and c) they don't manage their board and investors well.*"

> **Provide effective leadership**: Remember that leadership is both upward as well as downward to direct reports and employees. A good CEO provides leadership to the Board of Directors, company investors, and stockholders. There are several books written on this subject. A good place to start is *The Effective Executive - The Definitive Guide to Getting the Right Things Done* (http://www.amazon.com/gp/product/0060833459?ie=UTF8&tag=timeleadershi-20&linkCode=xm2&camp=1789&creativeASIN=0060833459), by Peter Drucker.

> **Create and sell a financial model**: Even with a good CFO, your CEO is the top fund raiser. It's important that the CEO defines alternatives and has a very clear view of how he/she will use the proceeds, including the option of not raising any outside capital at all. The CEO is the check and balance on the constant parallel pushes for more development, more marketing, and more growth.

> **Craft an operational plan and make it work**: Most founders are product guys. They need an operational CEO who knows the market and the marketing game. He/she must nail down a sales process that fits the domain and economy. This includes the tactical as well as the strategic. The CEO needs to know how to qualify and close deals, as well as who to sell to, why they should buy your product, pricing, and what your strengths are against the competition.

➤ **Communicate company values and culture**: Make certain that you as the founder and the CEO are on the same page on the mission, company values, exit strategy, and workplace model. Disconnects on how employees are treated or how decisions will be made can be disastrous, especially with family-owned or closely held ventures.

Executive recruiters are the old-fashioned fallback if networking doesn't work out, but find one who has long-term relationships with many experienced candidates and business executives. I have found that most startups and small businesses can't really afford to go this route (the average fee for a CEO is in the $40,000 ballpark).

Often times, you might find that the financial executives of other startups, or the Chief Financial Officer (CFO), are great candidates to run your technical startup. Obviously, they have the business knowledge you need, and they are especially attractive to potential investors in your company.

So, get out there and network today—online and offline—so that you can be one of the lucky ones who has been nurturing a relationship with some candidates and executive recruiters before the real need arises. Then, take a hard look at yourself in the mirror and decide whether it is time to make a change.

Importance of having a startup mentor

I definitely recommend mentoring for technical startups, and have been at different stages at both the contributing and receiving end of the process. These days, I often seem to hear from technical entrepreneurs who are struggling to find a mentor or complaining about their lack of effectiveness. Like any other relationship, it takes work on both sides to make mentoring work.

Every first-time entrepreneur or even an experienced founder stepping into a new business area needs a mentor. Nothing you have ever done raises so many questions or has the potential to be so fulfilling or risky as starting a new business for the first time. A mentor is a confidant who has been there and done that, and is willing to guide your steps.

Also, don't confuse a business mentor with a business coach. A mentor's aim is to teach you what to do and how in specific situations, unlike a coach who helps you develop your generic skills to decide what to do and how. The mentor helps the entrepreneur fill an experience gap, and a coach helps fill a skill gap. Both might be required.

Before you are ready for a mentor, you must know yourself. Have you assessed your strengths and weaknesses? What are your goals? Where are you heading? Unless you know these things, no one can help you. Also, you need to be prepared to take advice and criticism, if it is honest, helpful, and given in a friendly way.

Most entrepreneurs view a mentor as someone older and more experienced who takes the time to personally give guidance and advice, and who takes an emotional investment in your success. They don't think about this process as requiring an investment on their part, both in nurturing the relationship and really listening, without being defensive, to the advice given.

Brian Tracy, in **Earn What You're Really Worth** (http://www.amazon.com/Earn-What-Youre-Really-Worth/dp/1593156308), solidifies my ideas on how mentoring as well as other personal development activities can quickly increase anyone's value and income in business. Here are some key points on how to find and utilize the right mentor, which I have adapted specifically for entrepreneurs:

> ➤ **Set clear objectives for yourself in your business growth**: Decide exactly what it is you need mentoring on before you start thinking of the ideal person to work with. A successful financial executive probably isn't a good mentor to build and execute a great marketing strategy. If you don't have an objective, you won't know when you arrive.

> ➤ **Work, study, and practice continually to solidify the guidance**: The very best mentors are the most interested in helping someone who is willing to learn and grow quickly. This doesn't mean you should accept any guidance blindly, but it does mean that there is no time to make excuses, and an honest effort to understand and implement action items is required.

> ➤ **Don't ask for too much time or make a nuisance of yourself**: Remember, the best mentors are busy people, and they might be opposed to someone trying to take up a lot of their time. The best approach is to ask for small focused blocks of time, maybe just 10 minutes, in private and be prepared with real issues to discuss.

> ➤ **When you meet a mentor, you should lead the discussion**: Your mentor should not be driving your business or expected to provide critical feedback on actions taken or missed. It's most effective if the entrepreneur proposes the agenda and drives for specific insights, but never forgets to press the mentor for broader or related implications.

> ➤ **Remember the difference between a mentor, friend, and coach**: Expect a mentor to tell you what you need to hear, not like a friend who might tell you what you want to hear. A business coach is focused on helping you with generic skills, whereas a mentor's aim is to teach you based on specific situations. The same person can't be all of these.

> ➤ **On a regular basis, send a note to communicate progress and current tasks**: There is nothing that makes a potential mentor more open to helping you than your making it clear that you are following through and the help is doing you some good. This is also a good way to hand out and follow up on assignments to your mentor.

> ➤ **Keep the relationship positive and productive**: If a mentor proves to be unresponsive or on a different wavelength, bow out of the relationship immediately. Be aware that mentors are usually in a business position that can hurt you as well as help you, so don't waste their time or antagonize them.

When you consciously and deliberately seek out a mentor, you must look for someone who genuinely cares about you as a person and who really wants you to be successful in your venture or career. This emotional involvement and genuine concern for you are the keys to real mentor contributions.

Some people will say that they need to make all their own mistakes in order to learn from them. Yet, there is plenty of evidence that the fastest way to a successful business is by piggybacking on the counsel of men and women who have already spent years learning how to succeed. If you can't make a mentor relationship work, I worry about the rest of your business as well.

In case you think mentors are only for *wimps*, you should know that most great entrepreneurs are quick to give credit to their mentors. Bill Gates always revered the early guidance he received from Dr. Ed Roberts (http://www.tomshardware.com/news/Ed-Roberts-Altair-bill-Gates-paul-allen,10058.html), creator of the Altair 8800. Later, the great Warren Buffet (http://www.management-mentors.com/about/corporate-mentoring-matters-blog/bid/23238/Advice-From-Bill-Gates-Corporate-Mentor) became his mentor on many corporate matters.

In a reverse fashion, most of the recognized business gurus always found time to be a mentor. For a fortunate, surprisingly large club of CEOs, the late Peter F. Drucker (http://www.inc.com/magazine/20020901/24536.html) was the single most lucid, eloquent, and encouraging force in their lives. With experts like this willing to help for free, why should you be the one to go it alone?

Finding the right mentor for you is like finding the right investor—the chemistry and culture must be right, or it won't work. It's always appropriate to do your own due diligence to see if the background is appropriate for your situation, check domain credentials, and check references if you can. Some mentors charge for their services, and others might be willing to work for free.

In my experience, those who work for free are likely to be the least effective, give you the least attention, or will expect some other form of *quid pro quo*. People who do mentoring professionally will likely expect 1 or 2 percent of your equity or a retainer of several thousand dollars a year. Remember, as with many other consultants and experts, you tend to get what you pay for.

The best mentor candidates are the most experienced professionals you admire and from whom you can learn to accelerate your progress and avoid the deep potholes in the road ahead. Martin Yate, in his book *Knock 'em Dead - Secrets and Strategies for Success in an Uncertain World* (http://www.amazon.com/Knock-Dead-Secrets-Strategies-Uncertain/dp/1440506507), succinctly outlines the key criteria for choosing mentors:

➤ **Mentoring is not a group activity**: Mentors are not like lovers. You can have more than one at a time. However, my advice is to start with one, or certainly no more than one, in an area of expertise. It could make sense to have a business mentor, as well as a technology mentor, but a committee of your friends won't work.

➤ **The best mentors are older than you**: Although age and wisdom don't always go together, it is better to find a mentor older than you, because they will have skills you don't and the wisdom of greater experience. You need both. Gender doesn't matter, as long as they can garner your respect.

> ➤ **Let the relationship develop naturally over time**: Mentor relationships, like any other human relationship, don't happen overnight, and need to be nurtured on a person-to-person basis rather than remotely or anonymously. The best mentors will even introduce you to their support network, which can multiply the value.

> ➤ **The mentor should not have a direct reporting relationship with the protégé**: The protégé should be able to feel free to speak about issues that might be plaguing him/her, without fear of repercussions from a major board member, investor, or boss.

> ➤ **The mentor must be committed to being a mentor**: Mentoring is an incredibly important responsibility. If the mentor does not want this responsibility, he/she will view the time spent mentoring as a nuisance. Being committed means being available, listening well, and able to keep confidences. It probably also means receiving some kind of payment, as discussed earlier.

> ➤ **Find someone who will tell it straight**: Telling it straight means having direct discussions that are constructive, respectful, and specific. Both sides need the courage to stop if the relationship isn't working. Life is too short to waste their time or yours. In this context, it's also important to find someone who matches your values. A mentor is not a counselor—the first provides straight business guidance, while the second focuses on emotional and psychological challenges.

> ➤ **Pick a mentor with a background that matches your future interests**: Consider choosing mentors who have gone through the type of growth that you aspire to. If you yearn to be acquired by a fortune 500 company, find someone who started and grew their company to give you that perspective.

Remember that a good mentor doesn't relieve you of any responsibility in running your business. Be aggressive and take charge of your own decisions. Don't expect the mentor to do the work for you or even the research required to get a job done. In other words, don't abuse the mentor by asking them to be your boss or respond to every thought that pops into your head.

Most importantly, make sure that your selected mentor is not a critic. The dictionary definition of a mentor is *an experienced and trusted advisor* or *leader, tutor, or coach*. The definition of a critic sounds similar, *a person who offers reasoned judgment or analysis*. The big difference, of course, is that a mentor looks ahead to help you, while a critic looks backward to tell you what you did wrong.

We can all learn from both of these approaches, but in my view, the mentor is far more valuable than a critic. A mentor's goal is to help you build your strengths to avoid problems and pitfalls, while a critic feels compelled to point out your weaknesses.

The job of an entrepreneur is tough enough without a critic on your team, second-guessing your every move. Here are some tips on how to recognize whether a partner, consultant, or employee is a mentor or a critic:

➤ **Earns your absolute trust**: One of the key characteristics of a successful mentor relationship is trust. You should be easily convinced by actions and attitude that the mentor candidate has your best interests at heart.

➤ **Mutual respect**: You and your mentor must have total respect for each other and show professional courtesy toward each other. A critic is more inclined to offer advice through cynical witticisms, whether they consider you a peer, boss, or employee.

➤ **Able to communicate directly**: Your mentor must be able to clearly communicate their expectations and boundaries consistently, whether face-to-face or via e-mail. Critics often prefer to deliver their message to your friends and peers.

➤ **Similar ethics**: You and your mentor should adhere to the same ethical rules, as defined by your business and government communities. You will be uncomfortable with critics whose ethical positions are not clear or vary widely from yours.

➤ **Long-term relationship potential**: Mentors play important roles in the careers of most successful entrepreneurs. The relationships with good current mentors likely will continue and often grow into strong friendships. Most people cannot tolerate a long-term relationship with their critic.

However, try as you might to avoid them, we all have to deal with critics and the criticism they offer. Everyone reacts differently to criticism. Here are some tips on how to avoid any extreme reactions to criticism such as confrontations and angry debates:

➤ **Don't take it personally**: One reason people get angry at being criticized is that they take the criticism as a personal attack rather than a comment on performance. Alternatively, they think that the person criticizing them is trying to ridicule them. This is not always true.

➤ **Take suggestions from anyone**: Sometimes, people get angry when they are criticized by others who are younger or older, or not familiar with the subject. This is a bad move. Commit yourself to always looking only at the content and not who is offering it.

➤ **Don't reply immediately**: Don't push to reply to a criticism in progress. Allow the point to be made completely; then, think a moment before you start any response. First, find an agreement portion, ending with points you do not agree on.

➤ **Smile and don't get angry**: It always helps to smile when you are being criticized. This will help you create a non-confrontational debate and shows that you are confident in what you think.

Most critics I know think they are mentors, but I've never known a good mentor who is easily mistaken for a critic. If you listen to yourself, you can tell the difference. Are you asking forward-looking questions or making negative assessments about past events? It's hard to be a leader if you are always looking backward.

Also, be advised that your best friend is probably not a good mentor for you. Friends tell you what you want to hear. Mentors tell you what you need to hear. When the message is the same from both, you don't need the mentor anymore. In that sense, you should think of a mentor more like your advisor who has done all he can. You always need the friend.

I don't mean to imply that an entrepreneur needs a mentor more than a friend; it's just that friends are not normally positioned for double-duty as mentors. You need at least one of each and the ability to tell the difference.

How to assure a productive mentor-mentee experience

Every entrepreneur can learn from a mentor, no matter how confident or successful they have been to date. As I mentioned earlier, even one of the richest, Bill Gates (http://swiftcopywriting.com/?p=49), still values his friend Warren Buffett as his mentor. Yet, these relationships require special efforts on both sides to be productive and satisfying. Mentoring is not as simple as one person giving the other all the right answers.

Some of the best mentoring relationships don't involve monetary compensation, but none are free. The first cost is networking to find a mentor who is willing and able to give adequate focus to the relationship. In any case, it is a good form to offer compensation, such as a small monthly stipend, plus expenses, and perhaps a 1 percent ownership in your startup, to show your commitment.

From my experience, here are 10 basic principles for both the mentor and mentee to remember in getting the most out of any mentoring relationship:

> **Good mentoring requires building a relationship first**: A positive business or personal relationship between two people normally requires a high degree of shared values, common interests, and mutual respect. Remember that good relationships take some time to develop, so don't assume that your first discussion will seal the deal.

> **Agree on specific objectives and time frames**: Mentoring that consists of random discussions is not very satisfying for either side. I recommend one or more early discussions of mutual objectives, with a written summary of goals and expectations from the mentee to the mentor, with timeframes and milestones.

> **Make efficient use of time for both parties**: This means being respectful and diligent about scheduling and keeping appointments, and returning e-mails and phone calls. Don't attempt to multitask or allow constant interruptions during meetings. Book follow-up sessions with an agenda rather than fill time with random discussions.

> **Identify strengths and weaknesses early**: Both the mentor and mentee should put their cards on the table to avoid surprises later. Then, both should look for opportunities to leverage strengths and shore up weaknesses. This avoids wasted time and speculation, and provides the motivation to bring in other experts or mentors as required.

➤ **Mentor feedback must be thoughtful, specific, timely, and constructive**: An important aspect of a mentoring relationship is how the mentor provides feedback to the mentee. Formulate negative feedback in a constructive fashion. Using open-ended questions that start with *how* or *what* help the mentee to arrive at their own solution.

➤ **Mentees should avoid any defensive reaction to feedback**: The right response to most mentor feedback is a thoughtful question for clarification. Immediately responding with *reasons and rationale* to every feedback will be read as insincerity and will likely end the mentoring relationship quickly.

➤ **Practice two-way communication and candid feedback**: Mentoring is not a series of monologues and lectures from either side. However, candid feedback means not pulling punches when they are deserved. Both sides need to practice active listening and thoughtful questions. Constructive conflict is good.

➤ **Agree to deal with unforeseen challenges openly**: The most common challenges involve time and accessibility demands on either side, or the level of help expected. Both sides need to honor business boundaries and not stray into personal relationship issues. Agree up-front on how to end the relationship if other unforeseen circumstances arise.

➤ **Celebrate successes, and deal openly with failures.** This will help the learning process and build the mentee's confidence. With patience and time, the partners should develop a good rapport and become more comfortable with openly and freely conversing with each other.

➤ **Evaluate mentoring requirements on a regular basis**: The mentee, as the primary beneficiary, should be proactive in making sure that the review process occurs on a regular basis, perhaps quarterly. This allows for a frank discussion of unanticipated changes and the potential for discontinuing the process and declaring success.

The end of a mentoring relationship should be seen as an opportunity to review what did and didn't work and, more importantly, to reflect on the results so that every lesson that can be learned from the relationship is recognized.

Both the mentor and mentee should celebrate the successes, learn from failures, and conclude the relationship with positive feelings. To bring it full circle, mentees should now consider passing on their new knowledge and skills by entering a new mentoring relationship—as a mentor. This is the ultimate satisfaction.

Mentoring your team efficiently

On the other side of the coin, you as the technical entrepreneur and founder are expected to be a mentor to your team members. For many, this is a fun part of the job, especially as it relates to technical team members who might be following in your footsteps. Yet, as you start your business, time becomes an even more precious commodity, so you have to learn to do your own mentoring more efficiently. Rather than take an hour for every discussion, I recommend a process called 5-minute mentoring.

As an analogy, I've always wondered why every executive meeting has to be 1 hour in length, or longer. This is probably a tenth of your day spent on one issue. It better be a critical one, because you have a hundred others waiting. I believe you can be much more productive, as well as a more effective leader, if you approach most meetings as mentoring opportunities, and limit them to 5 minutes.

In a traditional meeting, another person presents you with multiple options, and you make the decision. With the 5-minute mentoring approach, the mentee asks for your support in their decision or asks for your insight on the considerations for them making a future decision. Which approach do you think is more fulfilling for them and best for your company in the long run?

The time limit has more to do with setting an expectation that the meeting is not to solve the problem, but coaching on the parameters and approach. If you are a problem solver by nature, this requires you to change your mindset from giving the *answer* to helping someone else understand the process, and come to an even better solution.

I have used this approach with high-tech roles such as software design as well as business development roles. It works, but in all cases, to be a successful mentor, there are some key things you have to do:

> **Be available always**: If you are *too busy* most of the time or locked behind closed doors, no mentoring relationship can work. It has to be evident to the mentee that this relationship is important to you, and you will make short periods of time available on a moment's notice as required. If you often make people wait, they will take extra time, which will make more people wait longer and later.

> **Adapt to each individual learning style**: Start by open listening. Some people learn best from anecdotal stories, and others need concrete pointers and step-by-step instructions. Respect each mentee's desire to grow and honor their individual style. Remember that 5-minute listening is not the same as 5-minute mentoring.

> **Respect discussion confidentiality**: Mentor discussions must remain confidential, so both parties can talk freely to each other without being quoted around the water cooler later. The mentee must not be afraid to show false starts or a naïve perspective.

> **Provide honest and constructive feedback**: Personal attacks and emotional comments are not appropriate, but people need real feedback to learn. Set the context by clarifying your goals and expectations on a regular basis. Critique the work and not the person.

> **Hold the mentee responsible and accountable**: Encourage the mentee to generate their own solutions and make it clear that they must accept full responsibility for their personal choices. Good people won't want it to work any other way. Most people learn best from making mistakes, so you have to let them fail sometimes.

I'm definitely not proposing the *old-fashioned* style of mentoring, where the goal was a one-way transfer of a broad range of knowledge or information. Here, the mentor was the authoritarian source, and directed all other aspects of the mentoring relationship. The mentee was a passive recipient and often had little say or control in the relationship.

Today's learner-centered mentoring is a dynamic and two-way relationship that involves critical reflection and full participation in short-period increments by both partners. The mentor assumes the role of a facilitator. The mentee becomes a proactive and equal partner, helping direct the relationship and set its goals.

The primary responsibility of a startup founder is to provide vision and leadership. Use 5-minute mentoring as one tool and stick to it with unwavering zeal. There's nothing worse than getting off course and entering areas that lead you away from the primary track. Your greatest contribution is maintaining focus and guiding the team. Give it a try. You'll get your time back and real respect.

Recognizing and hiring the smartest people for your startup team

The best way to reduce mentoring requirements on your team is to hire help, not just helpers. Helpers do what you say, while good help does what you need, without you saying anything. People who can help you the most are actually smarter than you, at least in their domain. Top entrepreneurs spend more time putting the right team in place to accomplish their objectives than spending time on any other components of their job.

A few entrepreneurs are so in love with themselves (narcissistic) that they insist on answering every question and making every decision. This is not only impossible, but also counterproductive. Effective entrepreneurs team with or employ people who can provide the answers directly, pertinent to their particular area of expertise.

True leaders also know how to move out of the way to let others do what they do best. If you're working too many hours and following up on every detail, you might want to look closer at your team to ensure that you've surrounded yourself with the right people.

In short, if you can find people with more passion, more knowledge, and more desire to succeed than you have, it will push you to be better and take the organization to new levels. Here are some key characteristics to look for:

> **Gets things done**: Smart people know what's required or can figure it out, and are confident enough to make decisions without you. Getting things done is crucial to running a business. Often, people with advanced degrees have academic smarts, but are not closers. You can't afford to make every decision or follow-up on every action item.

> **Recommend their own ideas**: How often do the people around you recommend sound ideas that you never knew were possibilities? If you're teaming with people who are smarter than you, you should be frequently surprised with their new ideas and solutions. You will be constantly learning from them.

➤ **Passionate and positive**: The smart people you want are as positive and passionate about your business as you are. They take ownership and responsibility for their actions. They convince you with their actions and questions that they understand the big picture. They speak confidently and deliberately rather than defensively.

➤ **More listening than talking**: Look for team members who are active listeners, where you can see yourself seeking them out for answers rather than always the other way around. It's great to team with inexperienced people who are growing so fast that you can envision working for them soon or having them take the helm of your business.

➤ **Avoid the narcissists**: Their energy, self-confidence, and charm make them look smart, but they resist accepting suggestions, thinking it will make them appear weak. They also don't believe that others have anything useful to tell them. Narcissists will take credit for all successes and always find someone to blame for their failures and shortcomings.

One of the most important jobs of every entrepreneur, and definitely one of the toughest, is to find and nurture people who are smarter in their roles than you. Resumes don't provide much of a picture in this regard. Supplement this with networking input, references, and your own personal interactions.

If you are looking for a potential business partner, count on building a relationship over several months before you really know the person. The business relationship at this level is just as important as a personal relationship before marrying (no overnight affairs). If you are hiring, make sure you have multiple interviews and input from multiple people on the team to balance your view.

In my view, one of the most important aspects of being a successful entrepreneur is surrounding yourself with people smarter than you. Don't let your ego get in the way. It's the best way for you to grow the business as well as yourself.

Another thing to look for in every hire is their ability to get things done. People who consistently get things done are called *go-to people*. As an entrepreneur, you need these people, and you need to be one if you expect your startup to be successful. This might be easier said than done, as resumes do not tell the story, and without real nurturing, the best people won't stay around long.

To highlight how rare this breed is, Jeffrey Gandz (`http://wwwold.iveybusinessjournal.com/article.asp?intArticle_ID=675`) of the Richard Ivey School of Business relates a quote from a new CEO in a large company, "*I have more than 1000 people in my head office organization, 900 can tell me something's gone wrong, 90 can tell me what's gone wrong, 9 can tell me why it went wrong, and one can actually fix it!*"

Finding and nurturing that one is the challenge for every company and every startup. I like his summary of how go-to people are different from other people, not necessarily because they have unique skills, but because of the ways these skills are configured and integrated with other leadership characteristics:

> ➤ **Know how business works and how to work your business**: They have what we might call *street smarts* as well as real intelligence. They have a special ability to help people get results, clear away road blocks, and resolve impasses that are frustrating people. Then, they use these skills to build support for required actions.

> ➤ **Politically astute without being politicians**: Unlike many political operatives, these people are seen as dedicated to the goals of the business rather than feathering their own nests. This leaves them with the reputation for being politically astute rather than being labeled with the stigma of being a politician.

> ➤ **Know how to use power when it's needed but seldom use it**: They recognize that people are persuaded by those that these people, in turn, can persuade. So, they open themselves up to recommendations from those they are trying to persuade. They recognize that people want recognition, so they reward people who get-with-the-program with attention for doing so.

> ➤ **Consummate negotiators, but getting it done is non-negotiable**: They are adept at seeing situations from others' perspectives, separating people from principles, building bridges between positions, and bringing people to their senses. However, they are laser-like in their focus on project completion, and never sacrifice deadlines for compliance.

> ➤ **Networks of reciprocation rather than deals**: However, these exchanges of favors and reciprocity are not conditional negotiation elements, but usually based on having done someone a favor without requiring anything in return. The favor is often motivated not by future consideration but by a genuine desire to help someone else.

> ➤ **Think out of the box while acting inside the box.** Go-to people are creative people who are constantly looking for better ways to get things done. Barriers are challenges, obstacles are opportunities for innovation, and the words *can't do* register as *how can we do*. They use the culture to change the culture and use channels effectively.

> ➤ **Analytical and intuitive, aggressive and patient, confident and humble, deliberate and decisive.** These sometimes paradoxical characteristics of highly effective leaders are present in abundance in go-tos. They escalate what needs to be handled at a higher level and don't feel that they have to resolve everything themselves.

While many resumes portray people as leaders, resumes are heavily weighted toward *initiators* (those who start things and develop new ways of doing things). Few talk about completions—driving things that they have initiated through to conclusion. You need both, and don't confuse the two.

If you are not that natural leader, remember that becoming the go-to person, even as the CEO, in your organization is very powerful in raising positive perceptions of your value. It's all about who you know, what you know, what you do, and how you can help. Best of all, it's fun to get things done.

How to turn your team members into an innovative startup team

Entrepreneurs are usually highly creative and innovative, but many innovative people are not entrepreneurs. As it takes a team of people to build a great company, the challenge is to find that small percentage of innovative people and then nurture the tendency rather than stifle it.

A while back, I read a book titled **The Rudolph Factor** (http://www.amazon.com/ The-Rudolph-Factor-Innovation-ebook/dp/B002D9ZL0K), by Cyndi Laurin and Craig Morningstar, which is all about finding the bright lights that can drive innovation in your business. The story most specifically targets big companies, such as Boeing, but the concepts are just as applicable to a startup with one or more employees.

The core message is that real innovation and competitive advantage are more people-based than product- or process-based. Every good entrepreneur needs a people-centric focus to ferret out creativity and innovation in his/her team and to build a sustainable competitive advantage.

I have observed that people who behave as mentors tend to have an uncanny ability to recognize and nurture people who have innate capabilities along these lines. Here are six of the characteristics they and you should look for:

> **Thinkers and problem solvers**: Innovators are naturally creative and love new challenges. Some might appear a bit eccentric to the people around them. They generally promote unconventional ways to solve problems and have an easier time than most at identifying the root cause of a problem.

> **Passionate and inquisitive**: These team members are passionate about their work and light up when talking about their role or a particular project they are working on. They often ask *Why?* even when it is not the most popular question to be asked.

> **Challenge the status quo**: They believe that questioning is of value and benefit to the organization. This is also how they discover what they need in order to solve a problem, so they aren't rocking the boat just for the sake of rocking the boat.

> **Connect the dots**: Innovators have the ability to quickly synthesize many variables to solve problems or make improvements. To others, it might appear as if their ideas come out of the blue or that there is no rhyme or reason behind their thinking.

> ➤ **See the big picture**: They tend to be natural systems thinkers and see the whole forest rather than a single tree—or just the bark on the tree. They might express frustration if people around them are having conversations about the bark rather than the forest.

> ➤ **Collaborative and action oriented**: They are not loners, and have the ability and confidence to turn their ideas into action. They act on their ideas, sometimes without knowing how they will accomplish them. The *how* is always revealed in time.

Your challenge is to go forth with this new awareness and thinking, and to find and mentor those bright lights that will drive innovation and competitive advantage. The next step after finding innovators is to integrate them into your team. A key aspect is establishing a team-based culture that is a safe environment to share and execute ideas.

In fact, this safe and nurturing environment has to extend beyond a single team to the highest levels of the organization. It should embody a style of leadership that is essentially a commitment to the success of the people around you and that opens the door for anyone in the organization to lead from where they are rather than waiting for the management to *do something*.

Innovation is at the very heart of every successful startup. Everyone wins when you look at things very differently and wonder *why*, not *why not*. What better way to extend this power than to surround yourself with more highly creative people? Then, you can make your technical startup a place of possibilities as well as probabilities.

Keys to motivation that every technical entrepreneur should know

One of the keys to maximizing the productivity of your team as well as yourself is motivation. It has been estimated that the average team member at any given time works at less than 50 percent of his/her capacity. Thus, mastering the art of employee motivation could double your chances of success over the average competitor.

While there are many books written on this subject, most entrepreneurs I know simply assume that their own vision, motivation, and drive will be adopted and maintained by partners and employees, based on a 1-hour inspirational talk by the founder or business leader, and supplemented by a reasonable salary and a dose of fear for good measure.

Unfortunately, it's not that easy. Motivation has to be a constant priority and tone, focused more on the positive emotional and internal needs of a person rather than on their opportunity to simply make more money. My review of the research indicates that many experts have settled on the four Rs for motivation (http://www.maccoby.com/Articles/4Rs_Of_Motivation.shtml), but I have found ten, and you can probably add a couple more:

- ➤ **Respect**: Every professional expects to be treated with respect. We all watch our leaders' body language, facial expressions, as well as their words, for indications of respect and disrespect. Show by your words and actions that you value their role.

- ➤ **Resources**: A team that doesn't have the resources to do their job will lose their motivation rapidly. In a startup, key resources include funding, facilities and tools, and the time to get the job done. The most important resource might be your help and support.

- ➤ **Relationships**: Positive social interactions with fellow team members lead to improved job satisfaction and motivation. Inversely, people who are negative and bring negative interpersonal attitudes to the workplace will destroy the motivation of others.

- ➤ **Responsibility**: New responsibilities, when done with respect and moderation, prevent stagnation and challenge people to perform at even higher levels. Most people will rise to the occasion, see their progress, and become even more motivated.

- ➤ **Recognition**: When you recognize and celebrate individual achievements, large and small, in front of peers, people feel wonderful about themselves. They feel more competent and eager to repeat the success or take on additional responsibility.

- ➤ **Rewards**: People need rewards to maintain their motivation, or they will start to feel that the recognition is all *show*, with no substance behind it. Cash incentives are a good start, but even intangible rewards, such as lunch with the boss, can be powerful motivators (http://www.amazon.com/Drive-Surprising-Truth-About-Motivates/dp/1594484805).

- ➤ **Reserves**: In the military, an important mission is always backed up by reserve forces. Having backup gives a team confidence, motivation, and a sense of value. In startups, when people are clearly willing to back up each other, everyone's motivation increases.

- ➤ **Reasons**: A good cause can be the most powerful motivator of all. Workers doing assembly-line tasks during World War II were highly motivated because they were helping win the war. Make sure that your team really believes their work has impact.

- ➤ **Reinforcement**: When a team member shows increased skills or results, following prior rewards, reinforcing that progress will result in a motivational multiplier. Reinforcement on a regular basis is recognition and rewards on steroids.

- ➤ **Recruiting**: People are more motivated when they see *new blood* joining the team. This gives everyone a sense of renewal, additional support, and a fresh perspective. Recruiting is the inverse of layoffs, which reduces motivation in everyone.

In reality, people motivate themselves, and all these dimensions are simply ways to accelerate personal motivation. The key to increasing anyone's intrinsic motivation is to align the support with things they value. Therefore, the first step is to get to know your people, talk to them, and ask them what they are passionate about. Don't try to guess the answers.

Doesn't it make sense to use these motivational elements to get that other 50 percent from your startup team? In addition, these elements will make your business a more enjoyable and exciting place for everyone, consistent with your own vision of being a technical entrepreneur.

Recognizing people who drain energy from your company

Every organization, no matter how small, has one or more people who are quite simply obnoxious, and they drain energy from everyone and can strangle your company. Sometimes, they are also intellectually brilliant, or closely related to the boss, so there is no easy way out.

In fact, they might even be the boss. So, if you find this article taped to your desk, it might be time to look in the mirror. At any rate, if you are stuck working in an office, at least you deserve some clues on how to recognize the different types and know it's time to run:

> ➤ **I knew that was going to happen**: This know-it-all has an answer for everything, and is proud to let you know, always after the fact, that they actually predicted ahead of time every calamity that has befallen the world and the office.

> ➤ **You wouldn't believe my latest conquest**: For the loudmouth, the word 'discreet' isn't part of his dictionary at all. His conversations at the water cooler or on the phone always seem to be audible across the whole office.

> ➤ **I'm so angry I could scream**: In my view, people with short fuses and anger issues ought to be banned from the workplace. People are always "walking on eggshells" to avoid creating another outburst, and office tension stays at an unhealthy high level.

> ➤ **Have you heard the one about…**: Every office has the joker, and he particularly likes to shock people with crude or off-color stories. He doesn't seem to take anything or anyone seriously, and especially loves his pranks on shy people who blush easily.

> ➤ **I'm so busy, I don't have time…**: The whiner will always be complaining about how busy they are and how many hours they put in, but you can never quite see anything they have accomplished. However, they always seem to find time to talk loudly on the phone or discuss the latest gossip.

> ➤ **I have no life**: Woe is me, and I'll be happy to tell you the gory details of all my lost loves, my amazing string of illnesses, and the strife in my family. These people will definitely suck the energy out of everyone.

➤ **I'm so worried about the project**: Always in a state of panic, these people bring stress to the whole office just by their hand-wringing, hovering over people's desks and nagging everyone to double-check for the dire consequences of possible mistakes.

➤ **I need a moment of your time:** We all love to help people, but when the request happens 10 times every day and for the same trivial issue, your blood pressure is bound to go up. It's not efficient to have two people doing every job.

➤ **I'm surrounded by idiots**: This person has an ego the size of a mountain and won't listen to anyone long enough to assess whether they are a genius or an idiot. In the long run, their statement will be true, because all rational people will have run away.

➤ **This world isn't fair**: This type is often associated with Gen-Y, but some people seem permanently afflicted as they get passed over for promotions. As Bill Gates said a while back to a high school graduation crowd "*Life is not fair – get used to it.*"

I'm sure I missed a few obnoxious types here, so help me out with additions and tell me how many of these you have in your office. I wish I could give you specific solutions and antidotes, but that's a bit tougher, and maybe the subject for another chapter or even a whole book. In general, survival requires large doses of tolerance, patience, and the ability to turn your ears off.

If it's your startup, you can't just ignore it. If you recognize several of these types on your team, you need to do something now, before they have sucked the life and energy out of your dream. Tolerance for you is not an option. People will follow your leadership, or lack of it.

Summary

The goal of this chapter has been to outline the major leadership challenges facing a technical entrepreneur in building a business, and how to prepare for them, as well as how to get the best help from mentoring and hiring smart people onto the team.

Now that you have the team that you need and the leadership required to drive it, it's time to look at some of the non-technical arenas that are key to driving your success in today's business environment. One of the most important of these is the advent of social media. In the next chapter, we will be taking a hard look at the do's and don'ts for social media. Let's go!

Do You Understand How Social Media is Changing the Business Landscape?

Everyone is talking about how social media can help you jumpstart your business at no cost, and experts are springing up on all sides to help you do this at a high cost. Yet a good percentage of small businesses still don't use social media at all. So who do you believe about how social media has changed the landscape, and what are the keys to success for any startup?

The reality is that most technical startups, and many other businesses, who claim to use social media, still don't have a clue of how to use it productively for their business. They randomly churn for hours a day on a couple of their favorite social media platforms, with little thought given to goals, objectives, or metrics, and ultimately give up and fall back to traditional communication and marketing approaches.

There are many "experts" out there telling you how to do it right, and offering their services for a fee. But very few are talking about how to measure your results, and the right metrics for optimizing your marketing environment. Using social media without measuring the results is not productive and not recommended.

This chapter will help you as a technical entrepreneur understand where and how to start using social media, as well as how to measure the impact, and make the required tradeoffs between cost and value.

Making the right use of social media

If your technical startup can't be bothered with social media, or has no plan to take advantage of it, then you are definitely at risk these days. But simply jumping in is not enough. Before you start spending money and time as a user, you need to understand how it can help you and your business. Using it randomly or incorrectly is a waste of your precious time.

Sherrie Madia and Paul Borgese have addressed the positives of this challenge in their book, *The Social Media Survival Guide* (http://www.amazon.com/Social-Media-Survival-Guide-Exponentially/dp/0982618514), which covers everything you need to know to grow your business exponentially with social media. They also identify clearly the five key social media mistakes that I often see, along the following lines:

> ➤ **Diving in without a strategic plan**: Don't start podcasting, blogging, tweeting, *friending* on Facebook, and posting YouTube videos until you know what your messages are, who will manage them, who your audience is, and how they and you are going to benefit from the content and relationship.

> ➤ **Not having a social media policy**: Your social media policy needs to outline how team members behave in the online universe during and outside of work. It should include education on style preferences and confidentiality. All messaging coming from employees should be aligned with your company's values and brand.

> ➤ **Failing to tailor the plan to your target audience**: Hone in on sites, tools, and applications your target audience is using. Is your audience out walking in the park without technology or are they technology lovers who never part with their BlackBerry or iPhone? Research your target market to find out who they are and how to reach them.

> ➤ **Producing weak, unfocused, or unhelpful content**: The same messaging rules that apply to classic public relations and branding apply to social media. Create strong, smart, well-thought-out content. Don't waste their time with self-serving promotion. Give them something they can use—tips, incentives, new ideas, fun, and inspiration.

> ➤ **Allowing your social media efforts to stagnate**: Gone are the days when companies could put up a website that sat on the screen like an electronic business card. Social media is about maintaining a dynamic conversation between you and your customers. Done right, it's not a one-off campaign by a handful of staff; it's a long-term commitment.

To avoid these mistakes and create compelling and relevant content, you need to focus your startup on the following initiatives:

> ➤ Develop a social media plan that targets your audience and business objectives

> ➤ Combine social media seamlessly within your traditional marketing plan

> ➤ Use social media to engage customers in new ways and sharpen your brand

> ➤ Find the right people to staff your campaign and curate its content and evolution

> ➤ Manage your reputation online and avoid the common mistakes of social media novices

> ➤ Measure the effectiveness of your efforts and expenditures—as well as competitors

> ➤ Turn your social media efforts into profit, rather than just another expense

According to the *Small Business Marketing Forecast 2012* (http://www.ad-ology.com/ smallbizrpt.cfm) from Ad-ology, social media for small business marketing has reached its tipping point. Just 10 percent said they would not use social media in 2012, down from 24 percent for 2011 and 39 percent for 2010. Lead generation continues to be the biggest benefit of social networking for U.S. small businesses. Other popular benefits were keeping up with the industry, monitoring online conversations, and finding vendors/suppliers.

Many companies believe that getting involved in social media is easy. They mistakenly assume that anyone who uses Facebook, YouTube, and Twitter for personal networking can do it for business. But personal versus business use requires two dramatically different skill sets. I recommend that you test the waters before you jump, but remaining on the sidelines won't get you there. Use the many resources available, like the Internet and this book, but now is the time for every technical entrepreneur to start.

How to begin using social media in your technical business

When my friend's small business was struggling a while back, I suggested he add some social media initiatives, and his answer was that he was *too busy*. His business has since closed, but his mindset is still out there. According to a study (http://www.ad-ology. com/smallbizrpt.cfm) of 1700 CEOs a couple of years ago, only 60 percent of companies today use social media for marketing, and only 12 percent of those feel that they are using it effectively.

What's the problem? It seems to me that there is abundant proof in the marketplace of the financial returns to both large and small businesses, the low cost of entry, and the ubiquity of social networks. Dell (http://readwrite.com/2009/06/12/social_ media_roi_dells_3m_on_twitter_and_four_bett) announced years ago that it had earned $3 million in revenue and a high ROI from using Twitter, and other businesses report daily on increases in web traffic up to 800 percent.

I suspect that a good part of the problem is that technical startups and small business owners still don't know where or how to begin. They don't know if they should move to social networks for lead generation, branding, customer loyalty, or for direct marketing and e-commerce. My advice is to pick one, start slow, and spread out as you learn. Here are some specifics:

> ➤ **Create a business profile on Twitter, LinkedIn, and Facebook**: A business profile starts with a business account using your company logo as your picture (avatar), rather than your photo or a picture of your cat. If you are in consulting, you are the business, so use a professional headshot. Don't mix your personal and business profiles or messages.

➤ **Focus first on creating content for visibility and credibility**: New relevant content weekly will dramatically increase your search engine ranking, and define you as a thought leader in your domain, and make your account interesting and attractive. Interacting with followers has value in the sense of listening to customers, but random and purely social interactions are a waste of time.

➤ **Develop a marketing strategy specific to this media**: Don't use the same message on Twitter that you developed for e-mail blasts and postcard blitzes. Social media demands two-way communication, rather than outbound only. Read everything you can about viral marketing. It's not free, since it requires unique marketing programs and events to talk about, so budget appropriately, but not excessively.

➤ **Start social networking with peers**: Pick a base, such as LinkedIn or Facebook, to be your community, and work the territory, much like you may have learned to work a room of peers at a tradeshow or convention, or local business organization. Find out what other people are doing, and what works for them. People love to share what they know.

➤ **Experiment with social media tools**: The basic tools are the platforms like Twitter and Facebook. But don't stop there. There is TweetDeck to help you use Twitter, and YouTube for video sharing. A most valuable tool is WordPress or TypePad for blogging. You need these to add the human element to your business or service.

➤ **Proactively learn from the experts**: Maybe it's time to sign up for a few free Webinars, or even invest in an expert consultant in this area. Successful people don't wait for their kids to teach them about new technologies, or wait to be the last one on the block to try new things. It's all available for free on the Internet, but your time is a valuable resource.

➤ **Define relevant metrics and measure**: That means first take some baseline measurements of, for example, lead arrival rate today, and costs associated with your current media marketing. If you don't have this baseline, you will never know if you are making progress. Then continue to measure and learn what works, at what cost.

If used correctly, I guarantee you that social media initiatives can improve your business with new leads by bringing traffic to your website, creating a buzz around your product or brand, creating inbound links to increase your search engine ranking, and improving loyalty and trust with your customers. How could you be too busy to work on these things?

Of course, if you found this book for technical entrepreneurs through your own initiative, I have to give you credit for being ahead of the pack. So loan it to a friend who is not so proactive. My challenge to you, then, is to kick it up a notch!

Even for those that are not too busy, an all-too-common question I get is "*Which is the right social media platform for my business?*" Is it Facebook, Twitter, LinkedIn, or one of the other 200 active platforms (http://en.wikipedia.org/wiki/List_of_social_networking_websites) vying for attention these days? The right answer is that not all of these are worth your attention, but it's probably more than one.

The *Tyranny of the OR* is a concept from the business best-seller *Built to Last* (http://www.amazon.com/Built-Last-Successful-Visionary-Companies/dp/0060566108/ref=tmm_hrd_swatch_0?_encoding=UTF8&sr=&qid=), by James C. Collins (Stanford Business School). Too many executives believe that things must be either A or B, and can't be both. The reality is that most businesses need to embrace the *Genius of the AND*, meaning they should use and monitor more than one of the available platforms, based on objectives.

If you are in the realm (http://www.hiscoxusa.com/small-business-insurance/newsroom/press/2011/hiscox-examines-social-media-usage-by-small-businesses/) of the 47 percent of small businesses who still ignore social media, you need to read the book by Dave Carroll, *United Breaks Guitars* (http://www.amazon.com/United-Breaks-Guitars-Power-Social/dp/1401937934). It highlights the story of how United Airlines in 2008 paid no attention to social media as Dave's story of his crushed guitar and poor customer service went viral around the world. United Airlines is still recovering from that debacle.

Thus your objectives for social media should at least include monitoring your online reputation on the three top platforms, and hopefully taking the minimum actions to turn any negatives into positives for the rest of us. Of course, the right approach is to be proactive along all the following fronts:

➤ **Reputation management**: You can't ignore the fact that Facebook alone now has over one billion users who may be talking about you, and there are fifteen other platforms per Wikipedia (http://en.wikipedia.org/wiki/List_of_virtual_communities_with_more_than_100_million_users) that have over 100 million users. You need to protect and grow your brand, so the first step is to know what's going on, and the best defense is a good offense.

➤ **Build your brand and expert visibility**: Engaging in social media and blogging on a regular basis is a low-cost way to achieve visibility, and become the go-to person for that topic and the voice that people trust in your industry. That's how you brand yourself as an expert in your niche and make your company the one that others seek out and turn to. Customers today trust those they know and those they see others trusting.

➤ **Increase customer leads and conversion**: With over 98 percent of the population (http://www.foliomag.com/2011/report-98-percent-u-s-online-population-uses-social-networks) now using social media, at least 30 percent look at business profiles on Facebook, Twitter, and LinkedIn before buying any product or service. Of those, approximately 70 percent said they wouldn't deal with a new company if it didn't have a social media presence. You need to be there.

➤ **Maximize customer retention**: It's a well-known axiom of business that efforts to retain existing customers have tremendous payback, compared to the costs of attracting new customers. Courting them with ongoing updates and special offers through their social networks is a natural way to keep their loyalty.

➤ **Proactive customer service**: Without social media, companies must rely on incoming calls and letters to address customer problems and concerns with products and services. Why not ask them for feedback before there is a problem, and watch what they are telling their friends, both good and bad?

➤ **Keep up with the competition**: Last year, Facebook's revenue from advertising was over $5 billion, which was a 40 percent year-over-year increase for the last quarter. Almost 40 percent of small businesses that sell on Facebook say it is their sole sales channel. Ignoring what your competition does is sure to limit your business longevity.

So what are the best social media platforms for small business, according to these industry leaders? It never hurts to look at where the big boys are. According to data from Inc. 500 companies (`http://www.openforum.com/articles/the-best-social-media-platforms-for-your-business`), the top three are Facebook (74 percent), LinkedIn (73 percent), and Twitter (64 percent). I recommend that these be the point of entry for every business.

Within these three, you should prioritize your focus based on the demographics that are important to your business. For example, if your customers are primarily young people, more will likely be found on Facebook. Professionals and B2B action favors LinkedIn. Twitter seems to be a mix of all demographics and business as well as consumer interests.

For the new platforms and all the rest, that's where tracking and testing comes in. Set some objectives, pick a likely platform, set some measurements, and do a 30-day trial. If you don't get results, it might be a mismatch for your target market. If you see progress, double down and add even more content or focus to continue the positive momentum.

So there is no one magic social media platform for any business, just like there has never been just one marketing channel for any business. The best marketing programs today for small businesses are the *genius of the AND*, including traditional print and video advertising, complemented by proactive efforts in a selection of the new social media domains. Don't put all your marketing eggs in one basket.

Differences between traditional and social media marketing

Even in the context of marketing, what every technical entrepreneur needs to realize is that the process and framework for making social media work is different from traditional marketing, and trial and error certainly doesn't work. Ric Dragon, an expert in online marketing, in *Social Marketology* (`http://www.amazon.com/Social-Marketology-Improve-Processes-Customers/dp/0071790497`), summarized the best set of steps I have seen so far for the new world:

1. **Focus on desired outcomes first**: Valid social media objectives for a business should include one or more of the following: increased brand awareness, lead generation, service and support, or reputation management. Obviously, the platforms and how you use social media would be different for lead generation versus service and support.

2. **Incorporate brand personality and voice**: Popular culture these days expects a more humanized brand voice, and constituents are listening carefully to the tone, vision, and expertise of that voice. Think about how you can project the voice you want, and make sure it is consistently used by all team members across all platforms used.

3. **Identify the smallest segments possible of your constituents**: Due to the information overload felt by consumers today, marketing at the generic segment level no longer works. Social media is the only one which allows you to be hyper-granular and drill down to micro-segments, to dramatically improve engagement levels and conversion ratios.

4. **Identify the communities for these micro-segments**: Traditionally, community implied a physical grouping, but today a community is characterized by what they value, more than proximity. More important than finding a community is creating one, with your blog and other social media engagement. The best communities then become your advocate.

5. **Identify the influencers of these communities**: Social media brings all the aspects of important influencers these days, including peer pressure, authority, credibility, and in some cases, celebrities. Because feedback from social media operates in real time, you don't have to wait months for results. You spend the months influencing the influencers.

6. **Create an action plan with metrics**: Good action plans include a listening plan, channel plan, SEO plan, and a content creation plan, with activities and metrics. Social media activities span the gamut from curation to gifting, building relationships and groups, blogging, service actions, to lead conversion. Pick the ones that fit your desired outcome.

7. **Iteratively execute and measure results**: Measuring is all about return-on-investment (ROI). This can be customer acquisition cost, revenue growth, profit, or whatever other parameters are key to your success. Iterate and expect to pivot, based on results, because you can't get it all right the first time. This is not trial and error.

In fact, marketing in the social media is fundamentally different from conventional marketing. The depth in which connections can be made with the audience or customers is far greater than it possibly can be with any other medium. The very nature of influence at this level means that the values and vision must be in tune.

Of course, with social media marketing, trial and error is not the only way to fail. You can fail by not being there at all (like the *United Breaks Guitars* story mentioned earlier), or making the big mistake (see *Red Cross Rogue Tweet* (http://www.huffingtonpost.com/2011/02/16/red-cross-rogue-tweet_n_824114.html)).

More positively, social media also offers many more ways to succeed. See the classic story of *Dell Makes $3M from Twitter* (customer retention), Australia's *Tourism via Facebook* (http://en.wikipedia.org/wiki/The_Best_Job_In_The_World) (large rewards), and Blendtec YouTube *Will it Blend* (http://www.grandsocialcentral. com/hustler-marketers/brand-managers/blendtec/will-it-blend-that- is-the-question) (brand building). It's time for you to learn the best practices of using social media in your company, and putting them to work before your competition puts you out of work.

The big three social networks for business

With the advent of social networking sites like LinkedIn, Twitter, and Facebook, Internet usage totally morphed from a serious business medium to a social and fun medium that still means business. Regular people now build technical business applications with *mashup* (http://en.wikipedia.org/wiki/Mashup_(web_application_ hybrid)) technology, rather than hiring programmers.

I've been a technology follower from the early days of the Internet, so a few years ago I decided to dive into this new world and check it out (who even heard of blogging or mashups ten years ago). I realized quickly that this new world isn't just for the social life of Gen-Y—it is a sea change for everyone in business, especially startups.

After any earthquake event, the first thing I recommend for anyone to do is to step back, get the lay of the land, and derive some guidelines for getting around efficiently, while avoiding personal injury. Here is a good characterization of the current big three in social networking for business:

> ➤ **Facebook is biggest, moving from social to business**: Currently, the biggest site in numbers is Facebook with over one billion active users. 50 percent of active users log on to Facebook in any given day. Their primary visitors in the past have been Gen-Y socializers, but the fastest growing segment now is business people, and discussion groups for business, like *Facebook for Business* with 56,250 members.

> ➤ **LinkedIn caters to senior business professionals**: The largest site traditionally targeted at business people is LinkedIn, with current numbers exceeding 259 million members. This one is a *must* for every serious business professional and executive out there today. You can join groups with your specific interests, participate in discussions or not, and highlight your business.

> ➤ **Twitter for business and networking is hot**: This site is for text-messaging on the Internet, with about 230 million unique visitors per month, and was first popular for social updates and gossip. Now it's the source of business leads and networking for thousands of people, and the source of the breaking world news for everyone. You need to be there.

Obviously, there are many others that you should evaluate based on your geographic location, type of business, and personal interests. Here is my perspective on a few of them:

> **MySpace is for artists, forget it**: The third biggest site (passed a while back by Twitter) is MySpace, with about 36 million users. They have groups for business and entrepreneurs, but the culture is primarily music and the arts. You will find business advertising there, but minimal business networking.

> **It's not all about numbers**: There are many more social networks that have good traction and a more specialized focus in the business networking world. Examples include Ryze, Plaxo, Orkut, RedWire, and Ecademy. In general, their membership is focused by geography, industry, or culture, so the value can be excellent.

> **Business networking today starts with social networks**: Social networking sites are more effective and efficient than attending all those boring business cocktail mixers and conventions. I'll even be so bold as to say that if you aren't on any of these sites, you are way behind the curve in business networking today.

> **Protocols for each site are different**: There is a hierarchy and a culture to social networking sites on the Internet, just like there always has been with professional business organizations and clubs. There are so many sites, so you need to choose wisely, and learn the rules for each. Most are free, so you can do serious business networking around the world without signing up for any of the fee services.

Maybe because the cost of entry is low, I see a swarm of startups today busy with add-ons, and building new offerings. It's a brave new world, for me an exciting challenge and fun to explore. But like every good explorer, I'm asking everyone I meet what's around the next corner. Are you there today, and what do you predict for tomorrow?

Steps to social media success for technical entrepreneurs

For guidance on this one, I'll put my money on one of the originals in the social media game, my friend Lon Safko, who has already published his third edition of the bestselling book, *The Social Media Bible* (http://www.amazon.com/Social-Media-Bible-Strategies-Business/dp/0470623977). In the book, and in his popular lecture series, he says you can do it yourself, and outlines five steps to success, which I have adapted a bit for startups as follows:

1. **Analyze existing media, social media, and your demographics**: Before you start, analyze existing media, demographics, and new social media alternatives for a fit to your rollout campaign requirements. Factor in the fundamental shift to *pull* marketing taking place across the world in media and advertising. See more detail on pull marketing later in this section.

2. **Understand the basic tools – the social media trinity**: Blogging (WordPress), micro-blogging (Twitter), and social networks are the trinity. Key social networks are Facebook and LinkedIn. Get to know the five W's of these and others—who, what, where, when, and why. Pick your fit.

3. **Integrate your strategy into the trinity**: Social media does not stand alone; it must be integrated into a balanced marketing strategy. Content is still king, so do the proper homework on what you blog, and the quality of the messages you deliver via social media. Put your social network links on your stationery, business cards, and e-mail.

4. **Assess and commit the resources required**: At this point you need executive buy-in, so decide what you do personally, assess your staffing and out-sourcing requirements, and commit the budget. This is the time to get creative, run pilot projects to look at ROI, and educate the whole team on objectives and activities.

5. **Implement metrics and analytics**: You can't manage what you don't measure. Determine the proper measurement tools and set up the measurement process. Only then can you determine your ROI. Manage your expectations, and analyze every marketing channel. *Lather, rinse, repeat* (http://www.amazon.com/Lean-Analytics-Better-Startup-Faster/dp/1449335675).

The best attribute of social media tools is that most of them are free. The down side is that many of them are limited, or have poor quality, and they come and go each day. You need to allocate a few minutes a day, or every week, to researching via blogs and websites like *Tech News World* (http://www.technewsworld.com/) the latest recommendations and reviews. This is not something you can learn once and forget about.

With social media, a key element of success is to focus on the message. Never *sell* or push out your message like conventional advertising. The trick is to listen first, add something of value to the conversation, and pull the customers to you because they trust you and want more. According to Lon, the keywords to remember are to be *sincere, authentic, and transparent.*

Now is the time to capitalize on this fundamental shift in power to the customer, who now has real control over your brand message. Companies now have to communicate, rather than just pontificate. Customers see what their peers are saying about you in blogs and product reviews, and how you respond to these, and this impacts their decision more than any advertisement.

But above all, don't forget to observe your competition and their social media activity. Luckily, you can see and measure online most of the things they can, and see which things work, and which ones don't.

Finally, remember that it takes time to establish and optimize your presence on social media sites. Use the five steps listed here to leverage your time effectively, stay one step ahead of your competitors, and enjoy the success that social media can bring your technical startup.

Some old and broken social media marketing uses

Isn't it frustrating to think you understand something new in business, like marketing with social media, only to realize that the landscape changed while you were looking at other priorities? For example, it used to be that marketing via social media meant buying banner ads on Facebook, or buying a position on search engine results, or sponsoring some blog entries, but these don't work anymore.

I just finished a book by Jim Tobin, *Earn It. Don't Buy It* (http://www.amazon.com/ Earn-It-Dont-Buy-Marketing/dp/1625351186/ref=tmm_pap_title_0), which asserts that *earned* social engagement drives far better business results than paid social exposure. Jim should know, since he is the president of *Ignite Social Media* (http://www. ignitesocialmedia.com/), of one of the best known social media marketing agencies. If you want to get current, here are a few of his bits of wisdom along these lines:

> **Nobody clicks on Facebook ads anymore**: Banner ads routinely average a 0.1 percent click through rate and Facebook manages to be about half as good as that. That's 99.96 percent of people not clicking on those ads. When the glass is only .04 percent full, you should start looking for a new container.

> **Where are the young social media users going**: They are going to Instagram, Tumblr, Snapchat, Kik, and other applications. Twitter was the fastest growing social network of 2012, with teens fueling the growth from 12 percent to 26 percent. In 2013, the visual web took over through Pinterest and Tumblr, with growth rates of 88 percent and 74 percent respectively.

> **You need influencers more than advocates**: Brands need influencers working on their behalf because they provide the third-party credibility and social proof that validates their products. 92 percent of people trust *recommendations from people I know* and 70 percent trust *consumer opinions posted online*.

> **Where did your friends go?**: SocialBakers (http://www.socialbakers.com/), a site that tracks data, reported in December 2012 that 1.4 million active users in the United States disappeared that month. Out of 160 million active Facebook users in the U.S. alone, it's a small percentage, but it is an early warning sign.

> **Maybe they just don't care**: *Pew Internet & American Life Project* (http://www. pewinternet.org/Reports/2013/Teens-Social-Media-And-Privacy/ Summary-of-Findings.aspx) reported in May 2013 that their focus groups found waning enthusiasm for Facebook among teens, that Facebook has become a social burden for them, and that users of sites other than Facebook express greater enthusiasm for their choice. LinkedIn has never been a focus for teens, while Snapchat interest continues to grow with teens.

> **New can turn old very quickly**: Friendster was a fad, Second Life was a fad, MySpace was a fad, and Facebook suddenly seems old school. Don't connect the latest platform, which may be transient, with the larger phenomenon of digitally enabled social conversations. If you can figure out why people care about your product, you'll have success regardless of the platform du jour.

Earning social media clout for your business, rather than buying it, seems to be all about engagement. Engagement occurs when customers and stakeholders become participants by sharing ideas with you, or talking to their friends about you, rather than merely viewing what you publish. Each participant becomes part of your marketing department, as other customers read their output, and become part of the conversation. It's the principle underlying viral marketing.

So how do you facilitate engagement and conversation with your solution? According to an explanation I first saw on Social Fresh (http://socialfresh.com/community-engagement/), it's really a cycle consisting of three key phases:

> **User to product (engaged user base)**: This part isn't new. In order to build any following, you need a solution that solves a real problem, not just technology that wows you, or great functionality with a painful learning curve. How engaged people are will depend on how much value they see, and how much they enjoy using the product.

> **User to brand (engaged audience)**: Once someone is engaged with your product, you'll want to get them engaged with your brand. This happens today when you talk to people through social media and responsive customer service. Get in the habit of having genuine conversations with your engaged users to create an engaged audience.

> **User to user (engaged community)**: Now you have an engaged audience of people who feel an emotional connection with your brand and product. Time to start connecting them with each other. You can do so using conversation platforms like forums, Facebook groups, or even build something yourself.

Many people would add another one—"user to after-sales service". Nowadays, users may complain online about your products and your company. So incorporating professional after-sales service into social websites should also be a key phase. It closes the loop, and makes users more engaged in their buying experience as a whole.

So that's how you earn customers through social media, rather than buying them with banner ads. But don't be misled, social media marketing to get customers and brand recognition through engagement still costs money (and time and effort). There is no free lunch. But don't spend your money on things that don't work anymore. That won't build any competitive advantage.

Steps to measure technical entrepreneur social media results

Jim Sterne, who has written many books on Internet advertising, marketing, and customer service, tackled the complex world of social media metrics a while back in his book titled *Social Media Metrics* (http://www.amazon.com/Social-Media-Metrics-Marketing-Investment/dp/0470583789). He has one of the first books on this subject, and he breaks the process down into nine steps which I like, as follows:

1. **Get focused and identify goals**: Social media is the realm of public opinion and customer conversations. If you don't have a clear idea of why you are there, anything you measure will be useless. He suggests you begin with the *big three* business objectives of higher revenue, reduced costs, and improved customer satisfaction.

2. **Get attention and reach your audience**: Measuring message delivery in social media is a lot like measuring it in classic advertising, so classic metrics apply. With social media, it is also important to identify how many people see your message as remarkable. That leads to the extra reach of word-of-mouth, commenting, and telling their friends.

3. **Measure respect and find influencers**: Your task now includes reaching the people who are key influencers, and understanding their impact. Therein lies the multiplier effect. Your message multiplier velocity and reach are the signals that your offerings have the right scope, spread quickly, and resonate with your target audience.

4. **Track the emotional sentiment**: Counting is fine, but analyzing the outpouring of millions of souls can reveal attitudinal shifts. Tracking public sentiment over time provides invaluable insight and gives you the chance to stay right on top of changes in the marketplace and your organization's brand equity.

5. **Measure customer response and action**: If they read it and like it, do they click through to your web site, or engage with your organization in new and different ways? Action is when people are drawn into a profitable and sustainable relationship with your company. That's where the money is.

6. **Get the message from your customer**: With the customer in control, you need to make sure you are getting the right message from the right people at the right time. That's real-time market research, and you need to measure how well you are hearing it and acting on it in your business strategy planning.

7. **Drive business outcomes and get results**: Now it's time to cycle back around to measuring what sort of business impact your efforts are having. Measure to see if you have an increase in revenue, a lowering of costs, and improvement in customer satisfaction. Then it's time to re-examine your goals to look beyond the *big three*.

8. **Get buy-in from your colleagues**: Some executives are slow to understand and embrace new communications methods. Use your results to convince them that social media is a vital part of your marketing mix, and deserves the resources necessary for proper implementation and measurement.

9. **Project the future**: Start now to look at where social media will be in two to ten years, and prepare for it. Don't let the changes takes your organization by surprise, or allow your organization to be the last to implement and measure you in the new world.

The tools to help you with all these actions are still evolving. You can scan the Internet for the many offerings to gather data, but the evaluation of the "why" behind the results is still largely manual. That's the insight you need to support your efforts to reach higher performance goals. The sooner you find these insights, the quicker you can make better decisions to positively enhance your bottom line.

How to balance social media costs versus value

Hopefully by now, you recognize that if you are a technical entrepreneur today, and not using social media to promote your business, you are missing out on a huge opportunity. But, contrary to what many people preach, it isn't entirely free. Most social media outlets don't require a subscription charge, but they certainly require an investment—in people, in technology, your reputation, and your time.

As I have mentioned before, there are hundreds of consultants out there who will take your money for guidance in this area, but I recommend that you start with some free resources on the Internet, or one of the many recent books on this topic. One I read a while back, *How to Make Money with Social Media* (http://www.amazon.com/How-Make-Money-Social-Media/dp/0132100568) by Jamie Turner and Reshma Shah, Ph.D., hits all the right points from my perspective:

> ➤ **There are risks as well as benefits**: As with many startup activities, you only have one chance for a great first impression. You can jump into social media with a poor brand definition, poorly focused content, unrealistic expectations of customer service, or be killed by malware or viruses.

> ➤ **Assess social media relevance to your product or service**: If your business is industrial B2B products, social media should be low on your list. Spend your time and money on other platforms. If you are selling to consumers, especially younger ones, your business won't survive without an effective social media presence.

> ➤ **Attracting key stakeholders requires sensitivity**: For some customers and many investors, a heavy focus on social networks and viral marketing may be a negative, rather than a positive. A balance of conventional and social communication and marketing is always advised.

> ➤ **Pick the right platform for your business**: Within each of the platform categories defined in this list, there is a right platform and a wrong platform for your audience. For example, LinkedIn is attuned to business professionals, Facebook is dominated by the social and upwardly mobile crowd, and the fading MySpace is for creative types.

> ➤ **Communication and writing skills are required**: Heavy texting experience is not a qualification for communicating via social media. In additional to strong journalistic writing and storytelling, you need business acumen, strategic thinking and planning, and the ability to do the right research. These days, video production is also a useful skill.

> ➤ **Make social media an integrated part of an overall strategy**: An integrated marketing strategy starts with an overall brand management strategy, delivered through online and offline communications, promotions, and customer engagement vehicles. Your Twitter and YouTube messages better match your print advertising message.

➤ **Find the right tools to analyze the ROI**: Return on investment metrics are not new, but the tools are different. Get familiar with current social media tools, such as Google Analytics, SproutSocial, and HootSuite analytics. Over time, put together the data you need to measure your progress on a weekly/monthly/yearly basis.

The key social media platforms today include communications (WordPress blogs, Twitter), collaboration (Wikipedia, StumbleUpon), and multimedia (YouTube, Flickr). In looking ahead, don't forget mobile platforms (iPhone, Android), and location-based services (Foursquare, ShopKick).

As with any resource or tool, you need to optimize your social media costs against a targeted return. That means first setting a strategy and plan for what you want to achieve, then executing the plan efficiently, and measuring results. It's not free, but it's an investment that you can't afford not to make.

How to make a real social media customer connection

As I visit the websites of many technical startups, as well as more mature businesses, I still too often see a *contact* page offering nothing but a sterile form for customers to submit, never to be heard from again. Social media connections, if they exist, are buried elsewhere or reserved for monitoring purposes only.

Social media is here, and is the preferred mode of communication by a large segment of your customers, so make it a positive differentiator for your business. Don't force them to use an automated phone response system, or a faceless unresponsive form. Customers are not all like you, and they have choices, so a *one size fits all* customer service is no longer a viable option.

There are now many resources out there to guide you in building social media into your business and improving your customer experience, including the book from multicultural marketing expert Kelly McDonald, *Crafting the Customer Experience for People Not Like You* (http://www.amazon.com/Crafting-Customer-Experience-People-Like/dp/1118360729).

Her focus is on crafting a customer experience that caters to people not like you, including social media aficionados, to bring in new customers and create a competitive advantage. Every startup these days must adopt this focus to survive and prosper. Here are some key recommendations I gleaned from her book to make this work:

➤ **Empower your social media front line team**: This front line team, often called community managers, are the *voice* of your company, and must have authority to make and carry out decisions that can make or break a customer's experience. That means forget using interns or outsourcing this function. You need insider *deciders* here.

➤ **Be proactive and put on your listening ears**: You absolutely must listen online, because that is where you will find the unvarnished truth about what your customers and prospects think of you. Asking the right questions will get you to that truth in a positive way earlier, rather than having to learn from damage control later. Many companies now send a short user-satisfaction survey to customers after every customer service interaction.

➤ **Respond online to feedback received online**: Before social networking, an unhappy customer might tell three people. Now an unhappy customer can easily tell three million. If these three million see no timely response, your problem can go viral. Respond online and let the positive vibes go viral instead. Don't force customers to go offline to your customer support phone or email for resolution.

➤ **Guide customers to the right social media channel**: As a startup, you can't be everywhere all of the time, so it helps to tell people through traditional channels, in a positive way, the best ways to find you. All social media channels are not equal, and customers are still learning, so they may also appreciate some guidance.

➤ **Connect members of your market to one another**: One vital aspect of relationship building requires that you become a true connector by introducing members of your market to one another, which will help them derive mutual benefit. A positive result could be a reputation that you put customer relationships first and sales second.

Providing the best customer experience to different kinds of people via different channels isn't just the right thing to do, it's the strategic thing to do. It will improve your business in several ways:

➤ Grow your business by bringing in new customers

➤ Give you a significant competitive edge, by better serving broader customer groups

➤ Increase customer loyalty and therefore customer retention

➤ Help differentiate you from other businesses or similar enterprises

➤ Give you a greater understanding of and insights to diverse customer groups

Although building social media into your customer experience sounds like work, don't forget that social media is a gift to every startup and small business. The conversations that once took place only between people in private settings now occur more and more in public online environments, across a world geography.

By eavesdropping on the right customer conversations, startups can identify their own strengths and weaknesses, as well as those of their competitors on a real time basis. Essentially, you can think of social listening as a free tool for market intelligence, consumer research, and customer service all rolled into one.

But all this only works if you are wired into the conversation, your customers know how to find the conversations, and they trust you to treat them as respected and valuable members of your community. Make sure your business is at the top end of this spectrum.

Summary

The goal of this chapter has been to help you as a technical entrepreneur understand where and how to start using social media, how to measure the impact, and how to make the required tradeoffs between cost and value received. The value of social media extends well beyond marketing, into requirements analysis, product feedback, and customer service.

Yet, don't be convinced that the use of social media supersedes the need for all the traditional business management tactics and requirements. It's just the newest of many elements of building a successful business. In the next chapter, we will take a look at many of these other elements that technical entrepreneurs often overlook. Take heed, do the work, and take the lead over your competitors.

9

If You Build It, Will They Find You, and Will They Use It?

Most technical entrepreneurs work hard on the proof of concept (technical), but skip any proof of the business model (revenue flow). In other words, once they are convinced that the product works, they assume customers will come, no matter what their price, sales channel, or marketing. These days, the technical side may be the easy part.

They soon find out that flexibility, visibility, and marketing are everything these days. You can have the best technology, but if the product misses the mark, customers don't know you exist, or they don't know how your technology solves a real problem for them, your startup will fail. Yet I see many entrepreneurs focus on the basics of customer interaction and marketing too little and too late.

This chapter outlines the alternatives for customer relationships and marketing in general, as well as the new rules required by social media and the overload of information bombarding potential customers via the Internet and traditional marketing sources.

The hardest part of building a successful business is not building a product, but building one that meets customer requirements, making sure they know how it benefits them, and making it available competitively. Here are some of the key lessons you don't want to learn the hard way:

Planning pivots – you may not get it right the first time

The popular view of a technical entrepreneur is someone with a big vision and a stubborn determination to charge straight ahead through any obstacle and make it happen. The vision part is fine, but more successful entrepreneurs have found that the extreme uncertainty of a new product or service usually requires many course corrections or pivots to find a successful formula.

The traditional mode of starting a company has long been to plan a serial process, where you complete all the steps, leading to the big bang launch of the company. I think it's time for a dramatic departure from this old model, to a new one called planned iteration or *Lean Startup* (http://en.wikipedia.org/wiki/Lean_Startup) methodology. With this one, you assume you won't get it right the first time, so you launch with a minimum viable product (MVP).

This idea was first articulated by Paul Graham in an old essay, called *Startups in 13 Sentences* (http://www.paulgraham.com/13sentences.html) in which he talked about making a few people really happy rather than making a lot of people semi-happy. One of his key points is that launching teaches you what you should have been building, and I agree.

All you old software development types will recognize the analogy to the traditional two year waterfall model of software development, which has been totally replaced with the Agile (http://en.wikipedia.org/wiki/Agile_software_development) iterative methodology. Agile assumes and plans for iterative development, where requirements and solutions evolve as more is known and markets change.

Don't mistake this for a license to launch an incomplete or poor quality solution. Your strategy today should be to define and excellently prepare the absolute minimum product that will excite a selected small segment of your intended customers, and roll it out to them as a Beta, early promotion, or even a give-away.

Then you assess feedback, adjust your offering, and iterate until you get it right (and have some very satisfied customers). Plan on multiple small launches, with iterations, rather than a big launch. Here are the advantages I see with this approach:

➤ **Faster time to market**: If you launch fast, you can be working with real customers in 4-6 months from your start, rather than 1-2 years. In today's fast moving marketplace, needs, competitors, and costs change rapidly, so even if you were right, two years later the wave has moved on. Equally likely, your first target was wrong, and you will need to adjust.

➤ **Show some traction before funding**: Let's face reality; the angel or VC funding process now takes 4-6 months of almost dedicated effort and time, and usually fails because you don't yet have a product or customer. By using a laser focused approach for the first iteration, you may actually produce something and get a customer without funding. Now investors will pay attention, since scale-up funding is less risky and has a time frame.

➤ **Fail fast and cheap**: Since you can predict that your first iteration will somehow miss the mark, speed and cost of pivoting are critical. We all know how hard it is to turn a battleship. With a minimum viable product, your startup remains much more agile. The planned iterations can then be applied more productively to enhance the right offering.

> ➤ **Find customers, partners, and channels early**: There is nothing like a real customer pipeline to convince you that you need partners and channels, and to convince partners, channels, and investors that you are real. Get out there personally and find that first customer. It will narrow your development focus, and adjust your strategy for you. Spend your time finding renewable sources of customers and iterate.

> ➤ **Use social networking to start the wave**: Costs are low these days to set up a credible website, so do some search engine optimization, start blogging, and start mining the social networks for interest. It won't cost you your whole funding pot to start some momentum, or to realize that your original strategy needs major tuning.

Think about it. Where did Google, eBay, and Facebook come from? They inched their way into public view before the first multi-million dollar funding rounds, and they have never had a big public launch. New product companies in the offline world start one store at a time, or in one geographic area.

Big bang product launches are the domain of big enterprises, and you can never match their clout and budget. The biggest advantages you have as a startup are speed and agility. Use them.

For the rest of us, Eric Ries, in his popular book on this subject, *The Lean Startup* (http://www.amazon.com/Lean-Startup-Entrepreneurs-Continuous-Innovation/dp/0307887898), lays out specific guidelines on how today's entrepreneurs can use continuous innovation to create radically successful businesses.

Eric espouses designing products with the smallest set of features to please a customer base, and moving products into the marketplace quickly to test reaction, then iterating. He does a great job in the book of making the case for management systems, rather than gut-level reactions, to make required course corrections (pivots), to dramatically improve the odds for success.

Pivots come in many different flavors, each designed to test the viability of a different hypothesis about the product, business model, and engine of growth. I agree with Eric's summary of the top ten types of pivots to consider. Don't try them all at once. I recommend that you pick one, put some measurements in place, and try it for at least a month before concluding that the change is working or not working:

> ➤ **Zoom-in pivot**: In this case, what previously was considered a single feature in a product becomes the whole product. This highlights the value of focus and minimum viable product (MVP), delivered quickly and efficiently.

> ➤ **Zoom-out pivot**: In the reverse situation, sometimes a single feature is insufficient to support a customer set. In this type of pivot, what was considered the whole product becomes a single feature of a much larger product.

> ➤ **Customer segment pivot**: Your product may attract real customers, but not the ones in the original vision. In other words, it solves a real problem, but needs to be positioned for a more appreciative segment, and optimized for that segment.

➤ **Customer need pivot**: Early customer feedback indicates that the problem solved is not very important or money isn't available to buy. This requires repositioning, or a completely new product, to find a problem worth solving.

➤ **Platform pivot**: This refers to a change from an application to a platform, or vice versa. Many founders envision their solution as a platform for future products, but don't have a single killer application just yet. Most customers buy solutions, not platforms.

➤ **Business architecture pivot**: Geoffrey Moore, many years ago, observed that there are two major business architectures: high margin, low volume (complex systems model), or low margin, high volume (volume operations model). You can't do both at the same time.

➤ **Value capture pivot**: This refers to the monetization or revenue model. Changes to the way a startup captures value can have far-reaching consequences for business, product, and marketing strategies. The free model doesn't capture much value.

➤ **Engine of growth pivot**: Most startups these days use one of three primary growth engines: the viral, sticky, and paid growth models (`http://larslofgren.com/marketingbasics/the-three-engines-of-growth-with-eric-ries`). Picking the right model can dramatically affect the speed and profitability of growth.

➤ **Channel pivot**: In sales terminology, the mechanism by which a company delivers its product to customers is called the sales channel or distribution channel. Channel pivots usually require unique pricing, feature, and competitive positioning adjustments.

➤ **Technology pivot**: Sometimes a startup discovers a way to achieve the same solution by using a completely different technology. This is most relevant if the new technology can provide superior price and/or performance to improve competitive posture.

Every entrepreneur faces the challenge in developing a product of deciding when to pivot and when to persevere. Ask most entrepreneurs who have decided to pivot and they will tell you that they wish they had made the decision sooner. In fact, a startup's runway is really not money, but the number of pivots they can still make. What are you doing to get to the required pivots faster?

Joining the new breed with a new mantra – nail it then scale it

I see more and more technical entrepreneurs who seem to have everything going for them—vision, motivation, passion, a good business plan, product, the willingness to pivot, and money, yet they can't close customers. Maybe it's time to look harder at the mantra of a new breed of gurus and successful entrepreneurs, including Steve Blank and Eric Ries, called **nail it then scale it** (**NISI**).

You can review all the specifics of this approach in a book by Nathan Furr and Paul Ahlstrom, appropriately titled *Nail It then Scale It: The Entrepreneur's Guide to Creating and Managing Breakthrough Innovation* (http://www.amazon.com/Nail-then-Scale-Entrepreneurs-Breakthrough/dp/0983723605), but I will present a brief summary of it here. I found their five phases of the process to be compelling, based on my own years of experience mentoring startups:

1. **Nail the pain**: Great businesses begin with a customer problem that has a big and monetizable pain point. Avoid the three big mistakes, of guessing but not testing the pain (on real customers), selecting a low customer pain (a solution is only nice to have), or selecting a narrow customer pain (a small number of customers willing or able to pay).

2. **Nail the solution**: Neither breakthrough technology nor maximum features will assure that *if we build it, they will come.* In fact, NISI recommends starting with the minimum focused set of features and technology that will drive a customer purchase. Success demands testing the solution early and quickly in the market, then iterating to get it right.

3. **Nail the go-to-market strategy**: In parallel with nailing the solution, you need an in-depth understanding of your target customer's buying process, the job they are trying to get done, the market infrastructure, and a stable of serious pilot customers. Do real tests with real pricing to see whether customers will pay you, without being pushed.

4. **Nail the business model**: Leverage your customer conversations to predict and validate your business model. For example, when you think about distribution channels, revenue streams, or the relationship with the customer, ask customers what they expect. Don't forget a viable financial model of costs, margins, customer acquisition, and break-even.

5. **Scale it**: Don't attempt to scale it until you have a proven repeatable business model that predictably generates revenue. Only then is it time to focus on the get-big-fast strategy, and the transformation of three key areas from startup to a managed growth company. These areas include market, process, and team transitions.

These pragmatics and points of focus can effectively counter three core myths that trap too many enterprising and capable entrepreneurs today:

> ➤ **Hero myth—why believing in your product leads to failure**: All too often, founders fall in love with their products or technology, ignore negative feedback from customers, and spend years building a product based on a vision that no one else shares.

> ➤ **Process myth—why building a product leads to failure**: Conventional wisdom is that after a great idea, the next steps are raise some money, build a product, then go sell the product. This doesn't work when attacking unknown problems with untested solutions.

> ➤ **Money myth—why having too much money leads to failure**: The old saying that *it takes money to make money* isn't so simple. Money allows entrepreneurs to execute a flawed business plan far too long, rather than staying focused on the market and adapting.

At the heart of it, to be a successful entrepreneur you have to be totally customer-centric, and learn to change and adapt as fast as the market. The pace of change in the marketplace is escalating, so entrepreneurs have to improve their ability to deal with change. That means you need to constantly be alert for a change in trends or culture, through regular customer surveys, interaction on social media, and a formal customer service feedback process.

At the same time, more entrepreneurs are jumping into the fray, and less money is available from investors. It's time for a new startup model. In my view, savvy *super angel* investors such as Mike Maples, Jr., and leading incubators such as Y Combinator, are already on this one.

Validating the business model

Proving the business model requires a different approach than proving the technical concept. For example, one CEO I know gave away his software product to the first ten customers. Customer technical personnel loved it, and it worked, so he was totally devastated when he couldn't sell one for a *reasonable* price in the first two months of hard selling.

So how do you go about proving the business model? It starts with a customer problem or need, and includes proving the technical concept, but starts earlier and goes much further, per the following key steps:

1. **Quantify problem cost-of-pain first**: Before you design your new solution idea, gather evidence and estimates of how much money a customer is willing to spend (if any) to solve the problem. Factor in your margin, and you will have an upper bound on your solution cost. You won't succeed with a product that is too expensive for the market.

2. **Prove the technical concept**: If the product doesn't satisfy the need, or it doesn't work, no business model can work. Start by testing the requirements on real customers, and providing *alpha* versions to get real feedback. Iterate and improve the fit until your test customers are delighted, not just tolerant.

3. **Use focus groups**: Gather some representative customer contacts, and give them your best sales pitch, including price, channel, and support. Then listen carefully to the feedback. Don't be discouraged if you don't get it right the first time. Changes at this stage cost almost nothing.

4. **Talk to domain experts**: Here is where your Advisory Board can help you in finding real people with deep experience in your product domain, and gather some unbiased feedback. Listen to potential angel investors, who have domain expertise, and aren't afraid to ask the hard questions on pricing and channels.

5. **Limited rollout**: If you have a physical product, try it in a couple of stores first. If you are on the Internet, try one city. This is tricky, since you have to do realistic marketing to see realistic results, but don't roll out the big viral campaign yet. Look at product costs, margins, commissions, and other expenses to make sure you still have a bottom line.

6. **Get a reference customer**: You should descend on that best customer candidate with everything you have. Don't give the product away, but make sure he or she has every bit of service you can provide. He or she better be so pleased that they are willing to provide a testimonial for your real marketing campaign.

7. **Sample trade show or user group**: If you use the big *Coming Soon!* sign correctly, people will stop by your booth for a look. Make sure they are real customers, and that they get the whole story (not just a technical demo), including the price and channel. Otherwise, their feedback has no value in proving your business model.

All this assumes you have done the right job first in assessing competition, establishing the sales and marketing channels, and optimizing costs. I see business plans with a great analysis of competitor's product features, but competitor's business models rarely get mentioned.

Over the last few years, the right business model has become the key to converting a good idea into a winning startup. Your business model can be your competitive edge, or it can be your soft underbelly. Test it out, before you dive in with the sharks.

The practical reality is that you must have an operational model that delivers value to customers at a reasonable price, with an underlying cost that allows you to make a profit. There are no *overrides*—for example, businesses don't thrive just because they offer the latest technology, or because everyone wants to be green, or because their goal is to reduce world hunger.

Pricing your product correctly

One of the toughest decisions for a technical startup is how to price their product or service. The alternatives range from giving it away for free, to pricing based on costs, to charging what the market will bear (premium pricing). The implications of the decision you make are huge, defining your brand image, your funding requirements, and your long-term business viability.

The revenue model you select is basically the implementation of your business strategy, and the key to attaining your financial objectives. Obviously, it must be grounded by the characteristics of the market and customers you choose to serve, the pricing model of existing competitors, and a strategy you believe is consistent with your future products and direction.

So what are some of the most common revenue models being used by startups today? Here is a summary, with some of the pros and cons or special considerations for each:

- ➤ **Product or service is free, revenue from ads**: This is the most common model touted by Internet startups today, the so-called Facebook model, where the service is free, and the revenue comes from click-through advertising. It's great for customers, but not for startups, unless you have deep pockets.

- ➤ **Freemium model**: In this variation on the free model, used by LinkedIn and many other Internet offerings, the basic services are free, but premium services are available for an additional fee. This also requires a huge investment to get to critical mass, and real work to differentiate and sell premium services to *convert* users to paying customers.

- ➤ **Cost-based model**: In this more traditional product pricing model, the price is set at two to five times the product cost. If your product is a commodity, the margin may be as thin as ten percent. Use it when your new technology gives you a tremendous cost improvement. Skip it where there are many competitors.

- ➤ **Value model**: If you can quantify a large value or cost savings to the customer, charge a price commensurate with the value delivered. This doesn't work well with *nice to have* offerings, such as social networks, but does work for new drugs and medical devices that solve critical health problems.

- ➤ **Subscription model**: This is a very popular model today for Internet services, calling for monthly or yearly low payments, in lieu of one value or cost-based price. Startup advantages include a more stable revenue stream, easier customer retention, and increasing customer investment over time. The customer advantage is a lower entry cost.

- ➤ **Product is free, but you pay for services**: In this model, the product is given away for free and the customers are charged for installation, customization, training, or other services. This is a good model to use to get your foot in the door, but be aware that this is basically a services business with the product as a marketing cost.

- ➤ **Product line pricing**: This model is relevant only if you have multiple products and services, each with a different cost and utility. Here, your objective is to make money with the portfolio, with high markup and low markup items, depending on competition, lock-in, value delivered, and loyal customers. This one takes expert management to work.

- ➤ **Tiered or volume pricing**: In certain product environments, where a given enterprise product may have one user or hundreds of thousands, a common approach is to price by user group ranges, or volume usage ranges. Keep the number of tiers small for manageability. This approach doesn't typically apply to consumer products and services.

- ➤ **Feature pricing**: This approach works if your product can be sold *bare-bones* for a low price, and price increments added for additional features. It can be a very competitive approach, but the product must be designed and built to provide good utility at many levels. This is a very costly development, testing, documentation, and support challenge.

> **Razor blade model**: In this model, like cheap printers with expensive ink cartridges, the base unit is often sold below cost, with the anticipation of ongoing revenue from expensive supplies. This is another model that requires deep pockets to start, so is normally not an option for startups

If you have real guts, you can try the Twitter model of no revenue, counting on the critical mass value from millions of customers to sustain your company. This model was popular back in the heyday of dot.coms, when investors were buying anything with a following, but is frowned on today. It definitely requires founders with deep pockets and investors willing to take a huge leap of faith.

In all cases, your business model interacts closely with your marketing model, but don't get them confused. Marketing is initially required to get visibility and access to the opportunity, but pricing defines how you will actually make money over the long term. A key challenge for every entrepreneur seeking funding is to convince potential investors that the marketing model will substantiate your positive revenue model, customers will buy the offering, and you have a viable business model.

Overall, I'm a huge fan of the **keep it simple (KISS)** principle—customers are typically wary of complex or artificial pricing. Your challenge is to set the right price to match value perceived by the customer, with a fair return for you. It's not a game show, so don't guess—do your research early with real customers. Your startup's life depends on it.

Creating a memorable website for your startup

Now that you have the product and the business model right, your customer needs to find you and quickly learn what you have to offer. These days, a first required step in that direction is to create a great website.

Smart people only visit and buy from credible and memorable websites. In the past, if your startup had a website presence, the company was credible by definition. In today's world, a website is necessary but not sufficient for credibility. Dreamers and gamblers have found out that if the website isn't validated as credible, it's probably a scam, and everyone loses.

Yet most startups I know experience the same shock of disappointment when they first open up their website to offer their *million dollar idea* product, and nobody comes. What validates credibility and makes your site memorable in the minds of consumers, and how much does it cost? Here are some key suggestions to get you started:

> **Put yourself on the site**: People buy from people. Until the company name is a famous brand, you are the brand. No name, picture, address, or business history only convinces customers that you are hiding, located in an un-trustable country, or don't have a clue. They will exit quickly.

- ➤ **Show evidence of your expertise**: Publish a regular blog, contribute to relevant social networks, and write a *white paper* on your technology. People respect people with relevant experience, so highlight your accomplishments and the credentials you have.

- ➤ **Highlight personal presence and testimonials**: Third parties are always more credible sources than you are. Highlight interviews and reviews from recognized industry sources and news sources. Include links to your profiles on LinkedIn, Facebook, and Twitter.

- ➤ **Create a positive online image**: Show your visitors some evidence of community involvement and charity efforts. Offer something that is really free with no strings attached, which would cause them to lose their trust in you. Set up an award and show winners.

- ➤ **Link to recognized brands**: If you can have an affiliate relationship with any recognized brand name or any connection to publicly recognized experts, highlight them and provide links to their websites.

- ➤ **Advertising presence**: The presence of a few related advertisements can actually improve your site credibility, since most credible sites have them. Of course, too many or obnoxious advertisements are especially harmful to a site's credibility.

- ➤ **Join relevant business associations**: Most will give you a membership graphic for your website, and an association link to give your business extra credibility. Don't forget the local Chamber of Commerce and Better Business Bureau.

- ➤ **Provide a privacy and security statement**: Display a logo such as McAfee Secure (`http://www.mcafee.com/us/mcafeesecure/products/mcafee-secure.html`) or Privacy Label (`http://www.privacylabel.com/`), in addition to specific policy statements on these subjects, to persuade your visitors and prospects to trust you.

- ➤ **Offer support assistance and guarantee**: Publish the terms of your support, return, and replacement policies. Be consistent, and provide contact information for both phone and e-mail access. Follow-up for customer satisfaction.

- ➤ **Professional user-friendly site design**: Studies have shown that consumers gauge credibility in large part based on the appeal of the overall visual design, including layout, typography, font size, color schemes, no broken links, and correct language usage. Don't forget basic Search Engine Optimization (SEO) so search engines improve your ranking.

These are all minimal-cost, survival marketing efforts. Beyond these, you will likely need to budget time and dollars (up to $50,000 is not unusual) for real marketing efforts to enhance your visibility and credibility, which include branding, promotions, give-aways, and free services.

Optimizing your website for the search engines

Now that you have a great website, the next step is to get it optimized for the search engines (SEO). A website not optimized for search engines is lost in the heap of a billion dead websites. Unless someone searches for your company by name, it won't show up in the first few pages of any search results. Of course, this website optimization will be only the beginning of your marketing efforts.

Search engines are programmed to rank websites based on their popularity and relevancy. These are subjective elements, but there are specifics that even a computer program can evaluate to set your ranking, and thus determine whether your site is alive and a good match to a specific search request. Yet, recent research (http://www.analyticsseo. com/blog/press-release-half-small-business-websites-are-not-search-engine-optimised) indicates that almost half of small business websites are still missing these basics, and thus are essentially dead to the search world.

The solution is keeping your site alive and vital, and following basic search engine optimization suggestions. Here are some high-value elements you need, if you hope to see your company on any page of results for relevant user queries:

> **Relevant and constantly updated content**: Websites that haven't been updated in the last couple of years can't possibly be alive. These days, the best way to provide fresh content is to attach your blog to the website, and add new entries at least a couple of times a month.

> **Create inbound and outbound links**: Contact related websites that are well known, to request reciprocal links. Another way to get inbound links is to review other site blogs and leave your comments with your link. Register your business in relevant directories and sign up in all local directories. Make sure you have no dead links on your own site.

> **Web page title tags**: You need to name every page of your website, and these names must contain your important search keywords. Check every page of your web site to make sure a title is predominantly displayed as the first line of a search result. Missing and meaningless tags will cause your site to be ignored by users, even if found.

> **Website keyword tags and description**: These are elements, normally added by your website designer, which contain one or two sentences that briefly explain to the search engine what each web page is about. These same tags and keywords should be used liberally in each page text to give that page a higher ranking.

> **Image attributes and sub-folder names**: Search engines process every word on your website, even optional internal names assigned to images (alt tag) and folders. Thus, even internal names of website elements must be properly named (eliminate computer-generated text) to amplify your search position.

> **Reduce page load time**: Eliminate flashy ads that delay entry to your site. Search engine spiders (also known as bots) take into consideration the page's size in kilobytes. Web pages that take a long time to load will discourage search engines and human viewers alike. The usual culprit is a picture or graphic that is larger than 20 kilobytes.

Completion of these tasks is not the full SEO job, but will keep your company out of the Internet dead zone. You can contract an SEO specialist at this level for a couple of thousand dollars, or you can do the work in-house, if someone on your team has some basic tools and web maintenance skills. SEO does not have to be a major expense.

Another alternative is to buy your way out of the zone with Search Engine Marketing (SEM). If you give Google enough money, their search engine will put you up as a preferred provider for any search keyword you buy. That may be a quick fix, but will definitely be more costly in the long run.

But, the cost of doing nothing is even greater. Websites that look like the walking dead to Google search, work like no website, which means that your business will suffer. Work on a good website is never done, but there is no time like the present to wake up and get started.

In summary, a startup with no website, or a website with no credibility, will kill your business. Use the tips outlined previously during the first three months to get in the game and count on much more time and money if you intend to stand out. Make your website not only credible, but incredible!

Organic versus paid search results

Probably every one of you who has a technical business and a website have been approached through e-mail or personal contact, and asked to spend money on paid search results (appear on the first page of search results, right hand column, despite low SEO rank). What most people don't realize is that, according to new research (http://searchenginewatch.com/article/2200730/Organic-vs.-Paid-Search-Results-Organic-Wins-94-of-Time), 90 percent of search engine users rarely look at the paid results.

Paid search engine ranking (PPC) is buying advertising for your business from Google or another search engine company. Their computers then cleverly merge your ads with search results when users search words imply an interest in your products. If you sell widgets, and a user is searching for widgets, your ad will appear on the first page of search results for widgets.

This is NOT the same as Search Engine Optimization (SEO). SEO is not placing ads, but tuning your website so that it is more highly ranked by Google, and featured in the first page of results, not in an ad beside the results. PPC is sometimes called *buying your way into search results*. Both have the same end goal of getting people to your website.

With PPC, the goal is for the search user to not only see your ad, but to click on it to get to your website (click-through), and buy your widget (conversion to sale). In this context, there are many parameters and concepts you need to understand before you buy advertising:

➤ **Cost per impression (CPI)**: This cost model is the most like traditional newspaper and television advertising, where advertisers pay for each ad appearance or page-view (impression) on a search result page, even if the user pays no attention. For Google, this is pay per impression (PPI), or pay per mille (PPM) per thousand impressions.

➤ **Cost per click (CPC)**: In this more popular model these days, advertisers do not pay for each appearance of the ad, but only when a user clicks on an ad and is redirected to the advertiser website. For sites displaying the ads, this is called pay per click (PPC).

➤ **Cost per action (CPA)**: Another alternative was added a couple of years ago to mitigate the problem of people clicking just to get paid (click fraud). It pays only if a customer clicks through AND takes a further action (conversion), such as buying a product or filling out a web form. The display side is called pay per action (PPA) or pay per lead (PPL).

➤ **Keyword research and budget forecasting**: All these models start with the advertiser choosing the right search keywords to match user searches. Popular keywords have higher costs. PPC experts charge you to research, analyze, and estimate hit ratios, to optimize your success and set a campaign spending budget for you.

➤ **Campaign setup and ad copy writing**: There are many additional variables that the inexperienced marketer may not even think to consider: competition and positioning strategies, budgeting, match types, search and content syndication, and ad copy testing, as well developing the best ad wording and layouts.

➤ **Tracking and performance reporting**: Advertising is all about getting the most results for the least cost. You may be getting great traffic, but poor conversions. Other PPC experts will track your campaign from click to transaction, providing you with detailed reports on and return on investment (ROI).

If you do all these things right as a search results advertiser, you will make money from selling your product. If you do all these things right by displaying other people's ads on your website or blog, you will make money from advertising—like Google and Facebook, who offer services for free, and still make millions in revenue.

But either way, it requires big numbers to work (traffic), click-through rates are small, and the pay per click is tiny. Until your traffic is in the millions of page-views per month, don't expect to live off the conversions or other people's ads. For credibility with investors, stick to the organic SEO model and other revenue streams until you have the high traffic to survive on PPC revenue.

Website ads are not a revenue stream for startups

One of the biggest red flags I see in many technical Internet-related business models today is advertising as the initial revenue stream, or a key part of it. If challenged, the founder usually cites the Facebook business model (free service to users and revenue from ads), but forgets that Facebook has had several hundred million in funding, and has been profitable only in the last couple of years.

The most challenging time is your first years, when your site is unknown and your page-views are low. Until you get a million page-views per month, your revenue will be negligible and advertisers won't be interested in your site. Don't count on that to fund your startup.

This is a tough business. It can be very successful like it now is for Facebook, but entrepreneurs usually underestimate how long it will take for page views to ramp. They might see early traction due to early promotions, or special advertiser deals, but then reality sets in.

To better understand these realities, let's clarify some terminology. Unless you live in this world every day, you are probably as confused as I was by the different advertising models, so let me outline the common ones:

> **Pay per click (PPC)**: In this most popular model, advertisers pay each time a user clicks on an ad and is redirected to the advertiser website. Advertisers do not pay for each ad view, but only when the ad is clicked on. For advertisers, this is called cost per click (CPC).

> **Pay per view (PPV, PPI, or PPM)**: With this model, you get paid for each ad view or page-view (same as impression). For advertisers, this is cost per impression (CPI), or cost per mille (CPM) per thousand impressions. Advertisers normally prefer CPC, since they don't like to pay when you ignore their ad.

> **Pay per action (PPA or PPL)**: This advertising model was added a few years ago to mitigate the risks of click fraud. Here the advertiser pays only if a customer has been delivered to a website and takes a further action (conversion), such as buying a product or filling out a web form. The advertiser side is called cost per action (CPA) or cost per lead (CPL).

Now back to the revenue realities. If a startup wants to get the attention of investors, it needs to show large growth, like $50 million in revenue in five years. Today, without highly specialized targeting, the rule-of-thumb expectation should be no more than $1 in advertising revenue per thousand page-views.

To get to $50 million in revenue you would need 50 billion page views in a year, or just over 4 billion per month. Facebook is far above this range now, now with over 1 trillion page views, but only the top 10 sites in the US are in the right ballpark, and all took several years to get there, and none of these have been startups for quite some time.

It doesn't matter that the ads themselves come in a myriad of shapes and sizes – banner, panel, floating, expanding, wallpaper, trick banner, pop-up, pop-under, or even video. Costs and payments vary by size, level of targeting, and volume. A current trend to increase revenue is to make advertisements more interactive, but the basic numbers haven't changed much.

The bottom line is that any online advertising revenue you project in the first couple of years for your startup will be heavily discounted by any savvy investor, and will likely cause your business plan to be rejected. Face reality.

Investors know that during this early period, you will likely be spending more heavily than you expect, to build page-views, rather than collecting revenue from the millions of users you won't have yet.

Building your startup brand

As a technical entrepreneur, it's never too early to start selling yourself and your idea. I hear lots of excuses from startup founders, like *I'm too busy*, concern over intellectual property security, can't afford an agency, and it's too early. The result is they get no feedback, no credibility, no visibility, and no investors until months later than they expect.

I'm definitely not lobbying here for promising things you can't deliver, or hiring a publicist before your first programmer. I'm talking about doing some real networking to test your elevator pitch, and get to know some potential investors before you ask them for money. How about talking to some real customers to see if they are as excited about your idea as you are?

You don't need an agency and you don't want a third party to be involved at this point. You need to do it yourself. Here is a list of ways that you can use public relations to benefit your startup, even before it is started:

> **Make yourself a spokesman for your domain**: Start writing a blog, speaking at local groups, and conversing at networking meetings about the need you see in the marketplace before you pitch a solution. People will soon see you as an *expert* on solar power, as an example, so your later solar power offering will have credibility by default.

> **Practice your message**: Publicists always tell you to stick to the crafted message, which was probably wrong anyway. If you start early, you can improve your message with every cycle, until you have an elevator pitch for your startup that resonates with the right people.

> **Even bad coverage is better than no coverage**: It's better to push the limits, or be a bit controversial, than not to be visible at all. Because of human nature, controversy gets people's attention much more quickly than total agreement. People forget your early mistakes if they haven't bought your product yet. For more perspective on this point, see the article *There is no such thing as BAD press!* (http://archive.redstate.com/blogs/dahmich/2007/jan/11/there_is_no_such_thing_as_bad_press).

> ➤ **Be unabashedly aggressive**: Don't wait for journalists to find you; they all publish their e-mail addresses and they're looking for something interesting to write. Give it to them. Start forum discussions on LinkedIn and Facebook, and send out regular tweets on your direction. Comment on other people's blogs, as well as writing your own.

> ➤ **Hand out memorable business cards**: When you leave your business card with another person, your memory and impact is tied to that piece of paper. Make it professional and unique, with a visual image that conveys your message, even without the words.

> ➤ **Keep in touch with your audience**: One networking introduction will likely not leave a lasting impression. Be sure to follow-up with key people by writing thank-you e-mails, asking for a personal meeting over coffee, or adding them to your monthly newsletter distribution.

At any point, hiring a professional to generate your PR may be well worth the cost, but it's not required. Try to think like a reporter, editor, or producer; analyze their audience; and come up with *the hook*. Don't forget your personal story as a possible hook—what you have overcome or left behind, and why you decided to become an entrepreneur.

Perhaps your product or idea addresses a social issue or event. If the hook isn't obvious, create one by orchestrating an event, holding a contest, or donating something to charity. The earlier and more you learn about marketing, the more effective you will be later. In a startup, you are the brand. Start building it early.

Creating a brand experience for your technical product with digital marketing

In reality, no matter how much you spend, viral marketing and word-of-mouth are not enough these days to make your product and brand really stand out in the relentless onslaught of new promotional media out there today. Innovation in marketing is perhaps more important than product innovation. Yet in many of the technical startups I see, the marketing content and budget are smaller than ever.

More than just spending, you need to create an *experience* in this digital age that sets you apart from the banner ads, e-mail blasts, and old-school websites out there today. According to a book a while back by Rick Mathieson, these have morphed into a digital universe of augmented reality, advergames, and virtual worlds that are highly personalizable and uniquely shareable.

His title, *The On-Demand Brand: 10 Rules for Digital Marketing Success in an Anytime, Everywhere World* (http://www.amazon.com/Demand-Brand-Digital-Marketing-Everywhere/dp/0814415725), characterizes the challenge of demanding attention from a new generation of consumers who want what they want, when they want it, and where they want it. Here are the new marketing rules I recommend:

➤ **Insight comes before inspiration**: Innovative marketing starts with customer insights culled from painstaking research into who your customers are and how they use digital media. Then it's time to innovate through the channels or platforms that are relevant.

➤ **Don't repurpose, re-imagine**: Digital quite simply is not for repurposing content that exists in other channels. It's about re-imagining content to create blockbuster experiences that cannot be attained through any other medium.

➤ **Don't just join the conversation, spark it**: Create new online communities of interest, rather than joining existing ones. Ask why it should be and why customers should care. Then give them a reason to keep coming back. Keep it real, social, and events-based.

➤ **There's no business without show business**: Remember Hollywood secrets. Your brand is a story; tell it. Accentuate the personalizable and sharable. Viral is an outcome, not a strategy. Make people laugh and they will buy.

➤ **Want control? Give it away**: Several companies, including MasterCard, Coca-Cola, and Doritos have let customers build commercials and design contests, with big rewards for the customer and for the company. That's giving up control, with some risk, to get control.

➤ **It's good to play games with your customers**: Games are immersive, but shouldn't be just a diversion. They need to drive home the value proposition. Don't forget to include a call to action, like leading people to the next step of the buying process.

➤ **Products are the new services**: Startups need to realize that products are the jumping-off point for building relationships with customers. Digital channels enable you to turn products into on-demand services that help customers reach their goals, and add value.

➤ **Mobile is where it's at**: In addition to thinking of mobile as a new advertising distribution platform, remember it's far more powerful as a response, or *activation mechanism*, to commercial messages we experience in other media—print, broadcast, and more.

➤ **Always keep surprises in-store**: Social retailing is the new approach, where real-world shopping allows customers to connect with friends outside the store, and try on virtual versions of fashions friends might recommend. Make your in-store services add value.

➤ **Use smart ads wisely**: The new generation of *smart advertising* enables the creation of an Internet banner ad to fit each viewer's age, gender, location, personal interests, past purchase behavior, and much more. The trick is to do this without being invasive.

Remember everything you do, or don't do, in the digital world is visible to your customers, and everything they say about you is visible on demand, all over the world. That means marketing can no longer be an afterthought or something you can postpone until later, when you have more resources. Without effective and innovative marketing, you don't have a technical business.

Using viral marketing effectively

Every time I challenge a technical business plan with little or no budget for marketing, I get the answer that they will be using *viral* marketing, which costs nothing. The founder explains that the product is so *buzz-worthy* that usage will spread rapidly through word-of-mouth only, meaning people loving it and recommending it to their friends.

First of all, Seth Godin (http://sethgodin.typepad.com/seths_blog/2007/10/ is-viral-market.html) pointed out a few years ago that viral marketing does not equal word-of-mouth. His view is that word-of-mouth is an unsolicited consumer action, positive or negative, which usually fades quickly, like a good or bad restaurant review.

Viral marketing is a deliberate marketing action, designed to grow attention at a compound rate, without further stimulus, by word-of-mouth. It usually implies an opportunity to win big, like a lottery, or experience something sensational, like an incredible video or free product.

At any rate, *buzz-worthy* and *viral* are marketing illusions that cost big money to create. In a business plan these are called marketing campaigns, which continue to rise in cost. Here are three elements of most viral marketing campaigns:

> **Hire brand evangelists**: Think of a brand evangelist team online as people blogging about your product or posting links to it in every forum. Brand evangelists offline talk up your product lines at cocktail parties or recommend your services to friends while watching their kids' soccer game.

> **Develop viral content**: Someone has to design and create those entertaining or informative messages that are designed to be passed along in an exponential fashion, often electronically or by e-mail. It's harder than it looks to exploit people's propensity to share humorous, enjoyable, or useful information, for example jokes, special offers, and games.

> **Seed viral activity**: People are more demanding and have more choices than ever before. This means spending more money on search marketing (SEM) to make it look like the buzz is working. It also means making the content appear omnipresent on the Web and in the marketplace, including dedicated video sites and blogs. In addition, special offers and competition prizes may be required.

As a result of the rising popularity of viral campaigns, the cost of developing one has increased significantly, and the increased *viral clutter* has made it more difficult to stand out from the crowd. However, despite this, viral marketing can indeed be more cost effective than traditional marketing when done well.

Seeding is the most expensive aspect of a viral marketing campaign, with some video sites charging in excess of $10,000 to be featured on their home page for one week. Only a few years ago a humorous video or unique toy could be seeded into a couple of relevant online communities, and it would be hugely popular. However, the cost of entry has gone up as the concept of viral marketing has become pervasive.

In general, a well-executed viral marketing campaign can cost anywhere from $100K to many millions. There is a reason that sites such as Priceline.com Europe and Facebook, which everyone believes were made popular by viral marketing, have spent at least $50 million each becoming a household name.

Some startups not only ignore this and don't budget for it, but they actually plan on the free viral marketing to generate enough revenue from click-through advertising to fund operations and future growth. That's a double death wish.

We have all heard of a few cases where viral marketing resulted in a message *spread through the Internet like a cold in a kindergarten*, but counting on this can just as quickly lead to the death of your startup. Unless you have very deep pockets, plan for some very significant marketing costs, maybe even comparable to your development costs, to kick-start your dream to get into the marketplace.

Above all, maintain a laser focus

In addition to all the specifics outlined so far, your technical startup needs to maintain a laser focus in the beginning to get market and investor attention. Google did it with search engines, Apple did it with a personal computer, and even Wal-Mart did it through low prices. A business plan I saw a while back to combine all the good features of several popular social networks on one site does not do it.

Trying to do everything at once probably means that none of the items will be done well. Plus it's almost impossible to craft a message that will make your offering stand out in the minds of customers. I can't think of a company that launched to superstardom with a broad focus. Can you?

Here is a summary of the "common sense" reasons why a laser focus is key to technical startup business success:

➤ **Time to market is critical**: It takes too much time to build processes and products to capitalize on a broad strategy. In the meantime, small competitors will appear and seize your business opportunities and steal your targeted customers.

➤ **Keep infrastructure costs low**: Every business needs some basic equipment and infrastructure, and ongoing development costs. Attempting to roll out the big dream internationally all at once costs lots of money. Getting more money is hard, but not as hard as building the big infrastructure and getting it right the first time.

➤ **Need to be nimble**: Every successful startup I know has had to *dodge and weave* or pivot quickly as they learn what their customers really want, and what really works in product design and marketing. Bloated products and the grand unifying *theory of everything* won't allow you to adapt quickly to market changes and mistakes made.

> ➤ **Innovate to market leadership**: Success requires market leadership in your product area, and it's easy to see that pushing more products and services dilutes your focus and attention. Market leadership isn't a one-time thing; it means continuous innovation, or you will be left behind.

> ➤ **Maintaining quality is key**: The more you try to do in parallel, the harder it is to maintain quality. Remember the old maxim that *you only get one chance to make a great first impression.* Customers are fickle and good quality and good customer service is hard, even with a focused product.

> ➤ **Personal bandwidth is limited**: When things become too messy and complex, and even you are not sure of priorities, people get disillusioned, tired, lose motivation, and tend to give up easily. A laser focus is easier to communicate, easier to manage, and more likely to get done quickly and well.

As with everything, there are two sides to every coin. When applied appropriately, focus will result in rewards exceeding your expectations. Conversely, focusing on the wrong things will result in a downward business spiral. Focus on exploiting strengths and achieving success rather than resolving weaknesses and avoiding problems. Don't get burned by focusing on the wrong thing.

Remember that most people can confidently and competently accomplish one thing at a time, and most customers are only looking for one thing at a time. After you saturate the market with your focused offering, then you will have the time and resources to broaden your offering.

Don't give up your grand vision, since no investor wants to buy a *one trick pony*. But also don't try to be the *one-stop shop* for all on day one. If you focus on your customers to build the right product, then make it visible and attractive to your target customers at the right price, they will come, and they will buy.

Summary

Hopefully, this chapter has convinced you that implanting and selling your dream product or service is an ongoing effort, not just a burst of speed and enthusiasm in the beginning. Success requires listening carefully to all constituents, and adapting your product, process, and marketing to optimize the experience for your customers.

This process of listening, adapting, and optimizing can't be done alone. You need to develop strong relationships with many people to make this happen. Who these people really are, and how to develop and nurture these relationships is the subject of our next chapter. Let's get started!

>10

Can You Build the Relationships Needed to Succeed in Business?

Previous chapters have covered the operational specifics associated with successful technical startups, from vetting the idea, incorporating the business, building a plan, finding funding, marketing, and more. Woven through all of these activities is the dependence on people relationships. So this final chapter is an important one, with a focus on strengthening the biggest weakness found in most technical entrepreneurs—building and using relationships, both business and personal. I have seen far too many technical entrepreneurs who can invent or build many innovative things, but can't or aren't interested in building relationships with the people who can make them successful in business.

A successful entrepreneur needs to build and nurture relationships with partners, team members, vendors, and most importantly customers. The principles are embodied in every aspect of the business, from finding complementary partners and team members, providing leadership and communication, marketing and sales, to the final merger or IPO of the company for the right price.

In all cases, the challenge is the same, finding people that you can work with and enjoy in the business relationship. The relationship has to have trust, communication, and respect in order to work. Otherwise, like a marriage, it will be doomed to constant conflict, second guessing, and unhappiness.

This chapter explores the fine line between competitors and partners, social and business relationships, customers and vendors, and provides guidance on where, when, and how to find the right partners for growth and strength, without unduly risking your business.

Don't work alone

You can't win as a technical entrepreneur working alone. You need to have business relationships with team members, investors, customers, and a myriad of other support people. Imagine a business with no customers or team members—no fun at all. From a more practical perspective, there just aren't enough hours in a day, or dollars in your pocket, to keep the business going without people working with you. And for people to work with you, you need both a business as well as a personal relationship.

That doesn't mean you have to be a social butterfly to succeed, or introverts need not apply. It does mean that you need to look, listen, and participate in the business world around you and network through all available channels, such as business-oriented social networks online (LinkedIn), local business organizations (Chamber of Commerce), and events or conferences in your domain.

I hope all this seems obvious to you, but I still get a good number of notes from entrepreneurs who have been busy inventing things all their life, but can't find a partner to start their first business with, and others trying to find an executive, an investor, or a lawyer.

What these people need is more relationships, not more experts, more blogs, or more books. So I thought I would drop back to some essentials in building and nurturing business relationships (most of these apply to personal relationships as well):

> **Nurture existing relationships**: We all know someone who claims to be a *close friend*, but never initiates anything. They never call, they never write, and wait for you to make the first move. If you don't follow-up on a regular basis with someone, there is no relationship, only a former acquaintance.

> **Build your network**: These are people of all levels that have been there and done that, meaning people who know something that you need to know. My best advice on how and where to get started is in the first couple of chapters of this book. Obviously, you don't need a thousand friends, but a few real ones can make all the difference.

> **Give and you will receive**: Relationships need to be two-way, and can't be just all about you. If you are active in helping others with what you know, they will be much more open to help you when you need it. The more you give, the more you get in return, both literally and figuratively.

> **Work on your elevator pitch**: This is a concise, well-practiced description of your idea or your startup, delivered with conviction to start a relationship in the time it takes to ride up an elevator. It should end by asking for something, to start the relationship. See *Chapter 5, When and How Do You Find Funding for a Technical Business?*, for more details on how to do this.

> **Don't skip all business social settings**: Face time is critical, even with the current rage on social networks, phone, texting, and e-mail. Studies show that as much as 50-90% of communication is body language. That's usually the important relationship part.

> **Nominate someone as your mentor**: Build a two-way relationship with several people who can help you, and then kick it up a notch with one or more by asking them to be your mentor. Most entrepreneurs love to help others and will be honored to help you.

> **Cultivate existing allies**: These are people who already know and believe in you, but may not be able to help you directly in your new endeavors. But don't forget that each of these allies also has their own network, which can be an extension of yours if you treat them well.

On the positive side, many attributes of an introvert lead to better business decisions, such as thinking before speaking, building deep relationships, and researching problems more thoroughly. Mark Zuckerberg, the founder of Facebook, is currently the most famous introvert entrepreneur, so don't let anyone tell you it can't be done. Mark has demonstrated that even introverts can develop the basic social skills they need for business.

One of Mark's secrets seems to have been to surround himself by extroverts such as COO Sheryl Sandberg, and people who have a complementary energy. But working alone doesn't get you very far. It takes a team to win the game of business, so take a look around you to see how far you have to go to get there.

Two heads are always better than one

If you are a first-time technical entrepreneur who started alone, I recommend that you partner with a co-founder with experiences, connections, and a skill set that complements but doesn't duplicate yours. Even experienced entrepreneurs need a partner to back each other up and improve fundability. The question is how to find that elusive perfect-fit partner.

First, I will admit there is no magic formula here, just like in real life when trying to find a relationship partner. But from my own experience and input from others, there are useful approaches that will improve your odds of success:

> **Define the ideal partner**: The most important step is deciding exactly what skills and experience you need to best complement yours. Start with your own judgment, but don't hesitate to ask for advice from a seasoned investor. Ideal partners here should not include your best friend or a family member.

> **Start the search with business networking**: Actively participate in local business groups and events, such as **The Indus Entrepreneur** (TiE) and entrepreneur forums. Join entrepreneur groups online, such as LinkedIn On Startups, Facebook for Business, and Twitter to find people with like-minded interests.

> **Join online dating sites for business partners**: Believe it or not, there are online websites that are dedicated to just this challenge. Examples include *PartnerUp*, *StartupAgents*, and *Cofoundr*. Don't forget the wealth of business blogs frequented by entrepreneurs and investors, where you make your interests known.

> **Use local university connections**: Call some professors and students at your local university to see whether they know any entrepreneurial students, alumnus, or professors who might be interested in jointly creating a real company.

> ➤ **Look for diversity in outside activities**: Major universities, such as Stanford and MIT, are flush with smart people from all cultures, many of whom would bring a whole new energy and creativity to your startup. Certain activities seem to attract the right kind of independent thinkers, such as rock climbing and ultimate Frisbee.

> ➤ **Talk to people at work**: If you have worked with someone at another company for a couple of years and realized that your work ethic, goals, and personalities are similar, that person may be a good match. Watch out for non-compete clauses and conflicts of interest with the current employer.

> ➤ **Move to the right geography**: If you live in the middle of nowhere, your chances of finding the right co-founder for your new high-tech startup are poor. Maybe it's time to consider relocating to one of the hubs for startups, like Silicon Valley, Boston, New York, or Austin. As soon as you find the partner, these are the places to find funding as well.

> ➤ **Get to know potential partners before committing**: Take your time. Personally meet with potential candidates in both formal and informal environments to check for a match in chemistry as well as interests. Ask every question you can think of and don't let emotions get the best of you. Co-founder is a long-term relationship.

> ➤ **Agree on role assignments early**: The last thing you need after all this work is partners stepping on your toes. Make sure you all agree on what you know, what you are good at, and what responsibilities are assigned to each. Get this in writing as a standard pre-nuptial.

> ➤ **Seek guidance from a lawyer**: Especially when dealing with co-founders that haven't worked together before, meet with a lawyer with all the partners present and tell him what type of company you are starting, who is contributing what, and other relevant information. Get it written down. Later will be too late.

As most founders come to learn, finding the right business partner or co-founder is among the most difficult yet most important things that new technical entrepreneurs need to do. Once they find a great partner, most of the ones I know stay with that partner through multiple startups. Of course, if you're the next Google, you may only need one.

Partner qualities to test before sharing equity

In the preceding section, I talked about how and where to find a co-founder. Here I will try to be a bit more specific on attributes that might indicate an ideal startup partner. Even if you are looking in all the right places, it helps to know what you are looking for.

In this context, I'm broadening the definition of partner from co-founder to *business partner*. The reason is that good attributes apply equally well to *external* partners as they do to internal partners, like a co-founder or CTO.

In all cases, the challenge is the same, of finding people that you can work with and enjoy in the business relationship. The relationship has to have trust, communication, and respect in order to work. So the following attributes have to apply to both sides of the partnership to work:

> **Enjoys working with other people**: Some people are too independent to be partner material. If you find it hard to trust others, love to work alone, always have to be in control, or insist on micro-managing, you probably won't find a partner who will satisfy you.

> **Does not need to be managed**: Good partners are people who are confident in their own abilities and are willing and able to make decisions, take responsibility for their actions, and provide leadership rather than require leadership.

> **Has a compatible work style**: Most entrepreneurs work long hours and weekends to get the job done. If you team with a partner who likes to sleep until late in the morning, and reserves the weekend for other activities, the partnership will likely not work.

> **Common vision and commitment**: It doesn't take long to sense someone's real commitment or vision and desired outcome of a joint project. Is your project seen by both as an end in itself, or a means to another end?

> **Similar values and goals**: If one of your core values is exceeding your customer expectations for quality and service, and your potential partner ascribes to the low cost, high profit mantra, a successful partnership is highly unlikely over the long-term.

> **Level of integrity**: High levels of integrity are important in business, but more important is your level of comfort with your partner's integrity. This is a critical element of a good relationship, but a tough one. This is probably the best place to apply your *gut* feeling.

> **Complementary skills**: If both of you are experts at software development, even though one loves design and the other loves coding, that still won't get the marketing done. Look at the big picture first of development, finance, and marketing/sales.

> **Passion for what they do**: The passion has to be in the business context—meaning result-oriented, customer-oriented, and sensitive to competition. In many cases, experts with academic or research credentials are not good partners for a business venture.

> **Ethical and diversity boundaries**: How the leaders of your company handle adherence to the spirit as well as the letter of the law will be seen by all employees, customers, and investors. Ethics and the view of personal boundaries should be explored fully.

> **No historical baggage**: Partner decisions are more important than hiring decisions. Thus you should do the same or more due diligence on educational background, previous work, and references. Look impartially from all angles and do the follow-up.

Beyond the core team of two or three startup partners, every startup should seek to *outsource* the rest of their strategic requirements to external business partners. It's faster and cheaper than building a large team in-house and usually more effective.

By using this checklist, you should be able to objectively match potential partners with your own needs and expectations. Then, as I suggested before, it's time to establish a formal agreement or contract to cement the partnership. With that, you will have a strong foundation for success, as well as a great working relationship for the next thirty years.

One of the first tough decisions that startup founders have to make is how to allocate or split the equity among co-founders. The easy answer of splitting it equally among all co-founders, since there is minimal value at that point, is usually the worst possible answer and often results in a later startup failure due to an obvious inequity.

Another common *failure to start* situation I see is one where the *idea person* insists that the idea is 90% of the value (and 90% of the equity). In the real world, the *idea* is a very small part of the overall equation. A startup is all about execution—meaning the equity should be allocated based on the value that each partner brings to the table in each of these dominant variables:

> ➤ **Experience running a startup business**: Running a new business starts with building a solid and credible business plan, working the investor funding process, and building an organization from nothing, with minimal resources. Successful Fortune 500 executives need not apply since most would not have experience with any of these tasks.

> ➤ **Domain expertise and connections**: If you are recognized as an expert in the business area of your startup, with a good reputation, and you know all the key vendors and customers, your value is huge. Building a product doesn't get it distributed and sold. Expertise can be marketing, technical, financial, or sales.

> ➤ **Pre-existing intellectual property**: Ideas are not intellectual property, until they have been converted into patents, trade secrets, trademarks, or copyrights. In many cases, one founder has started earlier and brings an important completed piece of work to the table, and that can have great value.

> ➤ **Sacrifice and time commitment**: A part-time commitment (less than 20%), for example working for the startup only on weekends, while holding down a paying job during the week, is obviously not the same as a full-time startup executive role, especially if the cash compensation is nonexistent, deferred, or at high risk.

> ➤ **Funding**: Providing the major funding source for an early-stage startup is a totally different dimension, but it usually trumps all the items above in demanding some equity. Funding without equity is possible as a loan, or as a donation, but normally people put in money to buy something that will have more value later. For purposes of commitment and business decision making, I always recommend that execution partners retain control of at least 50% of the equity.

An arbitrary, but perhaps rational, equity factoring approach would be to assign each of these five items as 20% of the total and allocate equity based on each partner's relative contribution to each. For example, if your rich uncle is providing all the initial funding but has no active business role, it might be smart to offer him a 20% slice of the pie.

Equity allocation is usually the first point in a startup where outside help should be considered (legal counsel, potential investors, startup advisors), as they may be able to provide experience and more importantly, an unbiased view that the entire team can trust.

An important key is *not* to dodge the discussion up front, come to some agreement quickly and write it down. If you and your potential partners can't get through this discussion in a timely fashion and come to agreement, then it's unlikely that your startup will ultimately survive anyway. Startup decisions only get harder later, never easier.

Even still, regardless of the initial equity split, you should seriously consider vesting your founders shares over at least two years. This means they will be metered out month-by-month, and a partner who changes his mind or defects early will not walk away with half the company.

The next big challenge for a multi-partner startup is the allocation of roles. Who will be the CEO, CFO, and CTO? The same variables apply, but here skills and experience are paramount. If you are an inventor and have the key patent in hand, that doesn't mean you should be CEO. Of course, holding key assets and money always provide leverage to management rights as well as economic rights.

All partners should never forget that their allocated shares are only the beginning and will be diluted proportionately when outside funding is later required from angels or venture capitalists. Investors will be quick to remind you that a small percentage of something is worth more than 100% of nothing. The same logic applies to splitting equity with co-founders.

Why you need business relationships with many others

After your relationship is set with the right co-founders and the startup team, it's time to expand your efforts to the many other key players required to build a successful business. These would include investors, lawyers, vendors, outside partners, and customers.

You won't have the time to carefully craft and nurture each of these relationships, so it's time to kick your relationship building capabilities up a notch. You need to learn the strategies to quickly assess new people and demonstrate the characteristics of a good partner very quickly to them.

Jan Yager, PhD, an author and speaker on this and related subjects, outlines well the requirements for good business relationships in *Productive Relationships: 57 Strategies for Building Stronger Business Connections, Hannacroix Creek Books* (http://www.amazon.com/Productive-Relationships-Strategies-Building-Connections/dp/1889262633). From my experience and hers, here are ten top relationship strategies for people in startups:

> **Create a favorable first impression**: You only get one chance for a first impression. Don't miss an opportunity for face-to-face communication where you can use body language that welcomes relating, estimated at over 50 percent of all communication. Limit the use of e-mail and texting for early interactions.

> **Avoid negative personality types**: By recognizing negative personality types, like the control freak, the blameless type, the idea thief, and the entitled, you will have a better chance of not taking his or her behavior personally. Avoid associating with them.

> **Proactively form relationships with positive types**: These are the people who will help you to thrive and prosper. They include real mentors, facilitators, visionaries, motivators, and negotiators. Of course, it still pays to keep your eyes open and carry your own weight.

> **Find a way to motivate others to want to get along with you**: Understand your own agenda, and figure out the agenda of others, hidden or obvious, to make it a win-win relationship. How can you appeal to others on an emotional level to work together? You do this by connecting your message, goal, or project to the goals and values of others that you need. Try to link your request to a clear and appealing vision the other person can fully support. Describe the task with enthusiasm, and express confidence in that person's ability to help you accomplish it.

> **Re-examine your attitude toward conflict**: Some conflict is inevitable. The key is how to deal effectively with it. Recognize points of view, respond to what happened, resolve what needs to be resolved, and reflect on the lessons learned. Then move on.

> **Deal with the back-off before it turns antagonistic**: Rather than have a confrontation, someone backs off. You can't make someone want to deal with you, but you can try to increase their motivation to deal with you—like getting together for lunch or trying to communicate in another way.

> **Benefit from harsh feedback about your work**: Receiving criticism is never easy. Try some recovery techniques, such as taking a deep breath, giving yourself time, and looking at the issue from their perspective. Keep your initial response short and sweet and in control.

> **Cope with the lonely at the top syndrome**: One of the prices that you pay for being a CEO is giving up a lot of the social relationships within the company. There is a line beyond which you cannot go. You cannot compromise what is right for the company just to be liked. Join associations or rely on your family for support and feedback.

- ➤ **Say goodbye if leaving is the best option**: Sometimes it's better to just move on, rather than endure extended pain. Even if you cannot quit this instant, you can at least start looking for a new job. Be proactive in planning for your next position.

- ➤ **Use social networking to improve your work relationships**: Savvy workers at all levels are using these sites to develop and strengthen their business relationships as well as to reconnect with previous business connections. Make your own luck by giving and seeking referrals.

Compounding the difficulty with even the best strategies in today's start up environment are two divergent concepts: a heightened degree of competitiveness and a greater emphasis on teamwork. This means you need even more emphasis on effectively engaging others and learning to deal effectively with potentially negative work relationships.

The startup world of the past, run by a couple of autocrats, no longer works. To succeed in today's collaborative, customer-driven networked economy, requires real business relationship efforts by everyone involved. Then the challenge is to utilize that relationship effectively and productively for your business.

Most technical entrepreneurs, and members of any small team, naively assume that the key to their success is hard work, dedication, and long hours at the business. In reality, their effectiveness is usually more related to how well they develop their work relationships with peers and business leaders. First they need to decipher correctly every relationship as a "workship", friendship, or foe.

"Workships," according to workplace expert Dr. Jan Yager, refers to those workplace relationships that haven't yet developed into full-blown friendships but are closer than mere acquaintances. In a related book to the one above, *Who's That Sitting at My Desk?*, *Hannacroix Creek Books* (http://www.amazon.com/Whos-That-Sitting-My-Desk/dp/1938998081), she explains the importance of mastering work relationships and provides specific guidance on building the right ones.

It behooves all entrepreneurs and all team members to recognize the positives and negatives of each type of relationship. More importantly, we all need to develop the right relationships and actively avoid those types that are not right for the business or not right for our career at a particular point in time:

- ➤ **Acquaintanceship**: Every business relationship, peer-to-peer, or inside to outside, starts as an introduction and formal recognition of roles. Too many relationships never advance beyond this stage, resulting in poor communication, no cooperation, low trust, and low shared productivity. Moving forward to workships is critical to the business.

- ➤ **Workship - Mentor**: This is a productive working relationship where one party who is more knowledgeable and/or experienced takes an active role in fostering the advancement of the other. When both parties contribute, it's a powerful and positive relationship that benefits both careers as well as the business.

> ➤ **Workship - Advocate**: Unlike the mentor, who is a coach and teacher, the advocate inspires you to be the best that you can be. The best advocates do this because they care about you as a person, not because of personal aspirations. Your business will benefit from the increased productivity, high morale, and skills growth.

> ➤ **Workship - Trailblazer**: The trailblazer is not overly competitive, but always is a few steps ahead and enjoys setting an example that you are inspired by, or motivated to follow. As a result, you are incented to be a trailblazer for others, which leads to stronger relationships throughout the team and a stronger startup.

> ➤ **Workship - Communicator**: The communicator is always researching the latest information and keeps you in the loop on what's happening in the business and why. Unlike the office gossip, information is always shared in a positive way, thus helping you to do your best at work and in your career. What goes around almost always comes around.

> ➤ **Friendship**: There are three conditions that accompany the transition from a workship to a more intimate friendship: a shared wish to move to the next level, expanding the work-based relationship to non-work experiences, and sharing issues requiring trust and discretion. Contrary to popular opinion, friendships are not inherently bad for business.

> ➤ **Romantic**: When the relationship is appropriate, condoned by the company, and welcomed by both parties, it can be positive from a personal and even a work perspective. On the other hand, it can cause enormous emotional and legal problems, not to mention pain, suffering, and business failure. Proceed to this level with caution.

> ➤ **Foe**: A *foe* relationship between two startup team members is always toxic to the business, so quick action from the top is required to save the business. Some foe relationships can be turned around to a productive workship or friendship, but all require first a shared wish by both parties to change. Workships and friendships can't be forced.

In summary, entrepreneurs need to be especially perceptive and sensitive to business and personal relationships, since they normally work with small, closely-knit teams, on innovative and highly unstructured environments. The quality of relationships with customers, investors, partners, and suppliers can easily be their sustainable competitive advantage or their death knell.

Unfortunately, too many technical entrepreneurs don't realize that all relationships are not the same. There are people you only recognize on the street, business friends, and then close friends whom you can always count on to help.

Another popular author, Tommy Spaulding, in *It's Not Just Who You Know* (http://www.amazon.com/Its-Not-Just-Know-Relationships/dp/0307589137), categorizes relationships into five levels, like floors of a building, and identifies the attributes of relationships at the different levels.

More importantly, he talks about the actions required to build a network of contacts at the highest level. I like his definition of the five floors of relationships, and as he states should spend 80% of your time getting 20% of your business relationships to the top floor:

> **Meet and greet relationships (first floor)**: This is where most business relationships start and remain. You need something specific from the other person—a loan, or product order, or help solving a problem. After you get what you want, you move on, with no giving or commitment.

> **Limited information sharing (second floor)**: But it's very basic information, the type you dispense out of social obligation or because it's a job requirement, not because you're offering some insight into who we are. Many people call these *close* friends, but in reality there is no trust, feeling, or giving going on at this level.

> **Emotional comfort level that goes beyond facts (third floor)**: You feel safe enough to voice opinions, discuss perspectives, and share feelings in making decisions. In business, positional authority remains the primary guiding force at this level, and most business relationships stay at this level or below.

> **Real same-page connection (fourth floor)**: This level allows conflict and resolution with no hard feelings. Here you get the introduction of *netgiving* as well as networking. Friends to the end talk about what's important to them and aren't afraid to discuss private matters.

> **Sharing the other person's state of mind (top floor)**: They become confidants, advisers, and cheerleaders who understand each other's needs and drives. Vulnerability, authenticity, trust, and loyalty are off the charts. It's a relationship based more on giving than on getting. There's only room for a few relationships at this level.

It's often said, *it's not what you know, it's who you know.* In business, there is another dimension, the level of your relationship, and the level of trust and giving established. Of course, relationships seldom fit neatly into a given level. They're far too dynamic, and may even move up and down floors like an elevator.

I recommend that you use the top floor as the reference point to think about your own business relationships. How many do you have at the top level, and what are you doing to actively develop more? Are your *close* business friends actually at the top floor, or merely at the second floor? Can you count on them for a real help or a big favor?

Tommy insists that building meaningful relationships without sacrificing integrity or treating other people as a means to an end will always help you achieve your goals and move beyond them, personally and professionally. These relationships must be based more on giving than on getting. That kind of giving gives you more than you could possibly imagine.

All relationships require hard work, patience, understanding, as well as tactics and strategies designed to make them blossom, just as you have tactics and strategies for marketing, selling, advertising, production, distribution, and customer service. Thus relationships are the basis for all the other keys to business success.

Don't look to a dating site for matchmaking business relationships

People looking for a quick fix for finding relationships often think of dating sites today. I've heard that there are over 5,000 dating sites online around the world, but I couldn't find one that focused on scientifically matching companies or people for business-to-business (B2B) relationships. That seems strange, since every business expert tells me that finding good business partners is just as tricky as a good marriage, without the sex.

Everyone agrees that successful business partnerships can provide cash for growth, reduce costs, provide new geographic markets, or bring whole new customer sets to the table. Bad ones will suck the energy out of your company and leave you wanting more. The thrill of the chase is always the fun part, but making it work is a lot harder.

Yet there are many similarities between finding a good business partner and finding a good personal relationship. For example, in both cases good relationships are key to effective communication, reaching a common understanding of requirements, win-win negotiations, and long-term satisfaction from joint efforts. As well, to find good relationships, both business and personal, the first consideration should be an analysis of the characteristics of the people involved. For business partners, your company objectives have to synchronize, and this requires adaptation by both parties beyond the honeymoon period. Here are some of the key elements to look for:

> **Principals on both sides need to be ready and willing to work with a partner**: Some executives prefer to operate in solo mode. If you have worked for yourself for a long time, such as living alone and making decisions without consulting anyone else, it may be hard to adapt to a shared decision-making environment.

> **Look for a match in operating style and work ethics**: A business partnership doesn't come with a no-fault divorce clause. During the *dating period*, look hard for those characteristics that suggest complementary strengths, compatibility, chemistry, motivation, and values. Consider a business *pre-nup* agreement.

> **Both sides should write down the shared objectives and vision**: If there is nothing to write down or the results are quite different, that's a big red flag. At this point, both need to put in some serious thought about common value systems and how integration will impact current operations and the *next generation*.

> **Agree on performance indicators measuring partnership effectiveness**: Every relationship needs to be mutually beneficial to foster trust and common commitment. If the value is channeled to one beneficiary, with more cost and effort to the other, the equation won't work for either.

> **Understand required changes to the current business model**: These need to be understood up front, since implementation will likely require staff changes, process changes, and a more complex communication system. Both sides need to evaluate the intangible impact of these.

Even with the best of efforts, in my experience a high percentage of partnerships don't work in the long run because the underlying entities have different long-term objectives. This means prior planning for an easy dissolution. Document early the partner agreement detailing what each person is responsible for, who makes what decisions, and how disagreements will be resolved.

In fact, I did find a few sites, such as *BusinessMatchmaker* and *BoardMyBiz*, which are a step in the right direction, but they still seem focused on letting you do most of the work (like LinkedIn and Facebook) to find the ideal partner.

How about finding the best fit for you through something like eHarmony's scientific approach to matching with 29 DIMENSIONS® of compatibility? I wonder how many dimensions of compatibility there are to a good business partnership? I know it's rarely love at first sight.

Should technical entrepreneur relationships ever be more than business?

We all have to communicate and collaborate with other people at work, but most of us start out instinctively trying to maintain an emotional distance from others in the work environment. In fact, most employee training courses recommend the distance if the work relationship crosses management levels, and most management policies strictly forbid fraternizing with the team.

Yet the *2013 Office Romance Survey* (http://www.vault.com/blog/workplace-issues/the-results-are-in-2013-office-romance-survey/) by Vault, Inc. found by polling more than 1,000 professionals at companies nationwide that 56% had participated in not only a friendship, but an office romance, and only 9% think that office romances are never acceptable. So I decided to start looking for some expert guidance on the pros and cons of this issue.

In the book referenced earlier *Who's That Sitting At My Desk?* Jan Yager, PhD in Sociology, a coach and speaker on work issues and friendship, outlines the potential benefits of *workships* (work relationships) evolving into friendships and romances as follows:

> ➤ **Improve communication and productivity**: Even casual friends at work are more likely to understand your requests, be convinced of the value of your ideas, and work in concert with you on projects. That's a win-win situation for both sides as more positive things happen more quickly. Warm feelings also make the work seem easier.

> ➤ **Offer support through tough times**: Positive workplace relationships can help balance some difficult issues you are facing outside of work. Even at work, if you are struggling with a difficult project, getting some help and support from friends there can easily make the difference between success and failure. We all learn more from people we trust.

➤ **Aid in self-esteem**: Workplaces provide day-to-day interaction opportunities that are a key to self-esteem for many. Friends are more likely to provide the positive feedback and accolades that we all need from time to time. Friends are also less likely to exhibit aggression and rudeness, which can lower the self-esteem of any receiver.

➤ **Can be a competitive advantage**: Despite accusations of favoritism, if your friendship with the boss is one of many factors in why you get promoted, that friendship may be a big plus for you at work. If you easily make friends with people at work, it means that you have good relationships skills, which is a key requirement as you move up the ladder.

Of course, there can be negative consequences to close friendships and romances at work as well:

➤ **Work-related betrayal**: According to most experts, romantic betrayals are the most frequent type of friendship betrayals, with work-related issues a close second. Betrayals at work run the gamut from telling lies, coloring the truth, plagiarizing work, to saying negative things to the boss. Of course, all these things can happen in any workship.

➤ **More emotional vulnerability**: Through friendship, you open yourself up to acceptance, being liked, admired, respected, trusted, and appreciated. You also open yourself up, as do others when they befriend you, to the greater possibility of disappointment, rejection, and misunderstandings. Success is the best antidote to emotional vulnerability.

➤ **Competition over salary, promotions, and position**: Sometimes friends share too many details on salary levels, work habits, and promotion expectations. This can cause feelings of unfairness and initiate emotionally competitive efforts. The result can be a loss of friendship and even loss of any working relationship.

➤ **Hard to keep work-related disagreements separate from personal relationship**: Work-related disagreements break up many romantic relationships, and broken personal friendships break up many businesses. In this new age of collaboration, unemotional different perspectives and disagreements have been proven to lead to better decisions.

If you are contemplating a transition from a workship to a more intimate friendship, according to Yager, you should make sure that it satisfies the following three conditions:

➤ **Make sure the move is a shared wish**: There are three distinct kinds of friends: casual, close, and best. A fourth category is more intimately romantic relationships. None of these four work well if they are *one-sided*, meaning only one of the parties is committed.

➤ **Be ready to reveal and involve your non-work experience**: Some people find that they have much in common in workplace duties and perspectives, but have nothing in common outside of work. Or they really don't want to share their personal life details.

➤ **Expect increased pressures from trust and discretion issues**: All friendships bring increased demands for your time and bring expectations and pressures during any changes in your life or at work. Make sure you both have the shared values in your personal life, as well as at work.

In my view and experience, the benefits of more ordinary friendship, not romantic or intimate, at work far outweigh the disadvantages. It's certainly more enjoyable and satisfying to spend your time with friends (men or women), rather than people you hardly know. Even from a business perspective, socializing at work today, contrary to a couple of decades ago, is considered collaborative and productive rather than a waste of time. The trend today is to *open* office spaces, even for executives, versus the private and quiet offices of yesterday.

Going further in the friendship direction to a romantic relationship is still almost always a negative at work because the emotional ties and tolls often override rational actions. As an example, I find that most Angel investors still decline to fund startup founders that are romantically involved, citing the high risk of emotional decisions and breakup.

Work relationships are in vogue, inside a company for collaboration and teamwork, and outside to customers and partners through social media for loyalty and interactive marketing. But all good things can be overdone. Make sure you maintain the right balance in your work relationships.

Great relationships are the key to scaling your business

Once you are able to achieve some real *traction* with your technical startup (paying customers, revenue stream), it may seem the time to relax a bit, but in fact this is the point where many founders start to flounder. All the skills and instincts you needed to get to this level can actually start working against you and you can fail to scale.

Investors often say that successfully navigating the early stages of a startup requires lots of street smart, guts, and luck. To successfully scale the business, there has to be a transition to *executive* mode in the more traditional business sense, where relationships are even more critical. Certain behaviors between these two modes are incompatible and can cause real problems.

Several years ago, John Hamm, who has a diverse background as a technology CEO, a venture investor, and a leadership coach/advisor, published some work on this subject in *Why Entrepreneurs Don't Scale* (http://entropyventures.com/scale.pdf) in the Harvard Business Review. Here is my interpretation of that work, incorporating my personal experience, identifying some strengths of a technical entrepreneur during early startup stages, which can become a problem for scaling:

➤ **Perseverance**: This is generally a required quality for a successful entrepreneur, but it can turn into an unhealthy stubbornness during the scaling stage. The key is to make decisions from data and feedback once your business has real customers and real products. Trusting your gut at this stage isn't good enough.

➤ **Absolute control**: During the early stages, you are the company and processes are not documented. You don't have much help, so you need a fanatical attention to detail. To scale the business, you have to find people who can do the tasks and delegate appropriately. Control freaks are doomed to failure.

➤ **Individual loyalty**: Most founders form very close relationships with the small team that gets the startup off the ground, and that is important. Scaling requires that you expand the team, probably with people you haven't known. You also have to deal with the inevitable personnel challenges, even within the original team. Total loyalty can be toxic.

➤ **Isolated and insulated**: Working in isolation is fine during the creative phase of the startup, where the founder is often the designer and architect, as well as the builder. Now this same individual has to step into the spotlight and meet with customers, analysts, and investors. Insulation from the real world will not work during scaling.

➤ **Tactical versus strategic**: Early stage startup founders have to think tactically. Even business school courses don't teach you to operate strategically, deal with people objectively, and create loyalty within a diverse workforce. These are areas where past stumbles are the best teachers. Investors don't want to fund your stumbles.

Every founder moving into the executive role has to step back and take a hard look at what works and what doesn't work. The best ones can do that and they adapt. Investors and advisors see this as a critical part of their role, and often are the *bad guys* who ask the founder to step aside while they bring in a *more experienced* CEO to take over the helm.

Unfortunately, some founders won't adapt and won't step aside. Even if they are pushed out, they can cause terminal damage to the business by negative versions of their strengths, now seen as stubbornness, unwillingness to give up control, testing loyalty, and hiding from reality.

Thus my best recommendation if you want to scale and to survive is to open up and work closely with an *outsider* that you trust, such as a respected board member, a coach, a mentor, or an investor. The key is to expedite your learning and take deliberate steps to confront your shortcomings. That way, you will become the leader your company needs, learn to stop floundering, and begin to fly.

The importance of great customer relationships

I often deal with early-stage technical startups, and many of these don't have any customers yet (but wish they did), so it's not surprising they still don't think of customers as their friends. More disturbingly, others do have customers, but the customer service program consists of an informal focus on *problems*, rather than a proactive effort to establish a positive relationship with friends.

The right time to put a formal customer service program in place with measurements is before the first sale of your product or service to a customer. You can't manage what you don't measure, and customer satisfaction these days is one the most critical success factors to every business.

A while back, I saw a great article on the Focus website, titled *12 Lessons From The Best Customer Service Companies* (http://www.comparebusinessproducts.com/fyi/12-lessons-best-customer-service-companies). It summarized some practical lessons that I recommend from companies with the best customer service around—both what to do and what not to do:

> ➤ **Keep it personal**: Yes, a certain amount of automation is necessary for efficiency, but customers should never feel like they are at the mercy of machines when all they really want is to talk to a human being.

> ➤ **Don't make the customer work**: Many companies build friction into their support systems by forcing customer to remember arcane account or customer numbers, e-mail addresses and passwords, before being helped.

> ➤ **Foster relationships**: When it comes to major, life-changing purchases, simply answering a customer's questions is not enough. To close large sales, a firm's customer service staff needs to build and foster relationships with customers.

> ➤ **Go above & beyond**: No small amount of customer frustration comes from the perception that companies are doing the bare minimum to satisfy them. Actions clearly above and beyond make the customer feel completely taken care of.

> ➤ **Be enthusiastic**: Another way to show customers that they're in good hands is to be really, truly, palpably enthusiastic, but not insincere or overwhelming about your products. Customers like to believe that businesses believe in the virtues of their offerings on a level transcending profit.

> ➤ **Be helpful without being annoying**: The overzealous floor clerk might think he's helping by following you from aisle to aisle, but in truth he is actually getting in the way. The challenge is to assist customers without stepping on their toes.

> ➤ **Even online retailers need phone support**: A mistake of online retailers is to assume *since we're online, we don't need a support number*. Web retailers typically direct all questions to a form that most people assume will never get answered by anyone.

➤ **Unabashedly seek to out-serve competitors**: Deliberately and un-apologetically strive to out-serve your competitors. Take stock of how the other companies in your industry interact with customers and seek out specific ways to do a better job of it.

➤ **Be prompt**: The reason so many people prefer phone support to online is not that online support is inherently awful, but it's often treated as less urgent. Let's be frank—who really expects to hear back from *support@someretailer.com* anytime soon?

➤ **Train rank and file employees in your customer service specifics**: Great customer service is not commanded down from the top by written edicts and policies. Every company known for outstanding service has made a conscious decision to train its rank and file employees in how to properly assist their customers.

➤ **Always innovate**: Contrary to some assumptions, customer service isn't all about direct business-to-customer interactions. Even the most courteous and professional staff can't rescue a stagnant company selling the *same old same old* year after year.

➤ **Create a desire to belong**: Finally, among the most powerful customer service techniques is creating a desire to belong. Customers with a desire to belong are fiercely loyal and provide positive testimonials and word-of-mouth advertising money can't buy.

Customer service, like any aspect of business, is a practiced art that takes time and effort to master. Treat your customers like your friends, be ready to show them a little extra love, and your business will always be remembered as the best.

I agree with John Spence, in *Awesomely Simple, Jossey-Bass* (http://www.amazon.com/ Awesomely-Simple-Essential-Business-Strategies/dp/0470494514), that in a world of nearly limitless product options and highly educated consumers with instant access to the price, features, and benefits of almost every product, delivering consistently superior customer service is one of the only differentiators left for creating loyal and engaged customers.

Here are the top ten suggestions from John and others for how to create a culture of extreme customer focus in your organization:

➤ **Create a customer service vision**: Much like creating a vision statement to direct the organization, you should also create a clear and compelling *customer service vision* that describes the level of service your organization aspires to deliver.

➤ **Exceed customer expectations**: Show a relentless commitment to exceeding, not just meeting, expectations. Customers can't tell you how to exceed their expectations, but they know it when they see it, they remember, and they tell their friends.

➤ **Continuous customer service innovation**: Many companies have an ongoing product innovation focus, but rarely think about customer service innovations. Define specific innovation objectives and rewards for improving the customer experience.

> ➤ **Create superior customer value**: Focus on creating superior value for your customers and they will love you. This means know your competitors, technologies, and alternatives available. Match your offerings to your target customers better than anyone else.

> ➤ **Own the voice of the customer**: The only critic whose opinion counts is the customer. Create strong, trusting relationships with your customers. Solicit feedback, communicate that feedback to the entire organization, and then be sure to take action on the feedback.

> ➤ **Be the expert on delivering superior customer service**: Find out everything you can about how to deliver great customer service. Steal the best ideas, benchmark against the top performers, and make improving customer service a core competency.

> ➤ **Train every employee to be a customer service champion**: Empower employees with the tools, training, equipment, and support they must have to deliver excellent service consistently. Reward and praise those who deliver, and deal quickly with any employee who does not embrace the service values.

> ➤ **Destroy barriers to delivering superior service**: Look at all systems, policies, procedures, reports, and rules. Wipe out anything that creates roadblocks or frustrations in the effort to delight and amaze the customer. Stupid rules that make it hard for employees to serve superbly can kill your business.

> ➤ **Measure, measure, and communicate**: Create a clear, specific, well thought-out, and over-communicated program to systematically collect and communicate the most important customer service delivery measurements to the people who can then act on them. Make it easy for your people to win.

> ➤ **Walk the talk**: Every level of the organization starting at the very top must be a living example of your service strategy. If you do not deliver excellent service to your internal customers—promptly returning phone calls, showing up on time for meetings, and acting professionally—there is no hope that your front-line people will deliver great service.

Sustainable competitive advantage was once based primarily on characteristics such as technology leadership, market power, economies of scale, and a broad product line. The advantage today has shifted to companies whose customer focus is superior. As a technical startup, you have the opportunity to lead. Use it, and don't lose it.

New technical product startups rightfully begin with a heads-down focus on creating the ultimate product—whether it's a new technology, a new look and ease of use, or a new low-cost delivery approach. Most then add customer service at the rollout, but very few really understand what it means to be truly *customer-centric*, and even fewer really achieve it.

In fact, a focus on customer relationships, often called customer centricity, means more than providing excellent customer service, although that's a step in the right direction. Customer centricity is a strategy to fundamentally align a company's products and services with the wants and needs of its most valuable customers, with the aim of more profits for the long term.

As I was reminded by Peter Fader's book, *Customer Centricity*, *Wharton Digital Press* (http://www.amazon.com/Executive-Education-Customer-Centricity-Essentials/dp/1613630077) from the Wharton School, brands such as Wal-Mart and Costco aren't really customer-centric. They do provide the right products at the right price to save all customers money (with good customer service), but they don't try to find their most valuable customers and nurture them to buy more or bring in friends.

Customer-centric means building loyal customers, like Apple appears to have done extremely well. It means recognizing that all customers are not the same, and that all customers are not always right. It means pursuing Fader's four tenets that can lead to even greater long-term success and profits than a great product at a low price:

> **Accept that all customers are not the same**: By recognizing the fundamental and inevitable differences among your customers, you can give your organization a strategic advantage over your product-centric competitors— who may know little to nothing about the customers who account for their success and survival.

> **Focus on individual customer value**: By understanding that there is real and quantifiable value to be found in individual customers, you can better focus your long-term marketing efforts on precisely those customers who will generate the greatest long-term value.

> **Quantify the value and cost of acquiring every new customer**: By working to quantify the value of each and every one of your customers, you can gain enormously valuable insight about how much you should be willing to spend to keep an existing customer and how much you should be willing to spend to acquire a new customer.

> **Personalize your offering to each customer or group**: By moving forward with a highly focused customer relationship management initiative, you can gather and leverage more information about your customers. This will allow your company to serve those customers in a more personalized (yet genuine) manner than any competitor can.

In reality, you don't need to get to know each individual customer. But you do need to segment your customers into homogeneous groups. Then you can decide on a marketing program, loyalty program, or a level of attention that is appropriate to each group, for acquisition, retention, and profitability.

Remember, this is not a one-time effort. The needs and interests of your customers are ever-changing, so you have to constantly re-align your resources to build mutually beneficial relationships. Don't focus only on your products and operational efficiencies, unless you already have the brand image and leverage to prosper with price as the key differentiating factor.

Success hinges on progressing past lip-service to the real work of building a customer-centric organization to execute the focus. That means setting up operational and financial metrics, educating team members, and rewarding the right actions.

Mergers and acquisitions for growth are special relationships

Every technical entrepreneur tries to maximize his startup growth by building and selling more product and services for the widest geographic area that he can support. This strategy is called **organic growth**, yet it alone may yield only a fraction of the potential you could achieve unless you add the additional strategies of partnerships and mergers and acquisitions (M&A) (http://en.wikipedia.org/wiki/Mergers_and_acquisitions).

Many entrepreneurs are paranoid about the partnership approach and think that M&A is only an alternative for large companies who are flush with cash. Both of these qualms are wrong and shortsighted. Laurence Capron and Will Mitchell explain why in *Build, Borrow, or Buy: Solving the Growth Dilemma, Harvard Business Review Press* (http://www.amazon.com/Build-Borrow-Buy-Solving-Dilemma/dp/1422143716), and I like their recommended framework for emerging firms to help build an optimal growth strategy for your company:

> ➤ **Evaluate internal development versus external sourcing**: Building through internal development, or organic growth, makes the most sense when you have a core set of skilled internal resources. Use external sourcing to fill in the non-critical gaps.

> ➤ **Add basic partner contracts or alliances**: Using contracts with partners for growth resources (*borrowing*) is best when you can both define the resources clearly and protect them with effective contractual terms. Don't use alliances for core competencies.

> ➤ **Invest in selective strategic alliances**: Borrowing by way of a more engaged alliance helps you obtain targeted resources when you and a partner collaborate through limited points of contact and have complementary goals for your joint activities.

> ➤ **Actively pursue mergers and acquisitions**: M&A is buying resources for growth. This makes sense when you anticipate needing the freedom and control to make major changes to enhance growth, with a credible integration path while retaining key people.

The real challenge here is balance. Too much emphasis on organic growth can become a straightjacket that leads only to incremental innovation and limited horizons. Too much reliance on growth via contracts and alliances makes you vulnerable to partners' actions and conflicts of interest. Overreliance on acquisitions drains resources and de-motivates internal teams.

In every technical startup, as well as in mature companies, there is no substitute for constantly maintaining a pipeline of alternatives. This requires constant focus, as well as maintaining the skill set to do things like the following:

> ➤ **Locating and not losing knowledge from within**: Startups often find it difficult to retain key personnel and to control proprietary ideas. Rather than push non-compete agreements on your superstars, it's more productive to create incentive systems and creative ways for them to work more independently, just for you.

> ➤ **External scanning for resources**: Startups can't usually afford a business development team, so that effort is just one of the measurements that should fall on every CTO and CEO. Here is also an ideal opportunity to use your external advisors and board to help identify external resources, potential partnerships, and acquisition opportunities.

> ➤ **Partial acquisition**: Budget relatively small educational investments at early stages to learn from a target firm without a full commitment, or without leading either partner astray. These can reinforce the operational and financial linkages through licensing or alliance agreements and allow the relationship to develop prior to an acquisition commitment.

> ➤ **Spin-ins**: This is a transaction whereby two firms agree on a set of milestones that would trigger a partnership or acquisition if the innovator achieves the specified goals. The initiator funds the innovators' development activities and gives them the flexibility to work independently.

There is no question that technical startups which manage the broadest alternatives for growth will gain competitive advantages. This selection capability is a skill and a discipline that every entrepreneur needs to nurture and develop over time. The world and current economic environments have changed. The past can be a deadly rear-view mirror. Look for new horizons.

Make your relationship connect deeply

A technical entrepreneur is often able to build an innovative product as a *lone ranger* but it's unlikely that he or she can build a successful business without the ability and effort to build relationships with many supportive players.

In addition to building relationships, the technical entrepreneur has to become a proactive leader who connects to customers and the team deeply, rather than just a bright light that struggles to be seen amidst the glare of a million other bright lights, by his team and by his customers.

Achim Nowak, noted business coach and author, in his book *Infectious: How to Connect Deeply and Unleash the Energetic Leader Within*, Allworth Press (http://www.amazon.com/Infectious-Connect-Deeply-Unleash-Energetic/dp/1581159242/ref=sr_1_1?ie=UTF8&qid=1359918351&sr=8-1&keywords=achim+nowak), talks about how technology today allows entrepreneurs to communicate and build apparent relationships at a furious pace.

They exchange more e-mails, texts, and tweets every day. Yet many know less and less about how to really connect and get people to commit to their business or product.

I've seen this all too often in my own work with technical startups. More noise always means more hours a day working, but it doesn't necessarily mean more business or more productive relationships. Nowak talks convincingly about how successful entrepreneurs connect deeply with others at the highest of four levels, with less effort and more results:

> ➤ **Level one – Talk at the social level**: Talk is the first of four levels of communication. It is the surface of many business experiences, and some people never get beyond this level of relationship. They don't engage with a measure of skill and ease at this level, which actively inhibits any resonation at a deeper level. You need to move past this level quickly.

> ➤ **Level two - Connect through personal power**: Every entrepreneur has personal knowledge and strengths that can get them past the social level in connection. These should include professional position, existing relationships, specific expertise, professional appearance, and passion for your cause or business. Use them effectively.

> ➤ **Level three – Shape the intent of the connection**: Great connectors don't just fall into conversations, they carefully shape them with conscious intent and tone. Action verbs are key to creating powerful intentions, and they unleash forward-moving velocity. Don't waste your precious time or theirs on long boring conversations at lower levels.

> ➤ **Level four – Energy conquers all**: Energy and passion is the realm where all resonating connections truly unfold. If an entrepreneur doesn't have it or doesn't show it, he or she will never be able to build deep connections and commitments from customers, partners, or team members. Everyone recognizes the visible and verbal queues of energy.

Technical entrepreneurs who understand how to connect and build relationships with people on all four levels are able to shape conversations with effortless grace and create infectious connections that are the key to business success in this age of relationships.

For many business people, the hardest part of establishing relationships effectively is dumping old habits and learning to ignore some old myths and common beliefs. Here are a few of the things you probably need to unlearn according to Achim for better business as well as social connections:

> ➤ **You need to find common ground fast**: Common ground is, in many ways, a wonderful thing, but is irrelevant when it is forced. Take your time to discover common ground and relish the many things that you do not have in common.

> ➤ **Avoid charged topics**: In today's media-saturated world, being comfortable discussing current and controversial topics is critical. In business, having the confidence to disagree, explore points of conflict, and learn new points of view builds real relationships.

> ➤ **Don't show the cracks**: In reality, not taking any risks in showing the personal cracks guarantees that you will be viewed as a business robot that nobody really wants to work with. The power of a vulnerable moment is a powerful connection.

> ➤ **Don't get stuck with a loser**: Some business people are so busy looking for the right connection, afraid of losers, that they are never really in any relationship. It is far more powerful to really connect with a few key people than to skim the surface with many.

> ➤ **I will, I will, I will be perfect**: The notion of perfection negates the wonders of all that is not perfect, such as the beauty of an awkward moment, the thrill of the unrehearsed encounter, and the delicious learning of solving a business problem.

Today, more than ever, people buy based on relationships and commit based on relationships, no matter how great the technology is behind your product. In addition, we are all human and we need good relationships to be healthy and happy. Maybe it's time to take a hard look at your people connections and use these tips to kick your results up a notch.

Summary

That concludes my guidance for technical entrepreneurs on how to succeed with those key aspects of building a business that don't come naturally to many of us. I myself spent many years focused on technology before I decided to broaden my perspective to the needs of building a business as a whole. Now is the time for you to do the same.

I found that building a technical business is not rocket science, and only requires a can-do and problem solving attitude to learn, practice, and adapt. If I can do it, and I can point to many others who have made a successful transition, then you too can take your technical solution from an idea to a successful business. There is no time like the present to get started. Go for it!

www.ingramcontent.com/pod-product-compliance
Lightning Source LLC
LaVergne TN
LVHW081340050326
832903LV00024B/1225